Film Blackness

BLACKNESS

FILM

American Cinema and the Idea of Black Film

MICHAEL BOYCE GILLESPIE

DUKE UNIVERSITY PRESS
DURHAM AND LONDON   2016

© 2016 Duke University Press
Printed in the United States of America on acid-free paper ∞
Designed by Heather Hensley
Typeset in Garamond Premier Pro by Graphic Composition, Inc.,
Bogart, Georgia

Library of Congress Cataloging-in-Publication Data
Names: Gillespie, Michael Boyce, [date] author.
Title: Film blackness : American cinema and the idea of black film /
Michael Boyce Gillespie.
Description: Durham : Duke University Press, 2016. | Includes
bibliographical references and index.
Identifiers: LCCN 2016010797
ISBN 9780822362050 (hardcover : alk. paper)
ISBN 9780822362265 (pbk. : alk. paper)
ISBN 9780822373889 (ebook)
Subjects: LCSH: African Americans in motion pictures. | Race in motion
pictures. | Motion picture industry—United States.
Classification: LCC PN1995.9.N4 G55 2016 | DDC 791.43/652996073—dc23
LC record available at http://lccn.loc.gov/2016010797

Cover art: Gary Simmons, *Erasure Series (#1 black)*, 1992. Chalk and slate
paint on paper. Collection of Peter Norton.

For Nathaniel and Benjamin.
My everythings.

CONTENTS

ACKNOWLEDGMENTS

This book is a product of years of thinking about the art of blackness. This is not the Atom Egoyan or Japanese New Wave book I once thought I would write. I blame many writers and artists for that, too many to list here. But I especially feel that Randall Kenan's *Walking on Water: Black American Lives at the Turn of the Twenty-First Century* was significantly responsible. Furthermore, I don't think I would be a scholar if not for Dr. Linda G. Zatlin at Morehouse College. My mentor, friend, and believer.

I am immensely grateful for my professors and advisors at New York University. My deep thanks to Ed Guerrero, Bob Stam, Sheril Antonio, Bill Simon, Bob Sklar, Noa Steimatsky, Chris Straayer, Isaac Julian, Kobena Mercer, and Manthia Diawara. Thanks as well to all my classmates in the Department of Cinema Studies at New York University for the profound and critical generosity. Special thanks to Alessandra Raengo. Our conversations about blackness were essential.

Thanks to the many interlocutors who have engaged with this material over the years. I have been blessed and inspired by their sharp readings, conversations, advice, information, and generous engagement with this work. Their insights continue to make me a better scholar. I owe deep gratitude to Cathy Davidson, Nicole Fleetwood, Erica Edwards, Paula Massood, Lokeilani Kaimana, Gary Holcomb, Dana Seitler, Ayesha Hardison, Charles "Chip" Linscott, Tess Takahashi, Racquel Gates, Tehama Lopez Bunyasi, Jason Sperb, Kara Keeling, Mia Mask, Keith M. Harris, Leigh Raiford, Amy Ongiri, Huey Copeland, Tavia Nyong'o, Richard Grusin, Courtney Baker, Fred Moten, Sharon Holland, Allyson Nadia Field, Astrid Kaemmerling, Rebecca Wanzo, José Muñoz, Nicholas Sammond, Samantha Sheppard, and Amy Herzog.

I feel very fortunate to have had the opportunity to share this work and receive feedback at annual conferences for the Society for Cinema and Media Studies and the American Studies Association. I also benefited from presenting portions of this work at the Alien Bodies: Race, Space, and Sex in the African Diaspora conference (Emory), World Picture conference, Black American Cinema Re-considered: The Contemporary Scene (NYU), the Black Cinema Now conference (NYU), Black Portraiture[s], the Association for Study of the Arts of the Present conference, and the African Literature Association conference. Finally, I am very grateful for the criticism and engagement I received at the Black Cinema House, Cornell University for the Voices & Visions in Black Cinema series, Brown University for the Cinema & Black Cultural Politics Lecture series, and the Cinema and Interdisciplinary Interpretation series at Columbia University.

This work has benefited from my having the opportunity to teach at New York University, Duke University, The New School, and Ohio University. Thanks to all my students, most especially the students in the School of Interdisciplinary Arts at Ohio University for their inspiration and rigor.

For their support, encouragement, and friendship, love to Charles Swanson, Darin Givens, the McCoys, Stewart Griffin and Jess Keyt, Zach Oden, Nicole Fleetwood, Nicole Kassell and Steve Yung, Dion Warrick, Dana and Cannon, Tess and Mike, Racquel and Kenny, Lokeilani, Paula and Matthew, Allyson, Cindy and Buddy Pound, Danielle Leshaw and Kevin Haworth, Deborah Willis, Gary and Kim Holcomb, Eden Osucha and Jason Middleton, Chris and Lekeshia Jarrett, Kevin Jerome Everson, Laura and Gadi Larson, Duane McDiarmid, Amy Bomse and Peter Limbrick, Lisa Robinson and Andre Fenton, Charles Smith and Lisa Quinn, Andrew Lampela, Jill Locke and Eric Vrooman, Lucius and Freida Outlaw, the 16th Street folks, the Alibi, Johnny's, the Union, Tony's, and Doma.

I am grateful for the support of my colleagues at several institutions, most especially my former appointment at Ohio University in the School of Interdisciplinary Arts, School of Film, and the Department of African American Studies. Special thanks to Bill Condee, Steve Ross, Robin Muhammad, Akil Houston, Ofer Eliaz, Marina Peterson, Andrea Frohne, Dora Wilson, John Butler, Paula Morrison, Charles Buchanan, Lorraine Wochna, Garrett Field, and Vladimir Marchenkov. Thanks also to my new colleagues at the City College of New York.

Working with Duke University Press has been a wonderful experience. My deepest thanks to Ken Wissoker for his friendship, support, rigor, and patience. His counsel was invaluable and his enthusiasm for the project sustained me throughout the writing process. Thanks to the anonymous readers for their invaluable assessment. Thanks also to Liz Smith, Elizabeth Ault, Heather Hensley, Judith Hoover, Carol Wengler, and everyone else involved with the editorial process and book design for their guidance through the production process. Thanks to Ricardo A. Bracho for indexing the book. Thanks to Wendell B. Harris Jr. and Barry Jenkins for discussing their work with me. Special thanks to Gary Simmons for permission to use his work as the cover image.

Much love to Daisy Williams Gillespie, Ralph Gillespie, and Myles Gillespie for my first dreams and lessons. For all the encouragement, love to Sam Scott, Janice Gillespie, the Howells (Bill, Linda, Burt, Alice, and Audrey), and Olive.

To Nathaniel Burton Blue and Benjamin Varda, you are my deepest joy.

To my favorite New York filmmaker, Annie J. Howell, I am grateful for the love and laughter. Thanks for bearing witness, thanks for the thrills, and thanks for inspiring me to believe. Always, till the wheels come off.

Portions of the introduction and earlier versions of chapters 1 and 2 appeared as "Smiling Faces: *Chameleon Street*, Racial Performativity, and Film Blackness," in *Passing Interest: Racial Passing in U.S. Fiction, Memoirs, Television, and Film, 1990–2010*, ed. Julie Cary Nerad (Albany: SUNY Press, 2014), 255–82; "Dirty Pretty Things: The Racial Grotesque and Contemporary Art," in *Post-Soul Satire: Black Identity after Civil Rights*, ed. Derek Maus and James Donahue (Jackson: University Press of Mississippi, 2014), 68–84; and "Reckless Eyeballing: *Coonskin*, Film Blackness, and the Racial Grotesque," in *Contemporary Black American Cinema: Race, Gender and Sexuality at the Movies*, ed. Mia Mask (London: Routledge, 2012), 56–86.

WE INSIST The Idea of Black Film

I am giving a reading at a bookstore in Spokane, Washington. There is a
large crowd. I read a story about an Indian father who leaves his family for
good. He moves to a city a thousand miles away. Then he dies. It is a sad
story. When I finish, a woman in the front row breaks into tears. "What's
wrong?" I ask her. "I'm so sorry about your father," she says. "Thank you,"
I say, "But that's my father sitting right next to you."

—SHERMAN ALEXIE, "THE UNAUTHORIZED AUTOBIOGRAPHY OF ME"

In the epigraph, Sherman Alexie dryly arrests an audience member's expectation and perception that his story be unscripted, a direct reflection of reality
in the barest of autobiographical terms. His narrative of this encounter with
this white woman exemplifies the collapsing of the distance between two fictions, one writerly and the other a sociocultural marker of being. Indian and
"Indian" are conflated, and the performative becomes reduced to unmediated,
existential accounting. In the absence of a consideration of verisimilitude, or
just literary form and style more generally, the woman's empathetic response
to Alexie's reading illustrates an inability to distinguish the author function
from embodied being. This epigraph evinces my concern for and investment
in the idea of black film. In a comparable sense, the woman's query and expectation correspond to the way that black film, and black art more broadly,
navigates the idea of race as constitutive, cultural fiction, yet this art is nevertheless often determined exclusively by the social category of race or veracity
claims about black existential life in very debilitating ways. But this book does
not merely equivocate about the debilitating ways of social reflectionist ap-

proaches. Accounting for black film in a manner that does not adhere alone to a focus on how cinema must oblige, portend, or emblematize social truth requires attention to cinema as an art practice with attendant and consequential questions of form and politics.

The belief in black film's indexical tie to the black lifeworld forgoes a focus on nuance and occults the complexity of black film to interpret, render, incite, and speculate. This misrecognition corresponds to Edwin S. Porter's *Uncle Josh at the Moving Picture Show* (1902) and the scenario of a rube who rushes the theater screen to protect his projected daughter's honor; in the context of this book's thesis the title would be *Uncle Josh at the Black Picture Show*. This book is about black film, or more precisely, the idea of black film. I argue that, as art and discourse, black film operates as a visual negotiation, if not tension, between film as art and race as a constitutive, cultural fiction.[1] I deliberately engender a shift to distinguish between the rendering of race in the arts from the social categories of race and thus forestall the collapsing of the distance between referent and representation.[2] This shift disputes the fidelity considerations of black film: the presumption that the primary function of this brand of American cinema entails an extradiegetic responsibility or capacity to embody the black lifeworld or provide answers in the sense of social problem solving. Furthermore the idea of black film cannot be tantamount to an ethics of positive and negative representation that insists on black film in the terms of cultural policy, immanent category, genre, or mimetic corroboration of the black experience. Black film must be understood as art, not prescription. This book does not insist on an aesthete's vision of a pure cinema, an art unsoiled by *incidental* or *extraneous* concerns for the cultural, social, and political. I am not arguing for a deracialized or postracial notion of black film. Film blackness means a rethinking of black film and especially the questions we ask about this cinema. In particular, this repurposing insists that to outline the idea of black film as an art entails addressing it as a practice that emanates from the conceptual field of black visual and expressive culture. This means that in addition to interdisciplinary collaboration with collateral questions that broach the art of blackness, I am framing the idea of black film in correspondence to literature, music, new media, photography, and contemporary art for a wider conception of blackness as the visualizing and creative production of knowledge that is one of the core values of the idea of black film. To be clear, instead of a book compelled by disinterest in the black lifeworld, *Film Blackness* is compelled by disinterest in claiming that the black lifeworld be the sole line of inquiry that can be made about the idea of black film.

As an example of how film blackness might offer a more inclusive and variegated investment in the idea of black film, I turn to Harry Allen's "Telling Time: On Spike, Strike and the 'Reality' of *Clockers*," not a review per se but an extended observation on Spike Lee's *Clockers* (1995). Opening with an account of his wife sighing while watching the film, Allen reads her response as a sign of disbelief, which mirrored his own frustration with the film. He also identifies a remark made by Ronald "Strike" Dunham, the film's protagonist, as emblematic of his overall impression of *Clockers*: "I ain't got the stomach no more for this shit." According to Allen, one of the film's irresolvable flaws entails "gaps in character motivation and logic" that result in a film that appears "alternately 'real' and contrived in ways that make you question the value, or reality, of what's 'real.'" While he pointed out how the film "cheats," Allen did recognize Lee's auteurist liberties and the "burden of representation": "Any filmmaker can use any filmic strategy to make a point, as long as that strategy is coherent. And Black filmmakers are burdened with the rope chain of 'reality' in ways white people simply aren't."[3] Though remaining fixed on what he considers the film's duplicitous quality, Allen notes that an additional shortcoming of *Clockers* is its failure to be a challenging enough mystery for the spectator trying to solve the question of who killed Darryl Adams. Yet this overture to a formal standard of mystery and noir detection is disingenuous, as the core thrust of Allen's contention with the film is founded on veracity claims about black film.

An adaptation of Richard Price's novel of the same name (1992), *Clockers* consequentially differs from the novel's primary focalization through homicide detective Rocco Klein with a shift to a narrative emphasis on Strike that amplifies the character's depth.[4] Aesthetically speaking, the film's color-reversal film stock remediates the light and shadow play of noir with a color palette of vivid grains that ominously evokes surveilling reportage.[5] Significantly the film's mystery of who killed Darryl Adams in truth suggests a narrative conceit of why Strike must be the killer. Thus, echoing the premise of Nicholas Ray's *In a Lonely Place* (1950) and the question of why Dixon Stelle (Humphrey Bogart) must be the killer rather than who killed the hatcheck girl, *Clockers* complicates noir form with an attention to black visuality, popular culture, and the narrativization of criminality. In other words, Strike must be the killer according to antiblack codes of criminality and not strictly by the procedural science of a murder investigation and noir justice.

Regardless, the rest of Allen's article is devoted to comments from an assembled roundtable of experts, three people identified as intimately knowledgeable about the film's subject matter, with the implication that they are capable of speaking with authority on the film: "'Ace,' a self-described on-and-off drug dealer"; "Luis Arroyo, Police Officer"; and "John Hanchar, EMT [emergency medical technician]." Each responded to the film through the analytic filter of his occupational and personal experiences as a way of measuring the "credibility" of various details, but most especially in terms of the characters and their actions. Noting the actions of film characters against his own drug-dealing experiences, Ace stated that much of *Clockers* was believable, but he pointed out that *clockers* was not a term used in the drug trade. Officer Arroyo found much that was realistic about the film but said the design of the interview room and the procedural behavior of the officers—their use of racist speech and their brutality—were unrealistic. The EMT found the morbid comic behavior of detectives at the crime scene realistic but thought the montage of staged gunshot victims in the title sequence was too graphic and bordered on fake. He conceded that the photographs might be staged or that perhaps he had just become "hardened" to such images. Each respondent's final question was "Your weapon of choice?" None was asked whether he knew that *Clockers* was a fiction film, yet their responses suggest they believe it was nonfiction, a mere reflection of a truth.[6]

My intention in offering this anecdote is not to scold Harry Allen and the respondents for making extraordinarily wrong claims that are endemic of a fringe opinion, a view that black film be primarily measured by an experiential truth or authenticity claims. Rather my intention is to illustrate something ordinary and common, the notion that a certifiably good or bad black film must be a matter of what one would credibly expect to experience in one's life, or in other words, that black film must correspond to reality itself. This logic operates with the presumption that the fundamental value of a black film is exclusively measured by a consensual truth of film's capacity to wholly account for the lived experience or social life of race. Rather than merely dismiss the indexical expectation with asocial or atemporal persuasion, this book promotes contextual and relational tendencies of the idea of black film. In the end, black film does not prosper as a diagnostic mission.

I briefly offered a few possible ways of approaching *Clockers* that addressed form and style (genre), aesthetics and materiality (stock), affinity (intertextuality), and narrativity (the conceit of a problem/crime and a solution). These offerings do not exhaust all the probable considerations of *Clockers*, but they are as vital and more immediately significant than veracity critiques. Moreover as *Clockers* is indeed a film invested in commenting on issues of the drug trade, inner city violence, black villainy, and black respectability, the real issue is that the film can be fully appreciated only as enacting the art of cinema *and* a social critique. Thus to ignore the former for the sake of the latter or to deny that the latter is mediated by the former denotes incomplete and imperfect criticism.

Film Blackness suspends the idea of black film by pushing for a more expansive understanding of blackness and cinema.[7] What do we mean when we say *black film*? Black directors, actors, or content? Charles Burnett, not Jim Jarmusch? *Within Our Gates* (Oscar Micheaux, 1920), not *George Washington* (David Gordon Green, 2000)? Is *Soul Plane* (Jessy Terrero, 2004) "more black" than *Ganja & Hess* (Bill Gunn, 1973)? What does the designation *black film* promise, and what does it disallow? Film blackness is a resolve to reaccentuate the values attributed to black film and generated by an abounding confluence of the art of cinema and black discursivity.[8]

Is It All Over My Face?

Film blackness demands more ambition for the idea of black film as a critical capacity and not agential authority. What if black film could be something other than embodied? What if black film was immaterial and bodiless? What if black film could be speculative or just ambivalent? What if film is ultimately the worst window imaginable and an even poorer mirror? What if black film is art or creative interpretation and not merely the visual transcription of the black lifeworld? As Ralph Ellison wrote in response to Stanley Edgar Hyman's analysis of black folklore in Ellison's *Invisible Man* (1952), "I use folklore in my work not because I am Negro, but because writers like Eliot and Joyce made me conscious of the literary value of my folk inheritance. . . . I knew the trickster Ulysses just as early as I knew the wily rabbit of Negro American lore."[9] Ellison exposes the violation of a critic's good intentions as an anti-intellectual engagement with the artist's choice of form and style that reduces the intertextual reserve of his work to solely the black lifeworld; the trickster is part, not parcel.

Blackness in this book functions as a term for art modalities that evince black visual and expressive culture. Film blackness particularly focuses on questions of intertextual consequence, visuality, performativity, cultural history, and the politics of cinematic form. Thus blackness functions as an interpretative and creative process that bears out what Kimberly Benston recognizes as an enduring lesson of black cultural nationalism: "[Blackness] is not an inevitable object, but rather a motivated, constructed, corrosive, and productive process."[10] Therefore film blackness denotes a reading practice devoted to the cinematic, the visual production of blackness (black visuality), and the critical ways that art disputes, distends, and aspires. This multidiscursive property of blackness signals the interpretative and performative capacity of the art of blackness as an aesthetic, cultural, and political engineering of craft.

Race as a constitutive, cultural fiction has always been a consequential element of American history and social life, and antiblack racism, white supremacy, and the Racial Contract are foundational and systemic features of American life. This resonates with the way the idea of race becomes engendered as a natural phenomenon. As Wahneema Lubiano observes, "What is race in the United States if not an attempt to make 'real' a set of social assumptions about biology?"[11] So then, in spite of the way race functions as a constitutive and cultural fiction, once it appears on the screen how could it be anything other than social fact, the way people are *raced*?[12] This misunderstanding of art enables a critical negligence and wish fulfillment that leaves black film as fruit from the poison tree or the idea of race as quantifiably, fantastically whole. This book insists that black film matters because it offers a critical range of potentialities for understanding blackness as multiaccentual and multidisciplinary. Film blackness renews the idea of black film as a highly variable and unfinalizable braiding of art, culture, and history. There is a rigorous pleasure and politics to this strategy that requires a consideration of what desires inform our conceptions of black visuality and the need to distinguish this pleasure from the dilemma of antiblack racism.[13] This requires engaging with a film as art on the grounds of what it does and as opposed to what it has been recursively predetermined to do as *of the black experience*.

The discursivity of *black* demands greater rigor than speculations of universal blackness. Stuart Hall recognizes that race as a cultural phenomenon cannot be simplified for the sake of maintaining the semblance of a stable racial category, for this would simply reiterate the essentialist manners of antiblack racism. In the context of my book's focus on the idea of black film, Hall's rhetorical query of the *black* of black popular culture echoes my emphasis on a critical investment that does not hinge on guarantees of a universal black subjectivity (or spectatorship).[14] Thus film blackness and its deliberate lack of a totalizing correspondence to a natural order of things or "transcendental racial categories" proffers a regard for discursivity instead of enduring claims of political and cultural obligation.[15]

The crucial cadence of *Film Blackness* is attuned to the critical dialogism of cinema as an enactment of black visual and expressive culture.[16] The term itself is meant to demonstrate a methodological prerogative to incite a discrepant engagement with the idea of black film.[17] Thus the concept of film blackness targets the idea of black film with a motivation concentrated on aesthetic, historiographic, and cultural consequence. With this agitated and churning interdependency of blackness, form, content, and the spatiotemporal magnitude of cinema in mind, this book contests hypostatic and canonical ideas of black film by complicating the conditional question of classifying black film and its social applicability or place in the social world. The vast modalities of black art, of which cinema is a part, often suffer the analytic impropriety of marginality, selective blindness, and indifference to the discursivity of race and blackness as potentiality.[18] *Film Blackness* insists on a redrawing of the lines of influence, appreciation, allusion, causality, reference, and exposition.[19] The discrepant engagement of this book calls attention to cinema's capacity to pose distinctions and dissension in the place of diagnostic ceilings or the false intimacy of doing black film a favor by denying that it is a rigorous and flourishing art.

Nicole Fleetwood vitally considers the always already overdetermined nature of blackness in the visual field as its "troubling affect." She argues that this troubling is endemic to the process of visualizing black bodies. Her work is important for my thesis because of how she frames the objects of her analysis as providing "a lens to look at the affective power of black cultural production, or the calling upon the spectator to do certain work, to perform a function as arbiter, or decoder, of visual signs that become aligned with blackness."[20] *Film Blackness* demands a *certain work* of spectator, critical or otherwise, to revalue black film with the active labor of reading through and across blackness by treating each enactment of black film as discrete, if not ambivalent.

The Sum of Us

Black film does not and cannot satisfy identitarian fantasies of black ontology; instead it poses conceits, specificities, and contexts. *Film Blackness* persistently wrestles with the question of identity as something other than a fixed signifier. As Robyn Wiegman notes:

> If identities are not metaphysical, timeless categories of being; if they point not to ontologies but to historical specificities and contingencies; if their mappings of bodies and subjectivities are forms of and not simply resis-

tances to practices of domination—then a politics based on identity must carefully negotiate the risk of reinscribing the logic of the system it hopes to defeat. If rethinking the historical contours of Western racial discourse matters as a political project, it is not as a manifestation of an other truth that has previously been denied, but as a vehicle for shifting the frame of reference in such a way that the present can emerge as somehow less familiar, less natural in its categories, its political delineations, and its epistemological foundations.[21]

In the context of black film Wiegman's observations illustrate the tangential misunderstandings that enfeeble and excessively task the idea of black film. This is most evident in the ways that film blackness denaturalizes the authority of categorical claims by fixating on the contextual composition of the idea of black film. To demonstrate this, I turn to a film that disables the black identitarian essence impulse through a compounding of racial, gendered, and performative scripts.

An experimental short, Leah Gilliam's *Now Pretend* (1992) juxtaposes personal memoirs of black subject formation to John Howard Griffin's *Black Like Me* (1961), an account of his 1959 "transformation" and passing as a black man in the South. The modernist design of the film is structured by disinclinations and slippages with regards to personhood and black being. Instead of binaristic conceptions of being, the film poses a series of abstracted visualizations of blackness. It demonstrates an ambivalence toward veracity claims and identitarian prescription. The film opens with a shot of a shadow being cast on the sidewalk and pans up to reveal the back of a black woman walking, awash in the sounds of children playing. The kinetic handheld shots are in slow motion as the lighting casts her as a moving silhouette; then, with a cut to a black woman reading *Black Like Me*, the soundtrack features a reading of Griffin's account of an exchange with his doctor following completion of the final chemical treatment. As he leaves his doctor says, "Now you go into oblivion." The film cuts to a shot of an unknown figure walking in the evening through a field while carrying a flashlight that offers the only illumination. The figure's movement in the darkness and the light cuts to a black woman holding a mirror with the film's title within the frame. With a return to the kinetics of the opening sequence, the audio track shifts to a black mother talking of the effect of black consciousness on her sense of identity, while a voice slowed and accelerated whispers "Skin black" and a mother speaks of how letting her hair go "natural" became a confirmation of newness.

Gilliam orchestrates a braiding of blackness scripts in the sense of identitarian speculation, the Lacanian mirror stage, embodied masquerade, cultural standards of beauty, diasporic negotiation, and black femininity. In another poignant sequence from the film, a black woman walks through a park while carrying a ribbon. The text on the ribbon reads, "At what point did you realize the politics of your self/difference." The audio track returns to the mother reflecting on the politics that informed her parenting: "I wanted you to be a part of the larger world. But one in which you could keep your personal identity in a way that I felt I had not been able to do in the white institutions in which I had worked and studied." The mother's commentary shifts to her memory of the cultural politics of hair and her eventual decision to stop processing her hair. This account is accompanied by a montage that includes an unidentified black woman on a city street; two black girls wearing pillowcases on their heads to simulate long hair; ribbons laid over telephone wires, fluttering in the wind; the scene from *Imitation of Life* (Douglas Sirk, 1959) when Sarah Jane tosses a black doll; and a reenactment of the moment that followed the earlier citing of *Black Like Me*, when Griffin has returned home to shave his head and apply the final treatment of stain to his skin: "In the flood of light against white tile, the face and shoulders of a stranger. A fierce, bald, very dark Negro glared at me from the glass. He in no way resembled me. The transformation was total and shocking. I'd expected to see myself disguised but this was something else. All traces of the John Griffin I had been were wiped from existence." Intercutting shots of a black woman looking into a mirror that alternately features the words "identity" and "reflect," the film is further complicated by another reflection on the audio track of a woman recounting her experience of learning to speak properly (and convincingly) black in contradistinction to the pidgin spoken by her Trinidadian parents and the "sounding-white" accusations of her peers.

The film manifests an everyday abstraction of blackness as unsustainable in the strict terms of identitarian being. Through a multiplicity of voices and with reference to cinema, psychoanalysis, and the autobiographical voice, the film proffers and parallels multiple antagonisms surrounding the notion of black identity as something finite, something to which all might universally subscribe. Instead the film's avant-garde swagger compounds and plots blackness as the art of being, historiography, and cultural engineering. In the place of reinscribing categories, the narrator's voice articulates self-consciousness and the agential skill of recognizing the danger in accepting scripts from strangers.

Some scholars evade the complication of black film by pursuing a critical line that advocates for ethical judgments about film in a manner that suggests edicts on cultural policy. This type of criticism, anathema to the prerogative of the artist, insists on "good" black film along the tacit rhetorical lines of "good" black people. *Now Pretend* conceptualizes the *lived experience of race* in the necessary terms of complication and irresolution. The film's critical posture amply dissuades the impulse to wholly distill the cinematic apparatus to a reflectionist ideal.

In *Redefining Black Film*, Mark Reid attempts to remedy those issues that he believes deeply plague the writing of black film history and the reading of black film. He stresses that distinctions must be made between commercial film and those black independent films "written, directed, produced, and distributed by individuals who have some ancestral link to black Africa" and cautions against critical analyses that "[avoid] serious historical issues and [ignore] the polyphonic forms of black subjectivity." He prefaces his remedy in the following way: "Film histories that fail to distinguish black commercial films from black independent films tend to focus entirely on the commercial films. Consequently, they bury black film history by analyzing it according to 'relevant' theoretical criteria that are not applicable to black independent films. They also do not consider the particular cultural experiences of African-Americans. Other well meaning critics analyze black-oriented films according to the popular Marxist, feminist, and psychoanalytical approaches that appeal to the widest reading audiences—white male and female middle-class intellectuals."[22]

Reid insists that black film must be considered a practice tied to black subject formation that requires historical contextualization and a guiding attentiveness to polyphony. His thesis becomes troublesome with the absence of any real necessity to distinguish between the mainstream and the commercial other than to emphasize the importance of a black means of production, as if "for us, by us" is beyond reproach. Whatever Reid may intend in celebrating black people and black film becomes a treatise in the tacit terms of "the good black film" as "the good black." To pose film as black cultural production must avoid a conditionally narrow sense of purposefulness. To do so in a Marxist, feminist, and psychoanalytic way does not constitute accessing critical analysis as an exercise in white privilege. You cannot claim to read films dialogically and then refuse to see what the films are doing. How can you be willing to appreciate black film or film blackness when it is predetermined by such a prescriptive prerogative? Does any good really come from refusing to let art exceed your expectations?

Reid rightly raises the issue of a necessary rigor for the study of black film but then quickly states that it is inappropriate to pursue that "relevant" trajectory because it does not subscribe to the essentialist valorization of "for us, by us." He writes, "Critics and historians must analyze the independent film in terms of the filmmaker's efforts to create films that explore serious social issues and present balanced images of black women, men, and the African-American community. In developing such a cultural, ideological, socio-economic analysis of black film, critics and historians must describe how, by what means, and to what extent black independent filmmakers have chosen to be responsive to the needs of the black community."[23] This ultimately does a disservice to black people by suggesting that if there is some essence to be found, it is appropriate to think that film is the proper vessel for such a covenant. Being "responsive to the needs of the black community" does not mean you have to patronize this monolithic black community. Black film offers a vast array of possibilities for conceiving race in creative terms, and film blackness follows through on that promise without devaluing a lifeworld and overvaluing an art. Film blackness restages the conceptual casting of blackness as equal parts thought, élan, aesthetic, and inheritance. That is not a simple or exact matter, nor should it be. Reid's analysis may have been conceived almost twenty-five years ago, but the tendency to equivocate about the idea of black film with reference to a singular and fantastic black community or dampening readings devoted to black spectatorial prescription and perpetuating some notion of cinema's capacity to project black authenticity persist. If we must *see* ourselves, then let it be in mirrors and not on screens.

Darby English importantly considers "black representational space," the institutional/academic and cultural tendency to scrutinize black art in such a way that "can only be thought of as the effect of a politics of representation raging ever since 'blackness' could be proposed as the starting point of a certain mode or type of artistic depiction." In *How to See a Work of Art in Total Darkness*, English considers how the category of black art requires a "practical transformation" that ultimately bears out "the more difficult truth that the category 'black art' is now exposed as one among those many identity frameworks painstakingly constructed for use in a time whose urgencies are simply not those of our own."[24] In the context of American cinema film blackness recognizes this urgency but also understands that framing black film with an averred longing for a black truth benefits neither the art nor black people. What harm is there in watching a film as an invitation to think and be challenged rather than a perfunctory autopsy? I recognize the ideological hazards that English identifies as placing a cap on the creative and critical volition of art. Instead of substituting one grand theory with another, I am arguing for approaches that can account for resistances, capacities, and variables. Black film does not represent a closed hermeneutics; it represents a vast abundance.

Black Rhythm Happening

> Blackness is always a disruptive surprise moving in the rich nonfullness of every term it modifies. Such mediation suspends neither the question of identity nor the question of essence. Rather, blackness, in its irreducible relation to the structuring forces of radicalism and the graphic, montagic configurations of tradition, and, perhaps most importantly, in its very manifestation as the inscriptional events of a set of performances, requires another thinking of identity and essence.
>
> —FRED MOTEN, *IN THE BREAK*

The reprioritizing function of film blackness, a multiaccentual devotion to cinema and blackness, purposefully thrives on the searing and inscriptional capacity of blackness noted by Fred Moten. The "improvisational immanence" of blackness guides my conception of film blackness to enliven and amend the idea of black film as an *always disruptive surprise* that might pose new paradigms for genre, narrative, aesthetics, historiography, and intertextuality.[25] Film blackness thickens with the irreducible character of blackness and the radical capacity of black visual and expressive culture, a difference that ceaselessly devises and recasts.

Arthur Jafa's *Dreams Are Colder Than Death* (2013) richly demonstrates this sense of cinema's capacity to enact black visual and expressive magnitude.[26] An experimental documentary, *Dreams* focuses on the meaning of Dr. King's "I Have a Dream" speech fifty years later and whether the goals and ambitions of the civil rights movement have been achieved. The film asks, "Does the dream live on? And if so, what has changed?" The query centers on a sustained and prescient consideration of what blackness is, what the history of blackness is, and what the concept means to black people today. During the film's opening sequence there is a reverse motion shot of young black men appearing to fly backward from a public swimming pool. A sign of desegregation rolling back? In the midst of the gymnastics of black bodies cast from the water, Hortense Spillers's voice comes on the soundtrack: "I know we are going to lose this gift of black culture unless we are careful. This gift that is given to people who didn't have a prayer." Her "I know" is answered by Dr. King saying "I have a dream" on the soundtrack as her comments are ghosted by his "I Have a Dream" speech. In this prelude to the title sequence and the introduction of the film's premise there is the distance between a gift in peril and a prophecy. The film immediately signals departure from a static brand of documentary practice devoted to only the summation of historical detail. Instead the film intones a contemplative measure of the past, present, and future. It is an essay film in the sense of a nonfiction form of intellectual and artistic innovation whose black stream of consciousness is prefaced by Spillers's concern for the state of black culture.[27]

The film employs variant speeds to accentuate and amplify gestures and movements through and across time and ideas.[28] Furthermore the film offers an almost ceaseless montage of images that include black vernacular photography, contemporary art, galactic locations, dance, and news photography. Aesthetically the film frames its subjects in repose or moving as their commentary occurs as a voice-over. They are never seen speaking; they are always contemplative subjects whose thoughts circulate around them. This formal discontinuity of sound and vision or spoken word and the sight of a speech act gives the effect of a thought process in place of the staid voice-of-god narration.[29] In one significant sequence there is a radical sense of black political ventriloquism as Fred Moten formulates how as a result of the antiblack codes of America the black desire to be free operates as a conspiratorial act of theft, a criminal action. Moten's voice overlays a scene of the dancer Storyboard P performing his improvised choreography in the street, and thus there is a confluence of schemes: joyful, political, and performative.

A visual historiography of black thought, the film seethes with a productively agnostic impression of the idea of black history in progressive terms by considering the perception and conception of history in exquisitely visual and mosaic terms.[30] Geographically speaking the film is structured across the landscapes of Harlem, Brooklyn, Atlanta, Mississippi, and Los Angeles. The assembly of "uncommon folk and specialists," includes Spillers, Moten, Kara Walker, Charles Burnett, Melvin Gibbs, Saidiya Hartman, Flying Lotus, Nicole Fleetwood, Kathleen Cleaver, Wangechi Mutu, and black quotidian life. Together this group of visual artists, revolutionaries, musicians, academics, filmmakers, activists, everyday citizens, and the guiding eye of Jafa himself offer a history of critical resistance, philosophic practice, and black expressivity. But I would like to briefly focus on part of Moten's appearance. In the final section of the film his voice is paired with footage of him walking, and that is coupled with footage from a Trayvon Martin rally in Los Angeles. The slow-motion movement of a mass protest devoted to a black boy coded by a hoodie, murdered, and left to die in the rain with no shelter from the storm becomes punctuated by Moten's commentary that includes the following:

> When you say that black people are just an effect of slavery, you raise the question: Can black people be loved? . . . Not desired, not wanted, not acquired, not lusted after. Can black people be loved? Can blackness be loved? So what I am saying is that I believe there is such a thing as black-ness, and how it operates is that it is not an effect of horror. It survives horror and terror, but it is not an effect of these things. So it can be loved and has to be loved, and it should be defended.[31]

His comments are made in the context of a consideration of blackness and the object of black studies, a commentary that is interspersed throughout the film. This love signifies a critical devotion to recognize blackness in terms other than the determinism of horror. *Can blackness be loved?* Moten suggests that blackness is always already an act of faith with regard to the theological component of black studies. Instead this faith speaks to the potentialities of blackness as the immateriality of faith shadows and moderates the affective force of blackness. As an enactment of film blackness, *Dreams* demonstrates the rigor of black visual and expressive culture as a study of black thought and black performativity, a gathering and workshopping of ideas on black-ness as an act of noninstitutionalized intellectual labor.[32] The film pivots away from the narrative-interrupted recycling of a selectively remembered sense of Dr. King's vision to a dialogic envisioning of black praxis and freedom dreams.[33] *Can blackness be loved?* Moten's question, an exquisite explanation for *Dreams Are Colder Than Death*, resounds as a rhetorical call, a devotional affirmation, an act of revolutionary hope. In its dynamic devotion to a prac-tice of black intellectual montage, a multidimensional visualizing of black-ness, Jafa's enactment of film blackness amply testifies to the idea of black film as art and discourse.

I examine the intimacies and intricacies of film blackness not as an unbro-ken suite but as variant case studies with distinct consequences and inventive designs that collectively defer those compulsions that delimit the idea of black film and the art of blackness. I focus on four American fiction films as distinct enactments of film blackness, with attention to considering each across critical traditions of blackness and the arts. I chose these films for the complication and opportunity they pose for the idea of black film. Each proffers a distinct critical consequence, and my readings are focused on the conceptual mutability of film blackness as I locate each film within a particular discursive cluster that details how black film functions as a radical art.

Chapter 1, "Reckless Eyeballing," focuses on Ralph Bakshi's *Coonskin* (1975), addressing the film as an exercise in the racial grotesque. The film casts blackness as an absurd modality of critical dialogism with, among other things, the history of American animation, the New South ideal, vernacular cosmopolitanism, the blaxploitation film cycle, the cultural imperialism of Disney, and the countercultural comix of the 1960s. The film performs a radical resignification and critique of the stereotype as commodity fetish, especially the continued naïve and uncritical circulation of this iconography through mass media. Through a textual analysis devoted to one scene of *Coonskin*, I discuss the ideological texture of the film. *Coonskin* is a difficult film that challenges with the exaggeration and redirection of the cathected intention of stereotypicality.

Chapter 2, "Smiling Faces," considers Wendell B. Harris Jr.'s *Chameleon Street* (1989) and the ways the film stages racial passing in the key of racial performativity. The film's protagonist (Douglas Street) does not impersonate in the classical sense of racial passing pathologies. His passing as performative act occurs as a signifying menace, a threat to the categorical regimes of race and being. I also address *Chameleon Street* especially in relation to the "black film explosion" of 1991. This involves reading the film's inability to gain favor critically or financially or as an independent film, art film, or black film by recontextualizing it within the historiography of 1991 as a sign of dispute with the popular and delimiting assessments of black film.

Chapter 3, "Voices Inside," is an intervention in genre studies. With initial attention to the traditional consideration of noir and blackness, I build on James Naremore's discursive sense of "the history of an idea" and Manthia Diawara's "noir by noirs." Toward a reframing of noir I consider Chester Himes's discrepant engagement with "America" in the language of the hard-boiled detective tradition and the black absurd. My textual analysis of Bill Duke's *Deep Cover* (1992) examines the dialogics of genre form (noir) and the discursivity of race (blackness) as "modalities of noir blackness."

Chapter 4, "Black Maybe," focuses on Barry Jenkins's *Medicine for Melancholy* (2008), exploring the film's quiet accounting of blackness, the city, and historiographic rupture in the age of neoliberalism. I argue that the film's story of a black man and a black woman who couple for a day after a one-night stand is animated by issues such as melancholy, cosmopolitanism, love or desire or attachment, fantasy, gentrification, and the cultural geography of San Francisco. In this way the film's narrativized tracking of this couple focuses on the shifting cultural and racial textures of that city. Thus my diacritical reading of the film as fiction and chronicle considers the history of San Francisco as mediated by anxieties of black diasporic absence that are further imbricated by a romance conceit. In this instance of film blackness there is a complicated sense of how place impacts blackness in tandem with negotiations of futurity and the everyday.

With a deeply contextual concern, film blackness emphasizes how films are imbricated in a vital expanse of renderings, practices, and critical traditions devoted to blackness. The conceptual framing of film blackness fundamentally abides by this range for the sake of understanding that the idea of black film thrives as an enactment of black visual and expressive culture. This book is driven by the belief that the idea of black film is always a question, never an answer.

ONE

RECKLESS EYEBALLING
Coonskin and the Racial Grotesque

Man without myth is Othello with Desdemona gone: chaos descends, faith vanishes, and superstitions prowl in the mind. . . . It is the creative function of myth to protect the individual from the irrational, and since it is here in the realm of the irrational that, impervious to science, the stereotype grows we see that the Negro stereotype is really an image of the unorganized, irrational forces of American life, forces through which, by projecting them in forms of images of an easily dominated minority, the white individual seeks to be at home in the vast unknown world of America. Perhaps the object of the stereotype is not so much to crush the Negro as to console the white man.

—RALPH ELLISON, "TWENTIETH CENTURY FICTION," IN *SHADOW AND ACT*

"Fuck You. Shee-it. All right I'm going to give you an example. I heard that 350 of you white folks committed suicide by jumping off of the Golden Gate Bridge. And out of the 350 there was only two that was niggas . . . and one of them was pushed." The opening sequence of Ralph Bakshi's *Coonskin* (1975) is a joke delivered by two animated figures cast against the backdrop of a city sidewalk awash in the sound of sirens (fig. 1.1). These figures are so black that only the whites of their eyes and teeth make the sight of their face possible. They have the exaggerated physiognomy of distended lips and asses while dressed in hip 1970s urban clothes. Perhaps they are mutant cousins of the Disney blackbirds who in this case are too cool to care whether an elephant can fly. Hostile in its incongruent juxtaposing of suicide and racial violence (those who jumped and those who were pushed by persons unknown), the

FIG 1.1   A joke in the night. *Coonskin* (Ralph Bakshi, 1975).

joke directly addresses you white folks. An inciteful act of discriminate identification, the joke exceeds strictly humor, especially in light of its irrational incompleteness: For what does the joke serve as an example? Is this an example of poor taste, of mortality, of proclivities? The amusing repulsiveness of the joke occurs with the absence of discernible response cues as wit gives way to discomfort.

Following the cruel aside on suicide, the film cuts to a medium close-up of the right side of a black face, the face of Scatman Crothers (fig. 1.2). A man with a smile wider than his bowlegs, this shaded sage of American film and musical theater was known throughout his performing career as Mr. Bones, Smiley, Shoeshine Boy, Moses, Smoke, Big Ben, Reverend Markham (Pigmeat?), Duke, and Pop.[1] The majority of his characters do not have names but generic descriptors of slave naming and vernacular stardom. Yet he announces himself on this occasion with the sound of scat and the strumming of his guitar with an orality that does not subscribe immediately to the linguistic.[2] Nathanial Mackey recognizes scat as an act of improvisation that perhaps represents how black cultural production demonstrates the limits of conventional linguistics to account for historical trauma. Thus scat operates as a code: "I think of such things as scat, where the apparent mangling of articulate speech testifies to an 'unspeakable' history such singers are both vanquishers and victims of."[3] Amid this sonic ciphering of history, the lyrics rise to a naming: "Ah'm a Nigger Man." As Scatman sings, the film title appears to the right of his face as if the bluesman is singing the film into being. As the title sequence and the song

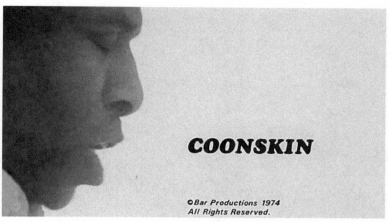

FIG 1.2 "Ah'm a Nigger Man." *Coonskin* (Ralph Bakshi, 1975).

draw to a close, the camera slowly tilts up, cross-fading into the beginning of the film. This tilt conveys a spatial measure of top and bottom and, tellingly, an *aboveground* and *underground*.[4] Just what is this film trying to do?

Coonskin has been known primarily as a "lost" film enmeshed in the lore of a cult film too daring and controversial for its time. The basic plot concerns two prison convicts (Randy and Pappy) who, having just escaped their cells, sit waiting in the southern evening just outside the prison walls for the arrival of a getaway car driven by Randy's friends (Sampson and Preacher), due at dawn.[5] Huddled in the shadows outside the scope of an arching spotlight, the young and impetuous Randy (Philip Thomas) stirs anxiously. In the absence of the "Once upon a time" standard, the older convict, Pappy (Scatman Crothers), says, "I just remembered. I use to know three guys just like you and your friends" (fig. 1.3). Thus begins the tale of Rabbit and his friends, Bear and Preacher Fox.[6] Pappy's vernacular storytelling is animated by the anthropomorphized figures of a rabbit, a bear, and a fox (fig. 1.4). The film shifts between live action and animation while also combining the two visual fields with the use of a Rotograph.[7]

The oral tradition gesture demonstrated by Pappy's story becomes the primary preoccupation of the film. Largely composed by animation, *Coonskin* significantly exposes the antiblack and fetishistic tendencies of the American imaginary so evident in the history of American animation and popular culture more broadly. Irene Kotlarz opines in regards to black representation in animation that despite the innocence of its form, "animation is important

FIG 1.3 "Once upon a time." *Coonskin* (Ralph Bakshi, 1975).

FIG 1.4 Brer Rabbit, Brer Fox, Brer Bear. *Coonskin* (Ralph Bakshi, 1975).

because the ideological force of its meanings can function precisely as an iron fist in the velvet glove of gags and sentimentality."[8] In *Coonskin* the presumed innocuousness of the form, the "just for fun" shtick of animation, provokes amusement and horror. In league with Ellison's mordant observations in this chapter epigraph, *Coonskin* demonstrates prickly knowledge of the distinction between madness curbed and madness rising in the film's purposeful trafficking in antiblack visual culture. This chapter focuses on how *Coonskin* as an enactment of film blackness disputes the crushing or consoling intention of antiblack iconography that Ellison describes.

Pappy's tale begins with Rabbit, Bear, and Fox having lost their home to foreclosure. They are subsequently forced to flee to escape the possibility of violent reprisals from the white citizens of a town that the mise-en-scène codes as southern. The trio's escape brings to mind the "Big Boy Leaves Home" scenario of an escape in the night due to quotidian clashes with white supremacy, although in this instance the trio must flee because Rabbit is forced to kill the local sheriff in self-defense after being thought responsible for the pimping of his daughter.[9] The fear of miscegenation and "the cult of true (white) womanhood" are derisively met by the impurity of a white girl who works in Darktown serving only colored clientele.[10]

Arriving in the briar patch of Harlem, they are confronted by the empty promises of their migration dreams. In Harlem they battle a duplicitous preacher, drug dealers, corrupt cops, and the Mob as their misadventures conjure up the "hayseed in the city" folly but with the twist of a rebel brand of cotton coming to Harlem. The figure of Miss America taunts them in sardonic vignettes over the course of the film. Rabbit attempts to keep the Mafia-controlled drug trade out of Harlem, and the film builds to the climax of a boxing match and the trapping (and eventual detonation) of the Godfather and his gay sons in a ringside Tar-Baby. The film closes with a cut back to live action and the approaching dawn as Randy and Pappy escape by car amid a hail of bullets, with Bear and Preacher at the wheel. Throughout the film New York City operates as the live-action backdrop for the escalating vernacular madness of the animated tale. The scripted and etched sear of animation in this profilmic tableau becomes further amplified by the recording of and eventual postsynchronization of sounds from city streets, bars, and restaurants.

In *Laughing Fit to Kill: Black Humor in the Fictions of Slavery*, Glenda Carpio questions whether the possibility exists for contemporary artists to untether stereotypes from their fetishistic moorings, even as she remains wary that such work risks ultimately reinforcing the lure of stereotypicality: "As the prominence of stereotype-derived art in the late-twentieth and early-twenty-first centuries attests, the idea of forever cleansing the American psyche of its racial fetishes may be not only a futile project but one that might fuel the power of the fetish all the more by making it taboo and therefore seductive."[11] The dilemma Carpio speaks of serves as the foundational question for this chapter and its examination of some of the ways *Coonskin* courts this risk of redirecting the force of antiblack iconography.

Coonskin represents the picaresque use of black vernacular culture from the antebellum and Reconstruction eras. The film stages slave folklore within a narrative resembling a blaxploitation film that parodically mimics Disney's *Song of the South*. Moreover the film strikes at the American imaginary and its dependence on "African Americanisms," what Toni Morrison calls "a fabricated brew of darkness, otherness, alarm, and desire that is uniquely American." The film vengefully redeploys aspects of this "fabricated brew" in a manner that perversely pivots on arresting antiblack visual culture for critical autopsy. This chapter echoes Morrison's own critical mission to examine the design of antiblack iconography and "avert the critical gaze from the racial object to the racial subject; from the described and imagined to the describers and imaginers; from the serving to the served."[12] *Coonskin* exhibits a bruising aversion particularly for those spectators and civilians untutored in how their innocuous pleasures have been cultivated by a legacy of white supremacist and antiblack terror. As well, the film addresses those who are hatefully indifferent.

My analysis focuses on reaccentuation in the context of art, race, and historiography. The writings of Mikhail Bakhtin are critical to understanding how the racial grotesque derives new meaning from old ideas. In "Discourse in the Novel," Bakhtin writes, "Every age re-accentuates in its own way the works of its immediate past. . . . Thanks to the intentional potential embedded in them, such works have proved capable of uncovering in each era and against ever new dialogizing backgrounds ever new aspects of meaning; their semantic content literally continues to grow, to further create out of itself."[13] By focusing on *Coonskin*, a film that complicates and contends with history and craft, I emphasize how the film stages the racial grotesque and compels new and timely encounters with those abhorrent American hegemonies focused on race, nation, and citizenship. *Coonskin* is always timely as the racial grotesque is never simply the anachronistic revival of a dead phenomenon but is also a creative practice attendant to the continued impact of racialization and white supremacy. In *Rabelais and His World*, Bakhtin considers the "carnivalesque" and "grotesque realism" in the work of François Rabelais, addressing the "material bodily principle" of medieval folk culture and detailing how the grotesque body, along with all manner of precious bodily fluids and orifices, performatively disturb and shock social hierarchies. Bakhtin stipulates, "The essential principle of grotesque realism is degradation, that is, the lowering of all that is high, spiritual, ideal, abstract; it is a transfer to the material level, to the sphere of earth and body in indissoluble form."[14] It is the indissoluble quality of this degradation and the irreconcilable tension of grotesque realism that drives my consideration of *Coonskin*.

Despite warranted accusations of homophobia and misogyny, this film has much to offer a consideration of antiblack visual culture. In fact it might provide an opportunity to understand (not forgive) its misogyny and homophobia by taking its antiblack critique into account. In particular I examine how the film's employment of the racial grotesque operates as both a parodic and a satirical critique of the affective economies of antiblack visual culture. Sara Ahmed frames emotions in terms of an economy or structure of exchange and transaction: "Affect does not reside in an object or sign, but is an effect of the circulation between objects and signs (=the accumulation of affective value). Signs increase in affective value as an effect of the movement between signs: the more signs circulate, the more affective they become."[15] Thus I consider how the film rhetorically mobilizes and parodically stages especially notorious aspects of American history attentive to the affective values of antiblack iconography. As a cumulative chain of recontextualizations, *Coonskin* disrupts the transactional web of antiblack nostalgia that has perpetuated and profited, in a material and affective sense, from black degradation.

Coonskin as visual historiography thrives on the ceaseless quality of history and also a sense of what Sianne Ngai calls "reanimation." In *Ugly Feelings*, Ngai analyzes three distinct figurations of animation and suggests that "racial stereotypes and clichés, cultural images that are perversely both dead and alive, can be critically countered not just by making the images *more* 'dead' (say, by attempting to stop their circulation), but also, though in more equivocal fashion, by *reanimating* them."[16] *Coonskin* reanimates the iconography of antiblack visual culture as a metapicture that cogently contests the rendering of blackness, national mythology, the circuits of pop culture, and cultural memory in the key of the racial grotesque.[17]

Here's a Little Story That Must Be Told

Before continuing with a closer textual analysis of the film, I focus on the production and exhibition history of the film and the importance of the narrative premise. Following the success of *Fritz the Cat* (1972) and *Heavy Traffic* (1973) with his Bakshi Productions Company, Ralph Bakshi began writing the script for *Coonskin* under the working title *Harlem Nights* after abandoning an adaptation of Herbert Selby's *Last Exit to Brooklyn* (1964): "I told [the investors] it was a remake of *Song of the South* set in Harlem. I told them I want to make the Uncle Remus stories and then I started to make my film. . . . It was a rope a dope. What these guys thought I was making and what I was making were two different things."[18] Born in Israel and a decidedly nonblack, Russian Jew who grew up in the Brooklyn neighborhood of Brownsville, Bakshi became the immediate face and target of the project.[19]

Billed as its premiere, the screening of *Coonskin* at the University of Iowa took place on 7 September 1974. The film then had a work-in-progress showing on 12 November at the Museum of Modern Art in New York City. The screening was disrupted by a protesting contingent of the Congress of Racial Equality (CORE) led by Al Sharpton and was followed by a disastrous question-and-answer session with a very combative audience and an unsympathetic Bakshi.[20] In the wake of the MoMA screening, Elaine Parker, the chair of CORE's Harlem chapter, commented, "It depicts us as slaves, hustlers, and whores. It's a racist film to me, and very insulting. . . . If it is released, there's no telling what we might do."[21] The film was beset by CORE-coordinated protests and nationwide pressure from the black press throughout the year leading up to its release. Its black actors were branded as "traitors to the race," and the black cultural nationalist creed of art as an implement of consciousness raising decried the film as a criminal act against black people: "This movie will not go on at the expense of the black community. . . . We charge them [Bakshi, Ruddy, and Paramount] with high crimes against black people—stereotyping and degrading blacks. . . . If you try to stop a factory from polluting the environment, is that censorship? *Coonskin* is a form of mental pollution."[22]

The film underwent numerous edits and dialogue replacement over much of 1975. This postproduction tinkering led to release delays that pushed the film further down the studio calendar.[23] The continued controversy and activist protest was the purported reason Paramount eventually dropped *Coonskin*.[24] Soon afterward, a distribution deal for the film was then negotiated with the independent Bryanston Distribution Company not long before the film's scheduled premiere.[25] Opening in August 1975 to a handful of bomb threats and smoke bomb incidents at theaters throughout New York City, *Coonskin* received a limited run throughout the United States and the United Kingdom, sometimes under the title *Bustin' Out*.[26] For most of the press, criticism of the film was cemented by the MoMA screening. Almost universally dismissed by critics and with an atrocious box office performance, the film was abruptly pulled from theaters after only a two-week run when Bryanston Distributors went bankrupt. In 1987 the picture resurfaced on video under the title *Streetfight*. Over the next two decades *Coonskin* primarily circulated on video-sharing websites, in bootleg DVDs, and on a much-heralded "ghost orchid," a Japanese laserdisc.[27]

Coonskin is often billed as the "anti–*Song of the South*" film. A live-action and animated adaptation of tales from Joel Chandler Harris's *Uncle Remus: His Songs and His Sayings* (1880), Disney's *Song of the South* (Harve Foster and Wilfred Jackson, 1946) contextualizes the transcribed slave tales into a family melodrama centered on the relationship that develops between Uncle Remus, an old black man, and Johnny, a young white boy. Uncle Remus tells the child the stories of Brer Rabbit, and these scenes of oral instruction subsequently trigger the film's transitions into animated versions of the tales that parallel the family melodrama by offering life lessons to Johnny.

Song of the South suffers from spatiotemporal indecisiveness: the setting might be a family estate or a plantation. The film hints at being historically set during Reconstruction, yet the time period bears a heavy antebellum inflection. These slippage problems that plague the Disney film echo those in Harris's work. James Snead notes the conundrum shared by Harris and *Song* as a compounding of "two fictions": "The reader/viewer is asked to believe two fictions at once: that pre-war life on the plantation was a time of happy conviviality between black and white; and that the upheavals of the Civil War have done little to change this state of affairs—the former fiction is balm for the credulous, the latter a refuge for the desperate, possibly even for those Southerners and Northerners hoping to efface by nostalgic denial a reality that could not be faced."[28] Abbreviated stagings of some of the Brer tales occur in *Coonskin* as the film's intertextual petulance supplements the fissured twoness of the *Song of the South* most immediately with the prison as new-age plantation conceit and Pappy as storyteller and foil to Uncle Remus. Pappy renews the vernacular specificity of the fables, a specificity that rises above the universal humanist pandering of Disney. In the case of *Coonskin* the profane restaging of Walt Disney's pet project signals something greater than the misleading "anti-*Song*" moniker. *Coonskin* deliberately resembles *Song*, but its deviation viciously signifies on more than Disney. The true crux of the film's menace must be understood as anti–New South.

The New South ideal that arose during Reconstruction framed the history of the antebellum Old South and the Confederacy in romantic and medieval terms of nobility: "'Lost Causers' equated themselves with the knights of medieval England. They had supposedly lived by their own unique and unbreakable code of honor; had administered their plantations in an enlightened and progressive manner, in the process of producing happy, smiling darkies who knew their place in society and were content with their servitude."[29] The New South and its fantastical design of Dixie would posit the antebellum past as a lost utopian cause. Dixie would be a place of racial harmony with a healthy integration of the new technologies of the Industrial Age to curtail dependency on an agrarian (i.e., slave-based) economy and thus would be the progressive prototype for America in the new century.[30]

Harris's *Uncle Remus* and the eight volumes that followed are significantly aligned with the New South revisionism of slavery. The stories are framed by a heavy romanticism of the South that evades the vernacular folklore's agency. This agential narration represents the way slaves used these tales to interpret their existential condition and survive. Lawrence Levine explains, "Such stories leave no doubt that slaves were aware of the need for role playing. But animal tales reveal more than this; they emphasize in brutal detail the irrationality and anarchy that rules Man's universe. In tale after tale violence and duplicity are pictured as existing for their own sake."[31] *Coonskin* amplifies the spatiotemporal particularities of these vernacular tales with an alienating and incriminating deliberateness.

Disqualifying the seditious quality of the folklore, Harris's Remus collections and the subsequent Disney adaptation act as infantilizing revisions of the black vernacular. Frantz Fanon notes, "It is perfectly obvious what these stories are all about. Br'er Rabbit gets into conflicts with almost all the other animals in creation, and naturally he is always the winner. These stories belong to the oral tradition of the plantation Negroes. Therefore it is relatively easy to recognize the Negro in his remarkably ironic and wary disguise as a rabbit. In order to protect themselves against their own unconscious masochism, which impels them to rapturous admiration of the (black) rabbit's prowess, the whites have tried to drain these stories of their aggressive potential."[32] Offering pop lullabies in the place of revolt, Harris's collections diminished the unruly blackness of the animal fables. Yet despite this abatement and pernicious suspension of the liveliness of the folklore, *Coonskin* exploits the untranslatable excess of the tales and their original intent and design. If for Walt Disney *imagineering* was a term meant to signify imagination and engineering, then in the case of *Coonskin* that term might denote its excoriation of the Disney platitudes of *Song of the South*. As a disobedient adaptation of *Uncle Remus: His Songs and His Sayings*, *Coonskin* disputes the veracity and nostalgia claims of the Disney film and its source.[33] Bakshi's film provocatively devises the mutual presence of Reconstruction and the Second

Reconstruction within its narrative.[34] This structural premise suggests shared features between the Reconstruction and post–civil rights eras as the association of the two coalesces around historical conditions, the persistence of white supremacy, and the legacy of antiblack iconography. In this way the simple truths of *Coonskin* supplant the sacredness of bucolic charm with blasphemous urbanism, positing trauma in the place of nostalgia with the force of the racial grotesque.[35]

Bakshi's combination of two modalities, live action and animation, in the service of a film dedicated to the profane staging of blackness inspirited by the racial grotesque compels a rather consequential point about blackness, liveness, and animation. Focusing on the "slippery mouth" syndrome of the stop-motion movement of the plastic mouths on the Claymation figures in *The PJs* to simulate speaking, Ngai observes, "*The PJs* reminds us that there can be ways of inhabiting a social role that actually distort its boundaries, changing the status of 'role' from that which purely confines or constricts to the site at which new possibilities for human agency might be explored."[36] These slippery gestures, what Ngai identifies as "surplus movement," connote something beyond the design of the figures' animators. For *Coonskin* the combination of live action and animation results in antiblack renderings in the everyday spaces of their conception. It would be a mistake to dismiss the animated figures in the live-action spaces as anachronisms or fallacious. The discordance signals an ideological circuit, a ceaselessness. Throughout *Coonskin* the animated figures bear the timeless tendencies of antiblack visuality, but with the difference of a blunt deflection evident in their slippery speech that defies their wretched form.

That Joke Isn't Funny Anymore

In the remainder of this chapter I focus on a pregnant pause (a little over two minutes in length), a moment of intermission within the film that functions as a mise-en-abyme or a textual and ideological summation of the film from within the film. This intermission begins in a break from Pappy's animated narrative, as he and Randy wait outside the prison walls for the dawn and their escape. Pappy implores the frustrated Randy to be patient and insists that he has to finish his story. As Pappy restarts his tale, the scene crossfades back to animation as the voice-over describes the high spirits in Harlem over the death of a corrupt cop who acted as muscle for the Mob. Emblematic of the mood of Uptown and against a full moon and rolling, misty clouds the central image in the frame is a strolling couple. The cel processing of their animated movement resembles the human locomotion schemes of Eadweard Muybridge, whereas the features of the couple are a tropic compendium of black stereotypicality familiar to the graphic arts (especially the legacy of American animation): bulging eyes, swollen lips, optic white teeth, and skin that is blacker than a thousand midnights. Clad in hip garb, they possess the fetishistic swagger of Carl Van Vechten's "nigger heaven," an interpretative measure of Harlem replete with opulent exotics and decadent primitivism. In midstride the couple's backdrop crossfades to the quotidian: a group of black men in a barbershop humming and handclapping in time. This sacred and secular dialectic episode of black expressive culture—one part amen corner and one part the Apollo—undercuts the foregrounded couple as they eventually fade away.

The syncopated breakdown of the chants and claps signals the rotoscoped arrival of a figure as rattling in animated appearance as the couple—an old, barefoot black man dressed in an oversized bowtie, one-button overalls, a frayed dress shirt, and a tattered, long coat. His ratty elegance evokes the "house negro," the slave who works in the plantation master's house clad in the master's hand-me-downs, a dutiful part of the master's family. Moreover the figure inhabits the minstrel pose of a comic mimic of upper-crust (white) status. He brings to mind one presumed coon in particular: Uncle Tom. Yet, as this Tom begins to speak, his oration quickly exceeds typical coonfare. With a direct address to the camera he begins, "Y'all remember when we use to run and fight for that empty white apartment? Shit, this nigger be sitting at home, heard some white folks would be movin' out ten blocks away and I'd run like a hurricane to get there first. By the time this sucker would get there, there would be three million brothers jumpin' all over the fire escapes and three million more Jews packin' and runnin' the other way. Shit, we all got apartments. Shit, we got the whole neighborhood, man." Continuing his direct address, he emphatically exclaims "Shit" and flips off the spectator ("Fuck you"; fig. 1.5). He then reaches up, grabs his shoulders, and with a hard pull and the shrill sound of tearing, strips off his skin. Throwing down this skin, his "coonskin," he shudders with laughter. The coonskin lies in a ghoulish heap of steaming carrion with hollowed eyes and a distended tongue. Where Tom once stood there now stands the body that was choked beneath: a soul brother clad in the accoutrements of "black is beautiful" and the cultural signifiers of soul as a style of black political culture (figs. 1.6–1.8).[37]

While Tom delivers his direct address, the background cuts between the

FIG 1.5 "Fuck you." *Coonskin* (Ralph Bakshi, 1975).

barbershop and two other scenes: Confederate soldiers in battle, and whites and blackface whites celebrating on a plantation porch. The textured tableau conscripts a cinematic staging of historical past, plantation revelry and Johnny Rebs rallying against Yankee aggression. Together the two scenes evoke the contextual history and ideological frames of Uncle Tom (figs. 1.9–1.10). The scenes are from D. W. Griffith's short *His Trust: The Faithful Devotion and Self-Sacrifice of an Old Negro Servant* (1910). The film, and the sequel that followed in the same year, *His Trust Fulfilled*, focuses on a plantation house servant named George who faithfully serves and protects "his" white family during the Civil War, when the master, a Confederate officer, is killed in battle. The blackface character intones the same specious attitudes of happy darkies, plantation bliss, and the noble cause of the Confederacy that would be fully realized in Griffith's *The Birth of a Nation* (1915).[38] The film acted as the cinematic realization of the New South ideal by providing a visual trans-literation of the ideal's view of slavery, the Civil War, and the necessary condition of the black. Griffith's war films exceedingly validated the white suprem-acist intent of the New South by providing a substantial narrative conceit and visual inscription. In this way the insert of these two scenes signal part of *Coonskin*'s critique of the legacy of American cinema and American history with the contradistinction of an unbound Tom.

Tom's self-evisceration utilizes the trope of the tear that is ubiquitous in animation, the comic gag of someone cloaked in the zippered skin of another: *Corporealist zippitous*. Yet this racialized sense of the tear and the coonskin

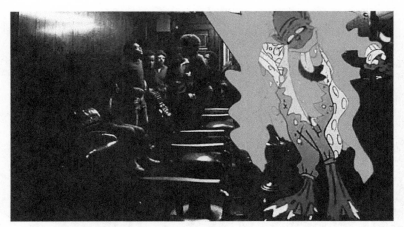

FIG 1.6 The tear. *Coonskin* (Ralph Bakshi, 1975).

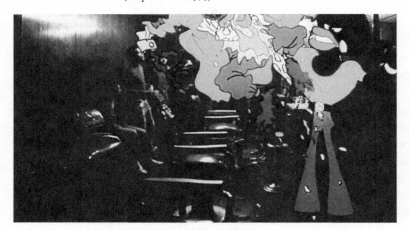

FIG 1.7 The coonskin. *Coonskin* (Ralph Bakshi, 1975).

FIG 1.8 The soul brother beneath. *Coonskin* (Ralph Bakshi, 1975).

FIGS 1.9–1.10 In the shadow of D. W. Griffith. *Coonskin* (Ralph Bakshi, 1975).

accomplishes more than an idle nod to the tradition of cartoon masquerade. A coonskin is literally a raccoon's pelt, but the visualizing logic of white supremacy metonymically links the coonskin to the skin of the black (the "coon").[39]

Importantly the coonskin illustrates the "crushing objecthood" of what Fanon understood as epidermalization, the visualizing process whereby black skin becomes overdetermined by the hegemonies of antiblack whiteness as the epidermal schema. This process regulates the visibility of race as a taxonomic impulse whereby skin functions as the definitive mark of racial being: "It [skin] is not a piece or component of the body but its fateful wrapping."[40] In *Black Skin, White Masks*, Fanon is met with the surveying look of a frightened white child ("Look, a Negro") and experiences a shattering of being indicative of the broader way that black skin circulates in the visual field as a sign of the abject. The epidermal schema instantiates skin as the connotative winding sheet of black being; it acts as the perceptual and effacing mark of the black: "On that day, completely dislocated, unable to be abroad with the other, the white man, who mercifully imprisoned me, I took myself far off from my own presence, far indeed, and made myself an object. What else could it be for me but an amputation, an excision, a hemorrhage that splattered my whole body with black blood?" For Fanon epidermalization produces an irresolute disorientation, a disjoining negation of being to such a degree that once the black attempts to exercise some measure of self-consciousness, he or she is met by fragmentation and a deeply cathected inferiority: "I was responsible not only for my body, for my race, for my ancestors. I subjected myself to an objective examination, I discovered my blackness, my ethnic characteristics; and I was battered down by tom-toms, cannibalism, intellectual deficiency, fetishism, racial defects, slave-ships, and above all else, above all: 'Sho' good eatin.'"[41] Fanon's psychic self-examination discovers a swirling catalogue of historical tropes that act as psychically available narrative triggers of black inhumanity.

Through epidermalization skin becomes the delimiting and tainted abbreviation of being. The coonskin tear imparts the distorting impact of epidermalization, as evident by the suggestion of an underneath as Tom loses his skin and forcefully derails the epidermal binding procedure. Tom's self-excoriation represents a graphic and repudiating struggle with the hemorrhaging cloak of abjection and the antiblack inscriptions of the epidermal schema. As an act of resignifying, the tear provokes a disarticulation of Tom. Once this Tom's masking of minstrel harmlessness is torn away, there remains a body denied. The soul brother now returns the gaze in the spirit of reckless eyeballing and thus intimates militancy and rebellion.

The somatic spectacle of the coonskin tear indicates a body sick with historiographic confliction. First, there is the incarnation of Tom as the abolitionist emblem proffered by Harriet Beecher Stowe's *Uncle Tom's Cabin* (1852). Second, there is the later derivation of Tom popularized by the blackface minstrel adaptations of Stowe's work that antithetically diffused its sociopolitical design to the point that it would eventually become an abject clown of the stage that connoted black buffoonery and monkeyshines more generally.[42] Third, there is the idiomatic expression "Uncle Tom," an ethical judgment of one who acquiesces to the antiblack tendencies of white supremacy with unadulterated subservience. This signifying sweep, comprising tragic piety, theatrical trope, and conjecture on blackness, provokes a simultaneity of ideological purposes that exacerbates the innate tensions of the Tom figure. In other words, the Tom tear illustrates a sign in a state of crisis, a sign riddled with contradictory duties that ultimately compels a graphic refusal. The tear denies the overburdening swell of crushing connotations that make up Tom's impossible contexture. The liminal suspension of Tom between historiographies with contesting motivations produces a resounding effect.

Tom's multiaccentual quality, the way it represents multiple forms and meanings, points to a figure emerging from the stasis of stereotypicality as a chronotope. For Bakhtin the chronotope represents "the intrinsic connectedness of temporal and spatial relationships that are artistically expressed in literature."[43] The meanings emanating from the *Coonskin* Tom are generated by multiple temporalities (e.g., the Civil War, Reconstruction, the 1970s) with distinct mediations of craft and social function. That is, this Tom possesses the chronotopic ability to infer history and discourse as a figural fiction that illuminates a dynamics of race and power.[44]

Tom's chronotopic quality exposes several ideological transparencies. He has been conscripted by several hegemonic purposes that stir the Tom icon beyond its designed implementation or social instrumentality. The noncompliance of this Tom does not assuage what Ellison recognized as the potential anxieties that the presumption of the stereotype's naturalness is calculated to quell: "Hence whatever else the Negro stereotype might be as a social instrumentality, it is also a key figure in a magic rite by which the white American seeks to resolve the dilemma arising between his democratic beliefs and certain antidemocratic practices, between his acceptance of the sacred democratic belief that all men are created equal and his treatment of every tenth man as though he were not."[45] Black stereotypicality serves as an enabling symbol for the belief that American democracy serves all in an equal or acceptable measure.

Furthermore the *Coonskin* Tom represents a rebel threat choked beneath an antiblack figural binding of Tom as the amicable and loving companion. The incongruousness of benevolence (Tom's form) and acrimony (Tom's speech) typifies the disavowed intent of much antiblack visual culture.[46] In the case of the *Coonskin* Tom the tear and the reveal of rebellion beneath disintegrate the enabling of the stereotype as normative and coherent. The film's acrimonious emplotment of the racial grotesque acts as a metacritical impulse to strike back ("Fuck you") and to disinter the liminal black figure from the deadening rhetoric of black inhumanity and white paternalism. With rebellion as a core value, *Coonskin* acts as a slow and brutal unraveling of that wholly American collusion of cultural nostalgia, antiblackness, and white supremacy—a collusion that sometimes best defines American democracy.

As a black body doubly occupied, the Tom infers a particular sense of Du Boisian double consciousness. For W. E. B. Du Bois double consciousness represents the black existential condition in America, with black personhood devastatingly mediated by an embodiment crisis. As Du Bois famously wrote, "It is a peculiar sensation, this double consciousness, this sense of always looking at one's self through the eyes of others, of measuring one's soul by the tape of a world that looks on in amused contempt and pity. One ever feels his two-ness—an American, a Negro; two souls, two thoughts, two unreconciled strivings; two warring ideals in one dark body, whose dogged strength alone keeps it from being torn asunder."[47] This crisis of being an American and a Negro, two seemingly irremediable categories of consciousness inhabiting one body, demonstrates how Du Bois's work pushes us "to see identity and race as both effects and cornerstones of visual processes, as both products and producers of visual culture."[48] Tom's performative negotiation with this conditional twoness typifies the complicated nexus of blackness, visuality, and nation. *Coonskin* exhibits an affinity with Du Bois in the way it exploits the distance between products and producers as a visual construction fraught with issues of historical intent and performative opportunity. The signifying fury of the film makes clear its familiarity with the history of race and the arts as a visualizing process.

There is another sense of twoness and liminality that emanates from the *Coonskin* Tom. As a body doubly inhabited and in graphic struggle with itself, the figure suggests a sense of the grotesque body. In *Rabelais and His World*, Bakhtin identifies the grotesque body as a prevalent element of the folk cultural practice performed in the carnivals of Medieval Europe: "The grotesque image *reflects a phenomenon in transformation, an as yet unfinished metamorphosis, of death and birth, growth and becoming.* The relation to time is one determining trait of the grotesque image. The other indispensable trait is ambivalence. For in this image we find both poles of transformation, *the old and the new, the dying and the procreating, the beginning and end of metamorphosis.*"[49] With the old Tom and the new soul brother, as well as the coonskin tear as the sign of a beginning and an end, this passage resonates with the distinct brand of rude incongruence and performative ambivalence enacted by *Coonskin*. Fundamentally the film's exercise of the racial grotesque stems from the paradox produced by the antinomy of human and nonhuman, the way that antiblack iconography, like the stereotype, acts as a fixed rendering of a person as a thing. As Leonard Cassuto advises, "To view people as non-human is an open invitation to the most fundamental and enduring category problems." Therefore the racial grotesque always strikes at the antithetical and constitutive core that informs the resulting regimes of antiblack truth and knowledge. Tom as a grotesque body is an ambivalent one as its contradictoriness and contrariness represent the instigation of "a constant intrusion on order, an anomalous agent of chaos."[50] The tear repudiates the *looking at one's self through the eyes of others* and signifies the vehemence of a human thing as a spectacle of negative reverence.[51]

The coonskin tear has a collateral relationship to the aesthetic and epistemological break toward a more radical sense of blackness insisted on by the artistic wing of the Black Consciousness Movement, the Black Arts Movement (BAM). The tear parallels the interpretative shift from biological determinism to a cultural politics of self-definition.[52] The art inspired by the period's engagement with the idea of a black aesthetic posed unadulterated critiques of America and richly artistic assessments of the black existential condition. Kimberly Benston notes, "We can see the Black Arts Movement, not as creed or even as method, but rather as a continuously shifting field of struggle and revision in which the relations between politics, representation, history, and revolution are productively revalued."[53] Devoted to the art of black cultural politics, the BAM rigorously challenged the meaning of race, the terms of liberation, and the means of cultural production.[54]

The soul brother figure signifies some of the BAM ethos because the tear is symbolic of the era's "politics of transvaluation" and the promotion of a new standard of art attuned to the political and cultural possibilities of black people.[55] This historical formation informs the soul brother's eruption of the recoded blackness hushed beneath the Tom. The period's tone of black cultural power and the refusal to expect anything less than black liberation are evident in the prerelease title of Bakshi's film: *Coonskin No More.*

The film's conversance with cultural nationalism informs its relationship to the blaxploitation film cycle, though it does not easily fit the general perception of blaxploitation films. As opposed to the exploitation subject matter of sex, drugs, and monstrosities of various kinds, blaxploitation films were often clumsily framed in response to black cultural nationalism. Some films were vague about any concrete or complex allegiance to the movement; many films aped the tropes associated with Black Power, the forbidden topic or taboo in the classic sense of exploitation cinema.[56] In various statements during the period between the MoMA screening and the eventual release of *Coonskin,*

Bakshi railed against what he termed the "Superfly type" and cultural nationalism more broadly.[57] In one telling sequence, the three the hard way of Bear, Fox, and Rabbit happen upon Reverend Simple Savior's black revolution church. As a follower of Black Jesus, Simple performs a tortured sermon on black dispossession in the shadow of white oppression as manifest in landlords, police, and pain. The sermon includes an interpretative dance by Savior while being struck by his coal-black attendants, who are costumed in white paper-bag hoods, with a wrecking ball, mace, club, and chain. Corpulent and nude, Savior gives the impression of a permed capon.

His theater of the oppressed, his mau-mauing confidence man routine, peaks with his being hoisted to the top of a luminous crucifix. Perched on the cross, he pulls out two pistols and shoots behind a trio of photos that drop down in the following order: John Wayne on the left, Elvis Presley on the right, and Richard Nixon in the middle. The hail of bullets produces confetti that crosses from the animated to the live-action reveling black crowd over Savior's chant of "Join the revolution." The sequence highlights Bakshi's problematic equating of the 1970s political culture of white conservatism and the Second Reconstruction with a reductive framing of black nationalists as merely "kill whitey" holy rollers.[58]

Marketed to inner-city audiences and driven by the finance principle of low investment and high return, blaxploitation thrived through a commodification of black cultural nationalism as pop phenomena.[59] Yet there are other values attributable to blaxploitation besides the strict terms of capital and industry. Kara Keeling contends, "Blaxploitation played a profoundly important role in adjudicating between a range of political positions vying for recognition as Black Power during the late 1960s and early 1970s and in presenting their resolution in the form of common-sense black nationalism."[60] *Coonskin* offers a very particular emboldened struggle against the Man that ultimately problematizes the blanket presumptions and values attributed to blaxploitation and all black films of this period. Bakshi's film, like other films of the time (e.g., *The Spook Who Sat by the Door* [Ivan Dixon, 1973], *Ganja & Hess* [Bill Gunn, 1973], *Wattstax* [Mel Stuart, 1973], and *Bone* [Larry Cohen, 1972]), were made possible by the popular cycle, but it and many other films exceeded what the industry, critics, and moviegoing public expected. What keeps blaxploitation vital is its ever-reverberating shock of black visual resistance, the possibility of a cinematic recoding of blackness. The execution of this recoding opportunity by *Coonskin* is indeed informed by a cultural nationalist muse, though the film cannot be classified exclusively in the categorical terms of blaxploitation cinema.[61] The film stages a radical sense of blackness with an amplification of the generative cultural nationalist traces of black cultural production rather than merely titillating pop posturing.[62] Within this tangle of pop political craft *Coonskin* thrives as a transgressive and productively bad blaxploitation object. As much as Bakshi disparaged and dismissed Black Power, the film cycle indeed enabled the possibility and informed the ideological function of *Coonskin* far beyond the "remake of *Song of the South* set in Harlem" pitch.

Darktown Strutters

Cutting from the soul brother, the next part of the *Coonskin* intermission bears out a key feature of the preceding tear sequence: the instrumentality of antiblack visual culture. This portion of the intermission is primarily composed of footage of a dance revue, a jazz orchestra, swing couples, and the comic styling of jazzed vaudeville as the performances span the 1920s to the 1940s. Tom's direct address mentioned how housing opportunities ("empty white apartments") and exiting Jews equal in number to arriving African Americans eventually led to the formation of a black neighborhood ("Shit, we got the whole neighborhood, man"). What is this neighborhood that experienced this diasporic changing of hands?

Tom's ribald account refers to the period in the early twentieth century when Jews gained greater access to housing outside of Harlem just as African Americans were leaving the Jim Crow South for the Northeast. Thus the jazz and dance montage depicts bodies moving to and moved by the promise of the Great Migration. The Harlem of *Coonskin*, the cinematic Uptown, suggests multiple intersections and imbrications of cultural histories and American urbanism.[63] This consequential aftermath of the historical flight Uptown would eventually lead the formation of a Harlem that Alain Locke tagged the Black Metropolis: "In Harlem, Negro life is seizing upon its first chances for group expression and self-determination. It is—or promises to be—a race capital."[64] With attention to this spirit of self-design, Richard Powell reimagines the Harlem of the 1920s and 1930s as more generative than merely vogue as it came to represent a geopolitical metaphor for modernity and an icon for an increasingly complex black diasporic presence in the world.[65]

The montage as visual historiography wrecks the presumption of black expressive culture as atrophied or without a tradition. Its focus on black performativity infers a connection to the Harlem Renaissance that historically corresponds with Tom's exposition. Bookended by the end of World War I and the beginning of the Great Depression, the Harlem Renaissance is characterized by a loosely aligned clustering of black poets, writers, dramatists, sculptors, painters, musicians, and dancers in Harlem. There are various opinions of the critical legacy of the Harlem Renaissance; William Maxwell offers the following assessment: "A self-conscious, Harlem-centered field of sometimes overlapping, sometimes contradictory attempts by black artists to link African American identity and history to the idea and material circumstances of an increasingly worldly U.S. modernity. These attempts occasionally took the (characteristically modernist) form of nostalgia for a superior premodern past, but the underlying force was on racializing the modern, and vice versa."[66] This proliferation of artists coincided with the conception of a black body politic attendant to emerging discourses on blackness and art practice. The Harlem Renaissance and New Negro trace of *Coonskin* evokes a history along with positing its place in that tradition.

The montage tellingly features one insert shot of modern dancers in front of a 1970s movie theater. Despite its clearly being of a different historical moment than the rest of the montage, this shot does suggest a historical scope. The historiographic irregularity in the wake of the coonskin tear articulates a tie to the agency and craft of preceding eras, whose own respective tears become framed as antecedent practices of resistance, forbearing acts of black modernism.[67] Although indirectly associated with the BAM's insistence on self-definition, *Coonskin* in this portion of the interlude suggests that it is part of a wider historical continuum.

Significantly, the sequence alludes to how jazz and dance acted as a performative challenge to the Industrial Age as a kind of stylized negotiation with new technologies. For example, Joel Dinerstein notes, "Through contact with Euro-American musicians and cultural elites, as well as with black workers and the urban soundscape, African American artists integrated the speed, drive, precision, and rhythmic flow of factory work and the modern cities into a nationally (and internationally) unifying cultural form: big band swing."[68] Thus in the hot house newsreel footage there are elements of the performances that gesture to the machine, industrialization, and mass production as the footage of vaudeville takes on a vernacular rendering of automation quality. Thus this portion of the intermission speculates on how music and dance grapple with the specter of the machine, with a performative commitment to innovation and improvisation as processes of redefinition.

Following on the heels of the coonskin tear, dance and jazz seemingly provide a brief respite from the furious semiotics of the racial grotesque. Yet black performativity as resistance to automation takes on particular relevance for the portion of the intermission that follows.

My Name Is Peaches

Before . . . our joy at the demise of Aunt Jemima and Uncle Tom approaches the indecent, we had better ask whence they sprang, how they lived? Into what limbo have they vanished?

—JAMES BALDWIN, "MANY THOUSANDS GONE"

From Harlem the film cuts again to the full moon backdrop. The foreground features the customary gag of the cartoon chase, yet this chase is far less satisfying in its zaniness and slapstick antics. The pursued is a screaming pancake. Scampering in close pursuit is a black woman firing a revolver. As each shot ricochets behind the pancake, it hoots and skips a desperate jig. A bountiful woman, the pursuer is crowned by a bandana and wears an apron over a red dress, dotted orange. It gives her the tenuous look of a field hand crossed with a harlequin. Eventually, after much circling, she leaps onto the pancake, flattening it dead. Chuckling, the woman rises from her crushing squat and reveals Aunt Jemima familiarly cast in the syrup-bottle pose (figs. 1.11–1.14).

The crux of this cartoon chase centers on a product assaulted by its trademark. Rosemary Coombe details how branding inspires brand loyalty by lending authenticity to its product and acting as an intimate mark that the consumer is acquainted with and subsequently seeks out. In this way the trademark "maintains and garners exchange value in the market, alluring consumers in its endless uniformity with promises of both standardization and distinction."[69] In the early twentieth century the Aunt Jemima trademark, as a result of the products to which it was indentured, came to represent the new mammy of the Industrial Age, a sign of domestic comfort, mass production, and modern commercial advertising. Like many racialized trademarks that came out of Reconstruction and off the minstrel stage (e.g., Uncle Mose, Uncle Remus, Mandy the Maid, Deacon Jones, Sambo), the way these commercial emblems inspired trust and the intimacy of brand loyalty is troubling.

The racial grotesque strategy of *Coonskin* poses Aunt Jemima in a way that deliberately disturbs the innocuousness of the trademark's dutiful service. If the Jemima trademark is imbued with a personality, then what happens when

FIG 1.11 A cartoon chase. *Coonskin* (Ralph Bakshi, 1975).

FIG 1.12 A cartoon chase. *Coonskin* (Ralph Bakshi, 1975).

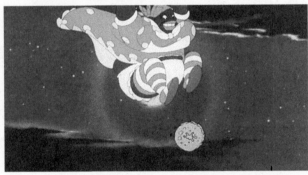

FIG 1.13 A trademark attacks. *Coonskin* (Ralph Bakshi, 1975).

FIG 1.14 The death of a product. *Coonskin* (Ralph Bakshi, 1975).

this embodied member of the household displays the capacity to murder the whole family as easily as she dispatched the flapjack? The historical precedent of slavery, the commercial exploitation of black bodies as laboring objects devoid of subject status, textures and historicizes Jemima's irritable play. Subsequently an emblem with personality that violently disputes the use of its labor raises the prospect of slave rebellion. The mammy intertext of Aunt Jemima exposes Jemima as brood of mammy, an icon that continues the tradition of domesticity and undesirable nurturer. But its circulation in the New South offers the consumer the added bonus of complicity with slavery in the form of branded utility.

The anti–New South ways of *Coonskin* expose the authenticating function of slavery for Jemima as the film again offers an instance of a racialized sign's instability as an occasion for the racial grotesque. As a fantastical prop, the Jemima trademark latently signifies historical erasure and the collusion between the New South ideal and white supremacy and American popular culture that Doris Witt points out is indicative of the fundamental liminality of Jemima: "Aunt Jemima was situated between two worlds: capitalism and slavery, technology and art, standardization and improvisation, money and love."[70]

The Aunt Jemima trademark's place in the American imaginary and commercial market is secured by what Lauren Berlant recognizes as an ideological indexing of values that propel the trademark's circulation: "[Aunt Jemima's] condensation of racial nostalgia, white national memory, and progressive history was a symptomatic, if not important, vehicle for post–Civil War national consolidation."[71] The pleasure that the Jemima trademark provides and the continued success it has achieved are possible only if this condensation is not made palpable. In this way the trademark is determined by a "lenticular logic," what Tara McPherson argues represents the process whereby imagery of the South is mediated through "a schema by which histories or images that are actually copresent get presented (structurally, ideologically) so that only one of the images can be seen at a time."[72] For the Jemima trademark this lenticular logic demonstrates how the mammy intertext cannot be occulted for it is the mammy that enables and confirms Jemima.

When one shakes a box of Jemima pancake mix, one does not expect to hear shackles, but "is it an accident that the proliferation of people of colour on food products historically associated with the slave trade (sugar, grain products — rice, wheat — coffee, tea and tobacco) is a mainstay of advertising?"[73] An industrialized mammy, Jemima represents not emancipation or historical reconciliation but the reiteration of slave labor in the nonagrarian mode of industrialization and mass production; the trace of slavery remains evident due to her look and continued exchange value as commodity fetish.[74] For *Coonskin* the racial grotesque exposes the historical trace of slavery as a ghost in the machine or *coon ex machina*, an "ontological residue" that cannot be prohibited or fundamentally denied.[75]

The scene's grotesque disruption or return of the repressed with regard to the Jemima trademark furiously speculates on how the mammy in the Jemima strikes back, disinterring the trademark from its ornamental status: "They have made you a shrine and a humorous fable, but they kept you a slave while they were able."[76] The seditious Jemima of *Coonskin* disarticulates itself from the hermeneutic regiment of the New South.[77] A trademark unbound, this Jemima has become a weaponized tchotchke, a mammy whose lullabies intone militancy and indictment. The unfinalizable liminality of the icon's new-old imagining is exposed; Jemima is now an uncollectible collectible, a vicious souvenir that can no longer be reclaimed as a viable "narrative commodity."[78]

Nobody Knows My Name

Cutting from the forthright Jemima, the tableau features a seated figure leaning against a lamppost. It is Miss America, a buxom and freckled sexpot in a red, white, and blue jumpsuit with high heels. Long blond hair blows across her face and a guitar lies in her lap (fig. 1.15). As a stand-in for "Liberty" and "America," she appears sporadically in vignettes throughout *Coonskin*, preventing the threat of black rebellion by direct and indirect means. Standing to her right is Tom, recloaked in the coonskin. Scratching his head, he then clenches his fists and begins to recite. Again the content of his address is incommensurate with his form in provocative ways:

> Ah'm the minstrel man
> Cleaning man
> Pole man
> Shoeshine man
> Ah'm a nigger man
> Watch me dance
> Ah've got the devil in me
> Ah've been waitin' on the employment line

FIG 1.15 Tom's blues. *Coonskin* (Ralph Bakshi, 1975).

Welfare line
Gasline
Since 9
Now Ah'm waitin' on the pawnshop line
Ah've got the devil in me
Ah've been shot on
Pushed on
Passed on
Gassed on
Red, white, and blued on
Now, Ah'm waitin' to turn on
Ah've got the devil in me
It's a man you see
Ah'm a natural blackface
Part of my race
And up my sleeve Ah'm holdin' an ace
That I won't die in disgrace
If I stop dancin'
And don't let you blow me anymore in the wind
Because I refuse to come.

The prose reprises the film's theme song from the opening sequence to close the intermission. "Ah'm a Nigger Man" functions as an acerbic counterpoint to the utopianism of *Song of the South*'s "Zip-a-Dee-Doo-Dah" ("My, oh, my, what a wonderful day / Plenty of sunshine headin' my way"). Written by Bakshi and performed by Scatman Crothers, "Ah'm a Nigger Man" mimics the comic self-degradation of the minstrel song and Disney's Uncle Remus, but with a blues inflection. Houston Baker notes, "Like translators of written texts, blues and its sundry performers offer interpretations of the experiencing of experience. . . . Even as they [the blues singers] speak of paralyzing absence and ineradicable desire, their instrument rhythms suggest change, movement, action, continuance, unlimited and unending possibility."[79] The affronting blues oratory of "Ah'm a Nigger Man" models a performative resistance to terror and disenfranchisement with the inimitable capacity of musical dissidence.

Similarly Clyde Woods defines the blues as an epistemological mode, a performative tradition of explanation and interpretation for the black lifeworld: "The blues became an alternative form of communication, analysis, moral intervention, observation, celebration for a new generation that had witnessed slavery, freedom, and unfreedom in rapid succession between 1860–1875."[80] So although seemingly a minstrel object, Tom's performance of "Ah'm a Nigger Man" reconstitutes him as a blues performer, a blues transgressor. Furthermore the delivery of the lyrics as prose has an affinity to the poetic style of the BAM. The repeated verse ("Ah'm a Nigger Man") is mobilized as a testifying call of blackness—a hailing of all blues people.

Driven by a commentary on de jure and de facto racial disenfranchisement, the first verse of the song opens with a connotative range of blackness. Each label associates blackness with services or labor before closing on the figure of the "nigger man." The descriptors are reified and embroiled in the synecdochic and metonymic impulses of the antiblack racist imaginary. The lyric "Watch me dance" is delivered with an aggressive smirk that is undercut by a brief shuffling soft-shoe to the hummed strains of "Old Folks at Home [Suwannee River]" (1851). This wistful invocation of the glory days of Dixie intrinsic to the New South is debunked by the blues challenge of coon form and seditious content. This antebellum ridicule is further evident in the reference to the riverboat pole man.

The line "Now, Ah'm waitin' to turn on" conveys a note of retaliation. This commencement or *turnin' on* is framed as an action or impulse that has long been "turned off" and dormant, which, once set in motion, will no longer tolerate being shot on, pushed on, passed on, gassed on. As the Narrator of

Invisible Man muses, "A hibernation is a covert preparation for a more overt action." The act of *turnin' on* could range from self-defense to decolonization of the mind, but it most certainly represents active resistance and details what is at stake for the "nigger man." Tom's blues recital as a provocation to be regarded echoes the sentiment of Ellison's Narrator: "I've illuminated the blackness of my invisibility."[81]

Who is the "nigger man"? Is he a perverse twist on the "I AM A MAN" marchers of the civil rights era? Is he merely a contemptible thing with no honor? His threat lies in his inability to be effectively neutered or contained by the narrativizing ritual of abjection. A defiant and willful rebel, the "nigger man" is, as Ronald A. T. Judy notes, always a *bad* one: "A bad nigger . . . is an oxymoron: rebellious property. In rebellion, the bad nigger exhibits an autonomous will, which a nigger as commodity-thing is not allowed to exhibit. There is little more dangerous than a willful thing; through the exhibition of autonomous will, the bad nigger marks the limit of the law of allowance by transgressing it."[82] Able to negotiate the racially stratified spaces around him, the "nigger man" gives the impression of harmlessness and anonymity ("natural blackface and part of his race"), and yet he is disingenuous ("And up my sleeve Ah'm holdin' an ace") in order to survive emboldened ("That I won't die in disgrace"). "If I stop dancin'" suggests that he is conscious of his objectification, but now he refuses to *dance* (literally and symbolically) and confirm the expectation of the entertaining and whimsical darky. This defiance comes with a mortal risk as the rebel Tom delivers the last verse looking directly at Miss America: "And won't let you blow me anymore in the wind / Because I refuse to come." Not simply an errant fellating pun, the line also alludes to the lyric image of "black bodies swinging in the Southern breeze" from "Strange Fruit" (1939), the Lewis Allen (Abel Meeropol) poem made famous by Billie Holiday.[83]

In one of Richard Pryor's comic segments in Mel Stuart's documentary *Wattstax* (1973) he illustrates the critical consequence of the satirical force that informs Tom's call to be valued. Pryor's joke results from giving voice to a person hitherto presumed to be a mute thing: "When they [white folks] found out niggers could talk, other than 'doh wah ho,' they got scared to death." The comic approximation of African speech ("doh wah ho") marks the joke as commentary on the legacy of slavery. Pryor continues as the joke illustrates not only that whites still associate modern-day blacks with African slaves—human commodities perceived as speechless—but also that their fear results in an explicit silencing, a refusal to hear, even when blacks do speak: "You know, like, one day, some whitey said 'Nigger, talk!' 'Well, motherfucker, I been wanting to tell you something!'" The surprised white man abruptly responds by saying, "I beg your pardon!," thus shutting down the conversation and punctuating Pryor's sardonic humor.

Like Tom's blues and Jemima's chase, the joke represents an expressive resistance that in the context of slavery shatters the antiblack presumption that the slave is a laboring thing that lacks value and voice. Satirically undermining the commodified slave, *Coonskin* exhibits the crux of Fred Moten's critique of Marx's hypothetical consideration of a speaking commodity that comments on its own use-value and exchange-value. Moten proposes, "The truth about the value of the commodity is tied precisely to the impossibility of its speaking, for if the commodity could speak it would have intrinsic value, it would be infused with a certain spirit, a certain value given not from the outside, and would, therefore, contradict the thesis on value—that it is not intrinsic—that Marx assigns it."[84] Just as in the case of the Jemima chase, Tom's blues act revaluates the terms of his worth like the rebranding of a commodity form that results in sedition and discord as its only marketable value.

With the moonlight serenade completed, Tom indignantly frowns and looks away dismissively with his arms crossed (fig. 1.16). Rebel Tom has articulated his worth and the history of a joke and a yoke. A cut to a close-up of Miss America's face highlights the smile she has held throughout Tom's protest (fig. 1.17). With bored indifference she robotically deadpans, "Help. Rape. Rape." At that, an accessory (in both senses of the word) rolls quickly from stage left and screeches to a halt. It is a wheeled stage prop of a gallows with a ready hangman's noose that drops around Tom's neck and quickly yanks him, lynches him, upward out of the frame (fig. 1.18). With the winding down of his struggling feet, Miss America giggles and begins strumming a folksy tune.

The conclusion of the intermission illustrates how the threat of Tom, a reconstituted freedman, becomes, in the white supremacist evaluative process, simply Gus, the white blackfaced male rapist of *The Birth of a Nation*. Tom's resistance becomes narrativized as a threat of sexual aggression. This black male rapist, once laboring chattel quantified by fecund yield, became a sexual beast to be vanquished by the disciplinary function of lynching.[85] Tom's death completes the New South lore of white male avengers driven by an enabling moral imperative whereby every windmill is a black man and every black man a dragon.[86]

FIG 1.16 "And don't blow me anymore in the wind." *Coonskin* (Ralph Bakshi, 1975).

FIG 1.17 "Rape." *Coonskin* (Ralph Bakshi, 1975).

FIG 1.18 Lynching. *Coonskin* (Ralph Bakshi, 1975).

> The film speaks for itself, which is what films are supposed to do. I wasn't lying.
> I may have told some truths that were unpleasant, but I never lied.
>
> —RALPH BAKSHI, IN ANDREW J. RAUSCH, "RALPH BAKSHI"

> Mr. Franklin: Because you see, my boy, hmph . . . slaves . . . ha ha ha . . . SLAVES!
> YES, that's it!! Slaves got options! Options, ya dig? I'm talking escape . . .
> revolt . . . death. *(Pause.)* Options. *(Pause.)* But cowards ain't got shit! Cowards
> only have consequences. *(Silence.)* Dig me? *(Silence.)* Do you dig me?
>
> —STEW, *PASSING STRANGE*

The *truth* of the film that Bakshi has insisted on over the years requires recognizing the depth of America's tradition of antiblack visual culture. The film addresses how purveyors and admirers of this iconography are complicit with regimes of antiblackness and white supremacy. *Coonskin*, rigorous in undiplomatic ways, scrutinizes the American imaginary with particular attention to the commercial and revisionist or nostalgic channels of vernacular cosmopolitanism. *Coonskin* is almost forty years old, yet it remains a slave film for modern times. As the line from *Passing Strange* surmises, *Coonskin* dispenses a range of options devoted to shattering the binding crush of antiblack visual culture with no regard for fainthearted, kumbaya posturing. The film's disobedient adaptation does not indulge the design of this iconography; rather the reanimating stain of *Coonskin* targets the historical consciousness of the spectator and the afterlives of slavery.

There are many who will never appreciate how unfunny *Coonskin* is intended to be. The violent pivot between subjectification and subjectivity is a humorless legacy. That *Coonskin* offends is incidental, and to dwell only on this completely misses the point of the film. The film requires an active spectatorship capable of addressing the legacy and design of this iconography as its tactic of the racial grotesque engenders a necessary ambivalence toward positive and negative readings. Importantly CORE's response and subsequent nationwide campaign against the film do not represent instances of knee-jerk reaction or "cultural reflex" that we can dismiss and belittle from the perch of our more sophisticated present.[87] The film has much to say about the Age of Obama, postrace, radical white (e.g., Tea Party, birthers), or perhaps Third Reconstruction times of the early twenty-first century.[88] Perhaps this is the perfect time for the majestic indignity of the racial grotesque to startle and thrive.[89]

The film's disorienting force, its own brand of mumbo jumbo and hoo-doo, operates as pathogen, cure, and rebellion.[90] As Darius James declared, "In *Coonskin*, Bakshi pukes the iconographic bile of a racist culture back in its stupid, bloated face, wipes his chin and smiles Dirty-Harry style. '*Now deal with it.*'"[91] The film continues to hold America accountable, perhaps more now than at the time of its release. The practice of the racial grotesque in *Coonskin* represents an act of film blackness outside the mainstream and prescriptive discussions of what blackness is and what it must do; it remains an exile on Main Street. If the problem of the twentieth century was the Du Boisian color line, then an additional problem may be the distinct restrictions placed on the art of blackness that both sides of this line insist on. For the sake of grotesque work like *Coonskin* and the idea of black film more broadly, this line will continue to inspire disturbing and profound crossings.

SMILING FACES
Chameleon Street and Black Performativity

In 1985 an article in the *Detroit Free Press* recapped the exploits of William
Douglas Street Jr., a black man and self-professed "Great Imposter" whose run
of various criminal acts of impersonation began in the late 1960s.[1] The article
featured excerpts from a jailhouse interview with Street, who at the time was
serving a prison term for unpaid loans he received while posing as a student at
the University of Michigan.[2] Upon reading that article, Wendell B. Harris Jr.
began research for a film project based on Street's exploits that would eventually become *Chameleon Street* (1989). Emblematic of the best of independent
cinema and alternative financing, Harris raised a $1.5 million budget with the
help of his family and black businessmen in the Flint, Michigan, area. He
spent three years visiting and corresponding with Street, writing the script,
shooting the film, and completing postproduction.[3] In 1990 the film won the
Grand Jury Prize at the Sundance Film Festival, and it opened in theaters a
year later. Harris, a Juilliard-trained actor, explained how he identified with
Street's masquerades in terms of acting:

> What I immediately saw when I read the first article on Doug was his
> ability to act, and act convincingly. That's the test of an actor: Does the
> audience believe? Part of the addiction that Doug has to the act of imper-
> sonation is the moment when he looks into somebody's eyes and he can see
> that he is pressing the right buttons to make them believe his performance.
> That's maybe the purest part of the high he gets from impersonating, be-
> cause he certainly doesn't look for money. In fourteen years he made less
> than four thousand [dollars] from the impersonations.[4]

Street's ability to "act convincingly" suggests something of how his imperson-ations operated to impress a belief and solicit a truth. But what constituted a *profit* for Street remains a rich puzzle. After all, if the motivation for his impersonations was a kind of material profiteering or net gain, that might offer a satisfactory explanation. Yet the return on Street's investment is not so immediately measurable. As the primary inspiration for *Chameleon Street*, the passing life of William Douglas Street Jr., the way he freely enacted and em-bodied multiple roles and negotiated with several cultural poses, signals some-thing more than the curious adventures of a charlatan and minor celebrity.

Street first received national attention in February 1971, when he was fea-tured in a UPI story that was picked up by newspapers across the country. The story recounted Street's attempt to try out for a spot on the Detroit Tigers baseball team by passing himself off as Jerald Lee Levias, also known as Jerry Levias, an NFL wide receiver for the Houston Oilers. Street had tried out for the Tigers two summers earlier and had even attempted to make the roster of the Boston Red Sox while impersonating a sports reporter for *Time* maga-zine.[5] His 1971 ploy as Levias was initially successful. He portrayed himself as an athlete who had grown tired of the NFL and now wanted to play the sport he had always loved. Street as Levias was considered a star tryout by the Tigers organization to such an extent that they flew him down to training camp in Florida. Upon arriving, Street borrowed money from a Tigers player, claim-ing that his finances were still tied up with the Oilers and that he would pay back the loan once he was on the team payroll. In spite of his mediocre play in the field, Street's ruse was discovered only after the real Levias contacted the Tigers and asked why they were circulating rumors about his NFL retirement. Street was not prosecuted. A few weeks after the Tigers ruse was exposed, he was prosecuted for passing bad checks at an Orlando hotel where the Minne-sota Twins were staying. He claimed he was a member of the team.

Shortly after the Orlando misdemeanor, Street returned to Michigan and committed a crime far less amusing. On 9 March 1971, he delivered a note to Gloria Horton, the wife of Willie Horton, a highly respected and admired Detroit Tigers all-star. Claiming to have tapes, photographs, and documents in his possession that detailed her husband's criminal dealings, Street's note stated that he would turn over the incriminating material to the authorities unless Ms. Horton paid him $20,000. The note threatened that if she at-tempted to contact law enforcement, she, her husband, and their children would be killed. She did contact the police, and Street was charged with extor-tion and underwent a court-ordered mental evaluation. He received twenty years' probation. Over the course of the 1970s and 1980s Street served various prison stints as a result of his continued compulsion to pose. His masquerades included impersonating a physician, lawyer, medical student, and college football player.[6]

As an adaptation of Street's history, *Chameleon Street* indelicately provokes the tradition of racial passing in literature and film with a keen disregard for the political, cultural, and social equivocations about racial identity that organize the passing conceit. Racial passing has often been considered as an ontological violation, an instance whereby someone poses as something he or she is "not" with regard to racial identity. Of course, what is understood as a fundamental aspect of racial personhood inevitably signifies something less than an indisputable or innate category and more a discourse that seethes with cultural, social, and political prescription. Street exemplifies what Elaine Ginsberg describes as the dialectical nature of passing: "Passing is about identities: their creation or imposition, their adoption or rejection, their accompanying rewards or penalties. Passing is also about the boundaries established between identity categories and about the individual and cultural anxieties induced by boundary crossing. Finally, passing is about specularity: the visible and the invisible, the seen and the unseen."[7] The film's protagonist thrives as a proficient quarreling with the power, privilege, and regulation of boundary crossing as *Chameleon Street* depicts the strategic opportunities generated by the discounting of the immanence of identity categories.

Chameleon Street details the wielding of race as constitutive cultural fiction, repurposing the racial passing tradition with the cruel play of a rebel cipher. As a result the film explores the limits of racial passing narratives with a disinterest in the more melodramatic tendencies of the mode that tacitly infer regulation and prohibition. As morality tales, these passing fictions devote a great deal of attention to how the racial passer suffers in his or her access to privileges previously denied. Thus the classic passing narrative is replete with the familiar and tragic melodies of "passing as betrayal, blackness as self-denial, whiteness as comfort."[8] Questions of power and knowledge are defused because the racial passer becomes the foregrounded object of pity and scorn while racial hegemonies are further naturalized and obscured. In this way Street as film protagonist irreverently resignifies the core impulses of the racial passing narrative.

The film's resemblance to a passing film is evident in its thematic anxieties around race, masquerade and authenticity, but the driving tenor of *Chameleon Street* obviously considers the substance of blackness in ways not dependent on self-loathing or racial dispossession because Street as film protagonist does not exhibit any interest in the disavowal of blackness for the lure of whiteness. Fundamentally Street's difference is an occulted tool that facilitates his success. As Cherise Smith succinctly notes, "To pass successfully, one must suppress one's own difference from, and perform the behaviors of, members of the dominant culture in order to appear like them."[9] Street's success occurs with a seditious impression of this suppression and emulation impulse. His passings transpire as epistemological challenges that distinctly amplify the way racial passing potentially displaces "the relationship between inside and outside, truth and appearance, identity and identity politics."[10] This is what makes watching the film like a spectatorial litmus test as whatever judgment we make of Street reveals the extent to which we concede authority to the conditional categories implicated in his masquerades.

How does one discuss a racial passing film whose protagonist has no allegiance to the more diagnostic conjecture of racial passing? How does one discuss a film whose protagonist demonstrates a deep disregard for the one-drop speculations of visuality and racial masquerade? Furthermore the film lacks any correspondence to the deracinated longings of the racial passing tradition. Instead the film's narrativization of racial passing moves beyond the rhetoric of racial phenotype and permanence by demonstrating the discursivity of race itself. The film unhinges passing from its classical moorings with a protagonist who enacts various impersonations of being as a *raced* passer compelled by a desire to be convincing, successful, and exceptional. *Raced* functions as a term for Street's modulating acts of identity as a measured motion or rhythm that is affectively attuned to place, race, and being.

Street is a raced subject whose blackness modifies the idea of race with each of his passing episodes and construes more than the ability to demonstrate expertise with a trade or occupation. This is because *Chameleon Street* insists on a shift from racial fidelity to identitarian disloyalty, racial passing to racial performativity. In other words, *Chameleon Street* as an enactment of film blackness demonstrates process rather than the idle cataloguing of lack or pathology.

The slippery protagonist of *Chameleon Street* traffics in what Lauren Berlant has called a "dissociative poetics": "Dissociation is at least four kinds of thing: an ordinary mode of affective delay; a state that manages destabilizing intensities by separating them; a condition of dispersed awareness, multiplicity and tangled intention intrinsic to the complexities with which incidents become events; and an effect of the pressure of the politicized world, a circuit breaker within the overwhelmed sensorium that is constantly snapping."[11] In the case of Street, the relational force of these dissociation codes determines the range and mapping of his performativity accents. Rather than portraying Street as misanthrope or social dropout, this detachment and disjuncture operate as a driving counter to the tangling choke of the social world and its compulsory sense of identity.

Supplementing Judith Butler's proposal of gender as a performative act rather than an inert category of being, Debby Thompson questions whether race is a trope. Focusing on how Anna Deavere Smith's performance art complicates the idea of race as strictly a static category of social being, Thompson suggests, "When an assigned identity is not re-cited and re-performed perfectly, then that identity can shift. . . . The subject produced through performative reiteration of norms can also somewhat re-perform those norms with a difference, and even, potentially constitute performative identities not yet normalized or even scripted or embodied."[12] Street deftly models a disobedient craft as his refusal to comply evinces artful disintegration. *Chameleon Street* resignifies the visual and textual logic of race, "the constructed, instable, reiterated, and citational discursivity of race."[13] As an enactment of film blackness, the performative enterprise of *Chameleon Street* indexes race through multiple strategies. This chapter focuses on four conjoined features of disobedience in the film, four strains of dispute resulting from the film's enterprise of racial performativity: diagnostic dispute, the menace of mimicry, the black modernist, and improvisational chaos. In addition I discuss the reception history of *Chameleon Street* in light of its poor circulation during the era of new black cinema. I argue that the film's indefinite place in the critical discourses on the idea of black film raises questions about black film historiography and black film scholarship.

Think Twice

> The film you are about to see and hear is based on the life experiences of William Douglas Street, Jr. and Erik Dupin. Many of the characters appear as themselves, while others assume fictional personae.
>
> —OPENING TEXT OF *CHAMELEON STREET*

At its start the film forecasts a thesis preoccupied with race and performativity.[14] Following the opening disclaimer, the first image of the film is an over-the-shoulder shot of a black man in a medical robe sitting in front of a desk.

Seated at the desk and facing the robed figure is a white man in a suit. The white man, a prison counselor, addresses the black man, yet to be revealed as Street: "Have you thought about what you're going to do on the outside?" The question seeks to substantiate whether the prisoner has been rehabilitated enough to be released. Indifferent to the formalities of the debriefing, the black man responds:

STREET: Umm.

COUNSELOR: Let me put it this way. Once you get out, will there be any more of these? [He picks up a newspaper article from a full file folder and shakes it at Street.]

STREET: No, no. I'm through, no more.

COUNSELOR: No more impersonations.

STREET: No, enough is enough.

COUNSELOR: I don't believe you.

STREET: Would I lie?

COUNSELOR: I don't think you're necessarily lying. I don't think you're in control of what you do or say. I think you behave in complementarity.

STREET: Okay.

COUNSELOR: Do you know what that means?

STREET: No.

COUNSELOR: That means you intuit what another person needs and then you become that need. Like right now you know that my job is to diagnose neurosis.

STREET: Neurosis are red. Neurosis are blue.

Street's pun serves as an aural cut to the beginning of the title sequence, a series of jump cuts composed of four close-ups of his face. Set in an indistinct space that suggests an underneath or a hole, each shot shows the face bisected by the illumination and shadow of high-contrast lighting that intimates a caul or the Du Boisian veil (fig. 2.1). His countenance ranges from agitated to bored, smug, and solemn. Throughout, the soundtrack features a voice at various speeds of indecipherability. The hailing of "Sit down," "Shut up," "Don't cross me," and "Look at him" are the only discernible phrases amid the aural buzz. The soundtrack then settles into a normal speed with the following prose: "The chameleon is about to invest. I think, therefore I scam." This final portion of the sequence shifts to flashes of color that pulse from red to blue to yellow with the title *Chameleon Street* flashing in a contrasting color within the frame blocks as the prose continues: "I think the air is sweet. I know not what

FIG 2.1 "I am Chameleon Street." Douglas Street Jr. (Wendell B. Harris Jr.) in *Chameleon Street* (Wendell B. Harris Jr., 1989).

I am. I am Chameleon Street." The title sequence closes with the sound of a heartbeat before the film properly starts with a voice-over: "Autumn 1978."

The opening sequence pivots on an abstracted address of behavioral psychology with the complementarity diagnosis. As a term for the way that social beings desire to be enhanced by another, complementarity suggests that individuals seek those who possess attributes that ultimately complete one's own self. The montage that follows the interview poses a clever response to the complementarity diagnosis. The prefacing of the "painter's primaries," or primary colors, by a black face generates a distinct hermeneutic triggering of the eye's physiological register of color. The diacritical encounter with the colors and countenances acts as black visual rhetoric (the black, red, yellow, and blue).[15]

Significantly this compositional shifting between color and colored converges around the punning reference to the Cartesian subject, "I think therefore I scam." Descartes's "I think, therefore I am" maxim illustrates belief in the fundamental self-evidence of an individual's truth of existence: the capacity to think. But for Charles Mills the Cartesian ideal engenders a normativity synonymous with the white existential condition, while the non-Cartesian sum signifies the significant dispute of Africana philosophy, a logic attentive to the black existential condition: "So it will be a *sum* that is metaphysical not in the Cartesian sense but in the sense of challenging a *social* ontology; not the consequent of a proof but the beginnings of an affirmation of one's self-worth, one's reality as a person, and one's militant insistence that others recognize it also."[16] Thus the black face, the new standard of color, in conjunction with the scam pun suggests a sense of raced self-evidence, a viciously signifying sum. Street's militant insistence operates as a protean joke that rebukes the perception or conception of his blackness.[17] Mercurial, unstable, and improvisational, Street as intuitionist encounters the Cartesian ideal with a black consciousness devoted to self-evident truth as performative.

Street's sum and joke grow heavier with the last line of the prose: "I am Chameleon Street." This embodying line announces the film's autobiographical conceit. The statement shares an affinity with another subterranean utterance: "I am an invisible man." Like the opening line of Ellison's *Invisible Man* (1952), the film's declaration represents "an existential moment [that] could be taken as *le degré zéro de l'autobiographie*: the encounter with a self that is only the presentation of its own mask and that does not exist outside of the unfolding autobiographical act."[18] Yet in *Chameleon Street* the speculative tendency of the biopic becomes an examination of the mask with no illusions of an ontological self that lies beneath. Focalized around the exploits of an undercover other, the film depicts an anti-autobiography, a scripting of unbecoming.

The first half of the film closely follows the real-life exploits of Douglas Street's passing escapades. The postindustrial Michigan setting lends a disquieting motivation for Street's compulsions. In particular the Flint locations lend a quality of dispossession to the film, with an urban setting marked by the trickle-down promises of Reaganomics, blight, economic recession, white flight, and the grinding down of the underclass. Beginning with the Willie Horton blackmail scheme and the subsequent celebrity attempt to procure a tryout with the Detroit Tigers, Street ultimately fails to fully charm the press and public.[19] Falsifying his press credentials, he lands an exclusive interview with a USC basketball star, Paula McGee (played by herself). But Street is neither Clifford Irving nor Jayson Blair, and his journalism pass is short-lived. He then passes as a Harvard medical student who transfers his residency to Wayne State Medical School. With a medical textbook tucked in his pants, Street quickly becomes recognized in the hospital as the "Harvard man" who can do no wrong. Only after a random background check does the ruse end, and Street is arrested.[20]

"I've got to get a new identity" is the only time Street refers to his passings as a matter of identity. Of course his measure of identity does signify devotion to a belief in concretized being or fixedness. Tellingly the line comes during the film's sporadically used transitional bridge of intercutting to the next scene with an unrelated scene: a shot of a train with the rattling sounds of acceleration. The linking of Street's performative rigor to the rails and momentum suggests escape velocity. The insert shot of the train re-mediates Paul Gilroy's chronotopic sense of the train's function in African American literature as a trope of black modernism and the themes of "movement, relocation, displacement, and restlessness."[21] The film's sense of propulsion is organized by sardonic brilliance as Street's spatiotemporal flow represents the unruly mapping of blackness as a dynamic system. In other words, his passings are concurrently acts of fugitivity and radical narrativity that defy diagnostic renderings of blackness. Just as de Certeau noted of the experience of train travel as being simultaneously "incarcerational and navigational," Street remains a manic and eternal voyager oscillating between mobility and immobility, order and disagreement.[22]

The Spook Who Sat by the Door

Yes, I know your little secrets now.
And I insist upon being not one of your clowns, but one of you.
And I shall stay with you, if I'm permitted to for a little while.
That's up to you of course.

—NINA SIMONE, *LIVE AT MONTREUX* (1976)

Sitting alone on a bench in a prison courtyard by the security door, Street is idly doing card tricks. The prison warden walks by with a group tour that momentarily blocks our view of Street. When the group passes, Street is gone. As a black prison guard trails behind, escorting a white woman, Street's voice-over observes, "Look at this brother here. He's so busy protecting the white woman he can't even be bothered by my escape." With his spectral disappearance, the scene completes the visual pun of the spook who sat by the door. In *The Spook Who Sat by the Door* (Ivan Dixon, 1973), Dan Freeman imparts the following advice to his revolutionary ward: "Remember, a black man with a mop, tray, or broom in his hand can go damn near anywhere in this country, and a smiling black man is invisible." This measure of race, visuality, and phenomenological presence alludes to blackness as invisibility, a state of being seen, then fragmented, delimited, and dismissed rather than merely a matter of being the unseen or not seeing. As Fred Moten explains, "To be invisible is to be seen, instantly and fascinatingly recognized as the unrecognizable, as the abject, as the absence of individual self-consciousness, as a transparent vessel of meanings wholly independent of any influence of the vessel itself."[23] Street's scripting operates as a form of strategic (in)visibility as he recodes the terms of his recognition and transparency as a force of black disobedience that adroitly exploits antiblack and white supremacist tendencies.[24]

A scene from later in the film illustrates another distinct strain of performative disobedience. Street sits in the living room as his wife does their daughter's hair. The daughter's demand for new toys quickly escalates, and he picks up one of her Barbie dolls. Daydreaming of a lover, Street spray-paints the doll's face black, then tosses the doll across the table: "There you go. Black Barbie." The contemptuous gesture immediately evokes blackface minstrelsy and black versioning, but in the precise terms of performativity the gesture illustrates Ellison's deft sense of blackness and the mask: "America is a land of masking jokers. We wear the mask for purposes of aggression as well as for defense; when we are projecting the future and preserving the past. In short, the motives hidden behind the mask are as numerous as the ambiguities the mask conceals."[25] Ellison argues that the mask, a sign of performativity and premeditation, possesses the capacity to navigate the antiblack ways of America. The Barbie scene highlights Street's threat in the land of masking jokers, cowards, and slippery motives.[26] As a masked performer, Street vigilantly regulates the time and space of his perceptible being in every moment of masquerade. In addition, the spray painting of the black Barbie puns racial passing and its classical hierarchy of white happiness and black lack, the way racial passing often acts as "a model for the cultural production of whiteness."[27] Street as a raced performer assumes an attitude of menacing mimic, and he fumes with disdain for whiteness and antiblack standards of normativity.

"The *menace* of mimicry," Homi Bhabha writes, "is its *double* vision which in disclosing the ambivalence of colonial discourse also disrupts its authority."[28] For Bhabha the menace of mimicry is generated by the provocation of the colonial authority's culture as the normative standard. The colonial subject's repetition and mimicry of this cultural standard is done as "a subject of a difference that is almost the same, but not quite." Mimicry does not ask the colonial subject to stop being a subject of the authority's rule. Mimicry asks the colonial subject to desire the discipline of subjection. The menace arises from the ambivalence necessary for the possibility of mimicry. This invitation to emulate deauthorizes the colonial authority's culture as either innate or natural. The capacity of this menace to subvert authority always exists because the colonial subject remains suspended between presence and absence, similar and dissimilar.

The menace of the film evolves as Street's performativity disputes compulsory measures of class, privilege or power, and access to knowledge. This

FIG 2.2 The doctor is in. *Chameleon Street* (Wendell B. Harris Jr., 1989).

deauthorization fuels his desire for the privileges of the authority he assumes. Ed Guerrero writes, "Street masquerades as a doctor, lawyer, journalist, and thus rebels by infiltrating [the] exclusive zone of elite professional castes kept out of the practical reach, and aspirations, of most black men."[29] While class aspirations and "the criteria of distinction" obviously inform Street's performative impulse, this impulse also exhibits a signifying contempt for whiteness.[30] His institutional gambits shuttle between exceptionalism and disdain for whiteness as standard. His actions offer a rhetorical query: What is the point in being an ethical black subject in an unethical, antiblack world? The film conveys a great deal of ambivalence toward an identity politics that would ultimately reinscribe race as a stasis of being. Street remains irreconcilable. While James Weldon Johnson's "ex-coloured man" eventually stopped considering his passing as a game and saw it as the betrayal of a birthright, Street's Talented Tenth dissident pose appears removed from the stakes of a "mess of pottage." Street manically shifts embodiment codes and deflects prevarications of his blackness.

One scene that exemplifies the film's evasiveness begins with Street cantankerous and bored while sitting on the couch with his daughter in his living room. Reaching above the couch, he removes a mask hanging on the wall next to a map of Africa, dons the mask, pulls out a knife, and calls his daughter to come and play. Circling around the room, he creeps behind her with the knife raised. Eventually, sitting on his lap, she asks him if something is wrong. Street mutters, "I'm insane," and begins cutting his arm with the knife. As his

FIG 2.3 "Does this tickle?" *Chameleon Street* (Wendell B. Harris Jr., 1989).

daughter passively looks on he runs the blade over her body before settling on her throat, asking, "Does this tickle?" (fig. 2.3). The teasing glide of the blade abruptly becomes a sharp cut across her throat, and play gives way to the gory spectacle of blood and a child screaming. Gabrielle, Street's wife, rushes into the room and screams, "Doug, what have you done?" The daughter yells, "Mommy, you ruined the game!" When Gabrielle complains about how difficult it is to remove the bloodstains, he acts annoyed and simply replies that the fake blood is supposed to wash out. It was just a game.

From the start artifice informs the premise of the psychotic driven to filicide. Positioned next to the map, the mask metonymically stands in for the dark continent of Africa. Yet it is not a tribal mask but a comedy mask unaccompanied by its tragedy counterpart, although theatricality abounds nonetheless. His donning of the mask and the play that follows evoke the tokenism of Diouana's mask in Ousmane Sembene's *Black Girl* (1966), where the mask is a symbol of dispossession and objectification and later an emblem for the conditional madness of the postcolonial subject and the haunting of the dead or improperly buried. The ritualized play of Street's mimed psychosis parodies the pathologization of a savage continent. Street is neither cannibal nor Trueblood, and his taboo of choice is a killer of sheep. Echoing Paul Laurence Dunbar, Street wears the mask that grins and lies, a mask of unending strategy and invisibility.

While serving another prison stint, Street bristles in another psychiatric scene:

COUNSELOR: Has anyone ever told you your sense of sarcasm is extremely strong?

STREET: Oh yeah. Has anyone ever told you that white people who get caught in the rain smell exactly like wet dogs? This is fact. Believe or not.

COUNSELOR: I beg your pardon.

STREET: Have you ever been standing in a crowd of white people and all of a sudden it starts to rain? It's a very particular odor, extremely aromatic.

COUNSELOR: You like to use humor as a smokescreen.

STREET: Look, I'm so far ahead of you. I know what you're about to say. I know what you're thinking. I know what you're writing on those evaluation papers. I know that you're wearing an incredibly cheap toupee. I mean I can sit here and punch all the right buttons and make you think that you're a genius for correctly analyzing this complex, exotic, notorious negro but— "notorious negro." That would be a good name for my autobiography. I've started writing my life story. . . . But you're not so far off. I give people what they want. When I meet somebody, I know in the first two minutes who they want me to be and I just cut the emotional cloth of my personality to fit the emotional clothing of whoever I'm—

COUNSELOR: Conning?

The Autobiography of a Notorious Negro could very well have been the film's alternate title, with its allusions to pulp engineering, a noir inflection that touches on how "the passing genre reads like the detective genre without the detective."[31] With its noir insinuations, *Chameleon Street* suspends the classical conception of crime or punishment and the sanctity of the law. "White people smelling like wet dogs" is a black vernacular critique of the "segregationist sensorium," the nonvisual ways (touch, smell, sound, taste) that segregation rationalized antiblack social hierarchies.[32] Overall Street responds to his counseling session as a mimic grown bored with his diagnosis. As a "notorious negro" (more Cross Damon than Bigger Thomas), Street straddles the classical division accorded to the black male in visual culture: "This schizophrenic way of representing black males as concentrated at the poles of celebrity and pathology leads to a dangerous array of perceptions and assumptions."[33] As the legacy of Richard Pryor attests, "that nigger's crazy" never had anything to do with a mental state. Conceding the diagnosis means recognizing an authority and sanctioning a script. Of course to do so would be anathema to Street's insistence on the improvised incarnations of his blackness. His mimic impulse as schizoid fury broaches being as a matter of anticipation and adaptation.

In a later sequence Street passes as an attorney with the Detroit Human Rights Commission. His legal mimicry results in the successful negotiation of city contracts with four white corporate lawyers. During the dinner to celebrate the closing of the deal, the fantastical and the pathological again converge as Street overhears two of the lawyers discussing tanning salons. He begins to question the lawyers about the tanning service. One nervously asks him about his interest, and Street responds that it is for research purposes. When pressed to describe what kind of research, Street replies, "White people." He continues, "It amazes me that whites avidly seek after all the accouterments of black style. You pickle your bodies in gallons of tanning lotion. You broil your pale flesh brown in the tanning spas at great expense and all the while maintaining such a marvelous contempt for black people. You wily Caucasians." Finishing his monologue, Street raises his glass to toast them. The absence of a reaction from them, as if he had never said a word, reveals that this monologue on duplicity, whiteness, and desire was an internal one.[34]

Street's wily comment is a sharp reading of fetishization and the ways of "racechange."[35] Moreover the "marvelous contempt" thesis relates to what Greg Tate identifies as "the long-standing, ongoing, and unarrested theft of African-American cultural properties by thieving, flavorless whitefolk" who desire "everything but the burden."[36] Masterfully versed in the ways of white folk, Street works hard at outmaneuvering racial privilege with the menacing scorn of an independent scholar hidden in plain sight. He does not like people, white folk in particular. He relishes showing up and ridiculing whiteness as the standard and instead gleefully circulates as a raced heretic genius.

The Young Mod's Forgotten Story

THE FORGER: You've seen my big Cézanne at the Metropolitan? Is that just a forgery, my friend? Is it not also a painting?

—*F FOR FAKE* (ORSON WELLES, 1974)

Are we in the embraces of a charming rogue? . . . The play of meanings thickens. There is the battle of wits against any authorized set of assumptions. But then there is the segue into his loving the game for its own sake, his desire to pull off a *masterpiece* of illusion.

—CLYDE TAYLOR, "TWO WAY STREET"

People ask me all the time, "What are we listening to?" I play the classics: Vivaldi, Hendrix, Debussy, Sly Stone, Sex Pistols, Ipso Facto.

—WILLIAM DOUGLAS STREET JR.

Street's performative raison d'être is mediated by an aesthetic ambition for what Clyde Taylor describes as *masterpieces*. Like a well-executed craft or a perfect art, the success of his masquerades communicates the substance of the line from *F for Fake*. At the close of the film Welles tells a story about an alleged encounter between Pablo Picasso and the legendary art forger Elmyr de Hory, in which the forger exclaims, "Do you think I should confess? For what? For committing masterpieces?" Street's masquerades too ignore the distinctions between art and forgery; there is the normative and there is glory. His brand of outsider art consistently tends toward acculturated performativity. Just as Welles's metacritical *F for Fake* effaces the categorical distinctions between documentary and fiction while deliberating on the construction of value in the art market, *Chameleon Street* dulls the veracity and identitarian claims that bolster some of the values attributed to the idea of black film.[37] Instead the film consolidates multiple fictions of embodiment and art with an eye for different measures of import.

Street enlists blackness as a discursive interlocutor. His insistence on elegance, style, and wit demonstrates his adaptability and cosmopolitanism. The phenomenon of black dandyism informs the proficiency of the film's protagonist, a savvy aesthete who does more than merely recycle conceits but practices passing as the performative art of racialization. "Black dandyism in the early 20th century," Monica L. Miller writes, "emerged as a sign that Black people now considered themselves modern, cosmopolitan, urban, part of a debate on how to reform, worldwide, conceptions of blackness and black people of the diaspora."[38] With the sartorial ways of the so fresh and so clean in mind, Street acts as a crossracial and intercultural auteur. His is a ceaseless tailoring of the cosmopolitan as the performative craft of black renegade chic.

The film's black modernist pursuit touches on what Henry Louis Gates Jr. notes about the passing life of Anatole Broyard: "The thematic elements of passing—fragmentation, alienation, liminality, self-fashioning—echo the great themes of modernism."[39] Therefore the life of Broyard requires an acknowledgment of the consequences of passing less ethically motivated for "it was not so much that Broyard *lived* a lie as that he *refused* to live a conventional fiction."⁴⁰ Street's refusal of a conventional fiction drives the aesthetic ambition of his dandy pursuit, a drive to be distinguishable. His chameleonism represents a prodigious ability to prevail by intertextual eclipse and thrive by constantly rendering obsolete the authority and knowledge of all interlocutors he encounters and cites.⁴¹

While Street is out having dinner with his wife, a drunken white man approaches their table; he presumes that Street's wife is a prostitute and available for purchase. When Street pushes him away, the white man throws his drink in his face while yelling, "Nigger! Get your nasty black hands off of me! Fuckin' let go!" Flustered and upset, Street regains his composure and addresses the drunk:

> You know that's a very nasty word. But you know what's, pardon the expression, fucked up is your grammar. *Fuckin' let go.* You can't say that. The rules of grammar apply to profanity as well. "Fuck" comes from the German root *ficum*, which means "to strike." It's a verb and it can be used in a variety of ways, both transitive and intransitive.... [Street proceeds to mime how *fuck* can be used to express simple aggression, confusion, apathy, ignorance, defiance, and authority.] See, these are all the things you could've used if you weren't so unbelievably coarse and crude and countrified. [Street looks at his wife.] That's alliteration, Babe. Remember, peckerwood, profanity is the last refuge of the ignorant, the insensitive, and the illiterate, but if you're going to use it, and I see you are, at least get the fucking grammar right, moron.

Street's dressing down of this white man occurs with an intertextual nod to Edmond Rostand's *Cyrano de Bergerac* (1897) and Cyrano's riposte to a stranger who insults his nose. Like Cyrano, Street attempts to defuse the humiliation of a slight with words. Unlike Cyrano, Street has less than remarkable swordsmanship and is beaten unconscious. His invocation of Cyrano refuses the hailing of the white man's "nigger" declaration. Importantly Street does not speak to the "nigger-naming" but to the use of *fuck*. The scene redirects antiblack racist speech as a matter of poor diction that requires elocution training by a skilled grammarian. "The rain in Spain stays mainly in the plain."

The longest impersonation sequence of the film entails Street's escapades at Yale University following his escape from a Michigan prison. During this sequence the allusive and intertextual measure of his aesthetic tendency is most evident. Arriving in New Haven, Street models himself as a buppie collegian before settling on the identity of a French-speaking exchange student

FIG 2.4 Pépé le Mofo. *Chameleon Street* (Wendell B. Harris Jr., 1989).

from Martinique named Pépé le Mofo. The rude hilarity alludes to Jacques Duvivier's *Pépé le Moko* (1936), a Moroccan-set film that centers on a Parisian jewel thief and bank robber (Jean Gabin) who must pass as an Algerian and reside in the "teeming anthill" of the Casbah to escape capture by the authorities. In place of the imperial vision of a debonair Frenchman forced to slum as a colonized other, the Yale sequence invokes the noir and colonial exoticism of Duvivier's film but with an equating link of white colonial authority and the exclusivity of the Ivy League.[42] In *Chameleon Street* the narrative recoding suggests an adaptation that stages Pépé passing as Jean Gabin, the menace of the gentleman other. An enchanting cinéphile, Street bypasses merely citational intention as he embodies these cinematic roles as an accredited artist of black being.

Street practices French by viewing Edith Piaf videos, reading Rimbaud, and watching *Beauty and the Beast* (Jean Cocteau, 1946), which he calls "getting my mind right." For a short time he even convinces a group of French Club students of his pedigree by comically rephrasing Zola's indictment of the Dreyfus affair. He simply says "J'accuse" and then randomly names a noun (fig. 2.4).

The malleability of Street's black dandy pursuit builds to the grand fruition of a costume ball with a French Revolution theme. He attends the affair immaculately attired as Cocteau's Beast and critiques the white crowd's chants ("Marat!") as a sign of their ignorance and lack of refinement. This black Beast throws shade and becomes ennobled amid the swirl of white dilettantes,

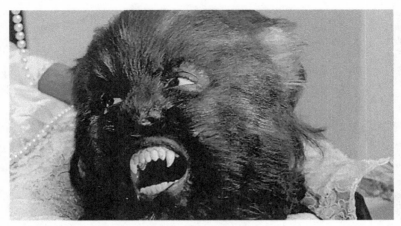

FIG 2.5 The Beast. *Chameleon Street* (Wendell B. Harris Jr., 1989).

repurposing the reductive binaries of savagery and race, beast and aristocrat. Gabrielle arrives at the ball dressed as Beauty. She does not immediately recognize him and only discovers that it is her husband when their names are announced as the winning costumed couple. A medium shot cuts to a wide-angle close-up of Street's face as he basks in his moment of fugitivity star time. The black Beast smiles wide and his canines sparkle as the king of the masquerade ball (fig. 2.5). The majesty of Street's Beast turns grotesque as the tightness of the close-up produces an unsettling fishbowl effect, the elongation of the image turning the salon setting into a funhouse. During the confetti-filled celebration, Gabrielle rips the mask from his face, exposing his "true" identity to the Michigan authorities waiting in the crowd. His makeup-smeared face appears as disfigured and profane as Dorian Gray's portrait (fig. 2.6).[43] In the end Street as the Beast repurposes the moral of the fairy tale: there is no truth inside; the cover is the thing.

Street's aesthetic aspirations mirror the art cinema designs of the film itself. One sequence in particular, shot from his point of view, symbolically illustrates the consequences of the film's auteurist manner. Street is discussing the entrepreneurial benefits of drug dealing. Mulling over the dealer's pitch, he asks, "The question is do I have to sell drugs in order to make money?" The supplier replies, "Look, brother. Do you want to philosophize or do you want to make some money?" The drug dealing consideration gestures toward the more popular permutations of the idea of black film at the time of the film's release. Of course the film's preference lies with philosophy over the "keeping

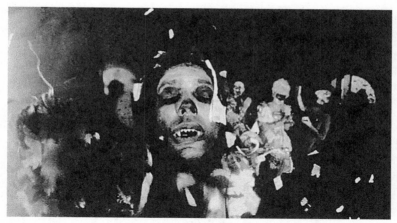

FIG 2.6 The Beast exposed. *Chameleon Street* (Wendell B. Harris Jr., 1989).

it real" profiteering of the hood film cycle in the early 1990s. Furthermore the film's inability to benefit from the new black cinema moment more generally illustrates the central problem of the industrial and academic collusion that produced a definition of black film that proved itself indifferent toward *Chameleon Street*.

All the Critics Love You in New York

The reception history of the film's commercial run (New York City, April 1991, to Boston, January 1992) details how *Chameleon Street* struggled with the prevailing notions of black film at this time. In September 1989 *Chameleon Street* premiered simultaneously at the Venice Film Festival and the Toronto Film Festival. It was described as "having enough contemporary black attitude on display . . . to draw the core audience of black college students and 'buppies' apparently targeted by the filmmaker" and an example of "what happens if you try to make a Spike Lee film without being Spike Lee. (Sometimes it doesn't even work if you are Spike Lee.)"[44] The Italian press gave the film the unfortunate moniker that would be recycled over much of the course of its commercial run: "the Black *Zelig*." After rejections from the New York Film Festival and the Museum of Modern Art's New Directors/New Film series, the film was accepted in the Sundance Film Festival, and Harris opted for a U.S. premiere there in January 1990.

The 1990 Sundance Film Festival was basking in the success of Steven

Soderbergh's *sex, lies, and videotape*, the 1989 winner of the Sundance prize for Best Dramatic Film. The film would gross $25 million and brought independent film to the attention of Hollywood and the general public. The growing appeal of this American brand of outsider or auteurist cinema pushed the circulation of independent cinema in the mainstream. Moreover the success of Sundance 1989 should be thought of as building on the general momentum of American independent film's circulation throughout the 1960s until the post–New Hollywood 1980s.[45] With expectations of another surprise and lucrative project (a "son of Soderbergh"), anticipation for the festival was quite high. This was especially the case in light of the field of films: Charles Burnett's *To Sleep with Anger*, the Hudlin brothers' *House Party*, Whit Stillman's *Metropolitan*, and the PBS project *Longtime Companions*. Melvin Van Peebles was even honored as a pioneer of black film.

Following a six-hour deliberation, the decision of the festival jury (which included Soderbergh, Armond White, Alfre Woodard, and Peter Wollen) was announced: Charles Burnett received the Special Jury Prize, the Hudlins the Filmmaker's Trophy, and *Chameleon Street* the Grand Jury Prize for Best Dramatic Film. The prestigious recognition was a moment of confirmation for Harris, who said, "I felt elated, I felt vindicated, I felt validated and I felt hopeful. At that moment, what I envisioned was a very quick distribution on a national level."[46] The recognition of *Chameleon Street* represented a moment when the idea of black film was notably enfolded in the discourse of American independent film in a way as important as Spike Lee and the circulation of *She's Gotta Have It* through the American art cinema and proto-independent circuit of the mid-1980s.

Much of the press and the independent film community in attendance disagreed with the jury, as many thought *Metropolitan* should have won. As a result the sense of a mistake having been made would become attached to the film. Writing on the awards ceremony, John Pierson commented, "Jaws dropped as Wendell arrived at the podium in his black sunglasses and Barry White–like basso profundo voice boomed out in the most memorable Sundance incident of egomania run amok."[47] Another critic wrote, "Except for *Chameleon Street*, the booty seemed to go to movies with obvious commercial potential."[48]

Harris sought a distribution deal for the film but had no success. Eventually he accepted an offer from Warner Bros., but it was not a distribution deal. Instead Warner Bros. bought the indefinite remake rights to the film before the film was tested on the market or even seen by the public. Still in need of a distributor, the film continued to screen at various festivals over the course of 1990, including the Black Independent Cinema Now program at the AFI/Los Angeles International Film Festival, the Munich Film Festival, and the Black Arts Festival in Atlanta. The film was well received by the festival audience in Atlanta and was cited in the press as "a black version of the Tony Curtis crowd-pleaser, *The Great Imposter* . . . [but] worth checking out in what promises to be a long and fascinating career."[49]

In late 1990 *Chameleon Street* became the first distribution acquisition of the newly founded Northern Arts Entertainment and initially opened on twelve screens nationwide early in 1991. In the financially and critically important New York City market, it received a fair review by Vincent Canby in the *New York Times* but failed to impress Georgia Brown at the *Village Voice*.[50] Her review, "The Word Is Lout," opened with a bizarre consideration of imposters by way of a comparison between John Guare's *Six Degrees of Separation* (1990) and *Paris Is Burning* (Jennie Livingston, 1990). The choice of imposter hints at the authenticity or legitimacy questions that the film and the director would endure over the course of the film's commercial run. Brown's discussion focuses only on those parts of the film deemed misogynist, ultimately framing these as representative of the whole film. Her scathing mischaracterization of the film acidly closed, "This general incoherence and self-indulgence makes watching Harris' movie powerfully irritating. Obviously I've missed entirely whatever moved the 1990 judges at Sundance to award *Chameleon Street* the prize for Best Dramatic Film. Two movies it beat out — *To Sleep With Anger* and *Metropolitan*."[51] *Chameleon Street* opened in New York City at Film Forum in April, briefly sharing the bill with *Paris Is Burning* (Jennie Livingston, 1990), a restored print of *Citizen Kane* (Orson Welles, 1941), and a repertory program devoted to the films influenced by *Citizen Kane* entitled "The Roots of Kane and the Children of Kane." *Chameleon Street*, a not-so-distant cousin of *Kane*, generated a very poor box office gross in its two-week run before it began a yearlong tour of the country on the art-house circuit.[52] The film did receive a very favorable review in the *New York Amsterdam News*, but the piece did not appear in press until two weeks after the film's run at Film Forum had closed.[53]

Crossing the country, *Chameleon Street* was met with criticism that had settled into a familiar composite, with comments such as "Impostor buffs should stick to *Zelig* and *The Great Imposter*" and "[Street is] a black variation on the character Woody Allen created in *Zelig*."[54] In particular Harris's directing skills received sharp criticism, for instance, "He has much of what it takes to be an interesting filmmaker—sophistication, intelligence, originality and wit. Now all he has to do is learn how to make movies."[55] The redundancy of the criticism was pervasive: "So while one understands why the Sundance jury passed up more accessible films like *To Sleep With Anger* and *Metropolitan* to give this film its top award, that doesn't make it any easier to sit through. Harris is definitely a talent to watch, but not necessarily this time around," and "enjoyable yet too contrived to pull off the sophistication of *Zelig*."[56]

In July the *New York Times Magazine* ran a cover feature devoted to the work of contemporary black filmmakers, entitled "They've Gotta Have Us."[57] *Chameleon Street* was not mentioned until almost a month later in a published letter of response to the article: "I appreciated the way [Karen] Bates let the black filmmakers featured in her article tell their own story. I appreciated the effort to historically contextualize the subject of black filmmaking. I was pleased to learn of black women directors other than Debbie Allen. But, I found the exclusion of Robert Townsend (who made 'Hollywood Shuffle' and this year's 'Five Heartbeats') a gross oversight. Wendell Harris ('Chameleon Street') and Michael Schultz ('Livin' Large) also merit discussion."[58]

The *Los Angeles Times* ran a small piece on the film whose clever title referenced the trials and tribulations of Harris and the film in the eighteen months after winning at Sundance: "Maybe He Should Have Impersonated a White Studio Boss."[59] The film received good notice in *Rolling Stone*, and a review in *The Nation* astutely concluded, "A film this sharp and intelligent deserves notice. . . . I caught it at New York's Film Forum, which booked it for a two-week run; it has also had some short runs in scattered cities, including Cleveland and Atlanta. But is this the best we can do for a talent as big as Wendell Harris's?"[60] The film continued to do poorly until its last reported theatrical screening, in January 1992 in Boston.

In the words of David Mazor at Northern Arts Entertainment, the film failed to garner "a champion."[61] In other words, the film lacked a major endorsement from critics, producers, directors, or the general public, although an article by Armond White suggests that at least one film critic did make an effort to champion the film. In May 1991 White's "Underground Man" appeared in *Film Comment* and opened with the following comment: "The virtues of Harris's debut are anathema to the current establishment—which is probably the highest praise a critic can confer." He also stated, "The film isn't 'ahead of its time' (there's really no such thing), but it will be fascinating to see whether the network of European-centered, white-focused film reviewers, production executives, and museum curators is ready for what *Chameleon Street* represents. Wendell B. Harris has made a real work of art, short on budget but long on film savvy." White admonished critics who labeled the film as derivative of *Zelig* and suggested that they failed to make a distinction between Jewishness and blackness: "Harris offers new social insight that goes beyond assimilation and conformity and scrutinizes the exercise of social power as a need inspired by American oppression."[62] The next month White wrote an article for the *Village Voice* entitled "Condition Critical." In it he rails against Georgia Brown for her "hostile review that gave short shrift to its [*Chameleon Street*'s] racial meaning." Significantly he also broaches the question of the *black* of black film: "People can talk about 'Black movies' without ever having defined 'white movies,' and Black artists wind up separated from the cultural mainstream. . . . The appellation 'black film' that turns up in current trend pieces has the same categorizing limits that made James Baldwin flinch 30 years ago over 'protest fiction' and 'problem fiction.' Labels are for control, not description. In film culture they are a way of denying Black moviemakers any pure artistic status while defusing their visions as special pleading."[63] White also wrote an article for *Essence* about the 1991 black film releases that singled out Harris's film, and an expanded version of his "Underground Man" was featured in *Sight and Sound*.

In November 1991 *Chameleon Street* and Harris were profiled in a segment by Elvis Mitchell for PBS's *Edge*, a short-lived show billed as a monthly television magazine devoted to American culture. The ten-minute segment contained an interview with Harris, clips from the film, Mitchell's own commentary on the film and new black cinema, and comments from several film critics (including Armond White), Steven Soderbergh, and a representative from Miramax Films.[64] Mitchell questioned the sincerity of Hollywood's openness to the current iteration of a new black cinema in light of the problems experienced by *Chameleon Street*. He suggested that the critical resistance to the film's content and form, coupled with distribution problems, represented a ceiling on black cinema. In particular the show lingered on Warner Bros.' purchase of the indefinite remake rights of the film, which Mitchell considered emblematic of the way *Chameleon Street* was ultimately perceived as outside the American film canon, and thus foreign.[65]

Russell Schwartz, executive vice president of Miramax, said, "It [*Chameleon Street*] is not obviously a black picture, per se. Which is also one of the good things about it. If it had any potential, it could work as a crossover picture." If you expand *crossover* from its capital context and consider it as the systemic or the pervasive, then perhaps the uncanny force of *Chameleon Street* crosses over too much. Guerrero reasons:

> Street's fantasy life . . . his frustrated ambition and intelligence, his dissembling in the face of [a] white professional class so eager to disavow its reflex feelings of racial superiority that it uncritically accepts him, all culminate in a dialectically shocking metaphor for the double consciousness, masked anger, and constant pretending that all blacks, to some degree, must deploy to live in a persistently racist society. And, of course, here resides the dark, troubled core of the film. Embellished by Harris's arty, *avant-garde* style and sardonic voice-over monologue, this is the unspoken and unspeakable truth that will forever keep *Chameleon Street* out of dominant cinema's mass entertainment markets.[66]

Guerrero precisely identifies the transactional failure of the film to profitably appeal to an audience that presumably would prefer not to be troubled by the performative tactics of blackness.

White wrote an homage (or eulogy) for the film in the wake of its sellout screening at the American Museum of the Moving Image in February 1992. He comments that the critical adversity *Chameleon Street* suffered was a sign of its distinction from the standard measure of black film: "*Chameleon Street* is a seriously talented person's attempt to find a means of expression he can call his own. And that, in the popular arts, is a heroic endeavor. It risks being unpopular, it risks not being distributed, and risks being misunderstood."[67] The film's reception history demonstrates a ubiquitous dismissal of the film's complexity that bears out Kobena Mercer's observations on the critical attention afforded black artists: "Black artists have not had their work taken seriously because the space for critical dialogue has been constrained and limited precisely as an effect of marginality."[68] Fundamentally the cultural imperialism evident in the critical reception of the film exhibits the debilitating premeditation of black film that by extension infers that black filmmakers cannot be auteurs and that black film is not art. Most of the criticism attests to what the film is not; none addresses the question of what it is. This egregious exercise in marginality with its insistent typological recycling illustrates what happens when a black film denies what were ultimately limited expectations.

Chameleon Street is not *Zelig, The Great Imposter, Six Degrees of Separation,* or *Metropolitan.*[69] The film's disappointing run cannot be adequately explained by its minor formal imperfections. A definitive and singular explanation cannot be culled from the many possibilities, including critical inattentiveness, poor distribution, independent film cronyism, unfortunate programming choices by exhibitors, antiblack racism, or white supremacy. The film experienced a cumulative failure to be appreciated or understood as an art film, independent film, American film, or black film. Moreover it suffered for being all these things at once, if not more. This valuation disavows the film's proficient intertext and therefore its distinct allegiance to auteurism and art cinema. Simply put, *Chameleon Street* was disavowed as a weird, uppity, black, arty thing lacking real value, as if a forgery. It was treated in many instances as though it embodied Douglas Street, the categorical trespasser incarnate, and thus endured a punishment spectacle like a passer exposed.

Phony Beatlemania Has Bitten the Dust

Chameleon Street did not comply with the ideas of black film advanced by the industry and film press. As a result the emerging historiography of a new black cinema proposed by academics during the 1990s also played a tacit role in the film's inability to appreciably be a black film in the available terms of 1991. In terms of black film historiography, the significance of 1991 cannot be overstated. Often called a "black film explosion," that year over two dozen films were released that were characterized as having "black content," a black director, or a black actor in a lead role. The narrativization of that year was part of a continuum of previously declared explosions: in 1990 (*House Party, To Sleep with Anger,* and *Chameleon Street* at Sundance), 1986 (the release of Spike Lee's *She's Gotta Have It* and Robert Townsend's *Hollywood Shuffle*), and the 1970s (blaxploitation). Nevertheless the number of films released in 1991 was unparalleled for several reasons. First, there was the release of two films that would become the highest grossing films by a black filmmaker at that time: John Singleton's *Boyz n the Hood* and Mario Van Peebles's *New Jack City.*[70] Other films released in 1991 include Lee's *Jungle Fever*; the sequel to the Hudlin brothers' *House Party, House Party 2*; Robert Townsend's *The Five Heartbeats*; the rerelease of Charles Burnett's *Killer of Sheep*; the Hollywood debut of the independent filmmaker Charles Lane with Disney's *True Identity*; Junior Vasquez's *Hangin' with the Homeboys*; the wide release of Julie Dash's *Daughters of the Dust*; Bill Duke's *A Rage in Harlem*; and Matty Rich's *Straight out of Brooklyn.*

This large field of films, along with their respective crossover appeal, was a lucrative prospect for the film industry but only by a dubious logic to account for the *black* of "black film." Take, for example, the following from a *Variety* article from 1990 entitled "Blacks Take the Helm":

> Black directors are making an unprecedented number of pictures this year, pictures that distributors hope to sell—like the rap and Motown many are scored to—in the mall as well as the inner city. Thirteen films by African-Americans are scheduled for release in 1991. Twenty other films starring black actors are slated for release, the most since the explosion of the early 70's, when hundreds of so-called blaxploitation features were made. But there's a difference this time around: While those earlier actioners featured black actors and were targeted to blacks, these new pictures are largely the product of black filmmakers—and many are expected to attract white audiences.[71]

The article acknowledges the historical continuum of black film, but the distinction it makes between the 1970s films and the films of 1991 exemplifies a "double displacement," what Michel de Certeau argued is a flaw in the conceptual logic of historiography that poses as "authorized to speak in the name of the 'real'" by proposing "a concept plausible or true by pointing to an error and, at the same time, by enforcing belief in something real through a denunciation of the false."[72] The 1991 iteration of black film is framed as a refutation of the 1970s version with the inferred binary of what constitutes a "true" as opposed to a "false" black film. Why is it these films that "featured black actors and were targeted to blacks" were not equivalent to those films "expected to attract large white audiences" just "like the rap and Motown many are scored to"? The entire period becomes quantified and dismissed by the logic that to target a black audience is exploitative but to aim for the lucrative crossover market of a white audience is good business practice. Furthermore the idea of black becomes ahistorically dependent on isolated incidents that are disaggregated from any sense of a historical continuum. But the industrial logic alone does not explain the placelessness of *Chameleon Street*. Certain tendencies of black cinema studies contributed as well.[73]

In "A No-Theory Theory of Contemporary Black Cinema," Tommy Lott broaches the designation problem surrounding the idea and criteria of a black film and black cinema more generally. Lott begins with a brief consideration of Thomas Cripps's *Black Film as Genre* (1978) and the deficiencies of sociological readings of black cinema. The temerity of Cripps's work is its insistence on black film as the marking of an anthropological truth: "To adapt Bronislaw Malinowski, black genre films have, like good tribal lore, expressed, enhanced, and codified belief; safeguarded and enforced group values; offered practical rules of conduct; and vouched for the efficacy of tribal ritual and gods. No other genre, except perhaps the American western, [speaks] so directly to the meaning and importance of shared values embraced by its audience."[74] Lott rightfully dismisses Cripps's position as essentialist. However, Lott also expresses skepticism for the Black British cultural studies inflection of black cinema evidenced by his dismissal of Teshome Gabriel and Kobena Mercer for, again, claims of essentialism. Lott articulates his position in precise ways:

> I want to advance a theory of contemporary black cinema that accords with the fact that biological criteria are neither necessary nor sufficient for the application of the concept of black cinema. I refer to this theory as a no-theory, because I want to avoid any commitment to an essentialized notion by not giving a definition of black cinema. Rather, the theoretical concern of my no-theory is primarily with the complexity of meanings we presently associate with the political aspirations of black people. Hence, it is a theory that is designed to be discarded when those meanings are no longer applicable.[75]

After discussing his strategy of disposability as an essentialism deterrent, Lott addresses blaxploitation and permutations of what he deems contemporary black cinema's "new blaxploitation" resemblance. His concern centers around a tenacious opposition to "aesthetic-based theories of black cinema":

> The attempt to reclaim and reconstruct a black film aesthetics that would somehow counteract the influence of Hollywood's blaxploitation filmmaking has, by and large, not been well-received by black audiences, although many of these films have been frequently presented at international festivals, in art museums, and in college courses devoted to film studies. How can we best understand the fact that films which aim to present a more authentic black aesthetic are largely ignored by and unknown to black audiences, while being extremely well-received in elite white film circles? Despite their admirable political orientation, such films seem to have achieved the status of art-for-art's sake, with mainly an all-white audience appeal.[76]

Lott's sense of aesthetics is compromised by his inability to address film form to any real degree. There is nothing to suggest that he entertains the need to deal with black films contextually or as individual texts, let alone as distinct enactments of blackness. Instead his black film aesthetic suggests speculations of a black ontology and an insistence on the role of a black audience in monolithic terms. His insights on the problems of procuring an audience are valuable, but considerations of box office gross and audience in regard to what he calls "aesthetically-minded black cinema" hinge on the continued essentialist slippage; equating the critical deliberation on filmmaking as an art practice becomes an exercise in authenticity. He correctly recognizes the negotiation between the "biological and cultural criteria of black identity" as a political act, but he cannot fathom that this negotiation does not mean a resolute act of black public policy. This negotiation must be unfinalizable to allow for the possibility of art and, importantly, the prerogative of the filmmaker as artist and the idea of black film.

Lott closes his essay with a calculated wish for the future composition of black film:

> I want to advance a theory of black cinema that is in keeping with those filmmaking practices that aim to foster social change, rather than participate in a process of formulating a definition of black cinema which allows certain films to be canonized on aesthetic grounds so as to occupy a place in the history of cinema. The theory we need now is a political theory of black cinema that incorporates a plurality of aesthetic values which are consistent with the fate and destiny of black people as a group engaged in a protracted struggle for social equality.[77]

It appears that Lott wants film to primarily be a vehicle for nobler race punditry, and never an art. He is right to push for a divestment from biological essentialisms, but not for the sake of circling into the trap of cultural essentialism. The call to repurpose black cinema as Third Cinema is a relevant proposal, but this proposition cannot be sufficiently appreciated in light of Lott's restriction on what might constitute a political vision.

Chameleon Street tacitly becomes something that Lott's position cannot imagine or appreciate. His antidialogical surmising remains dependent on the continued weightless phrasing of "the black experience." This is a disappointing and unfortunately too familiar trend wrought with conclusions so predetermined in their need to use film to offer pedantic guidance to black people that it would seem there is no real requirement to even bother watching the films. *Chameleon Street* poses a retort to the obligation charge of "the fate and destiny of black people" and thus requires a consideration that would not punish films for choosing not to engage in a notion of cinema as an instrument for compulsory blackness. *Chameleon Street* and many other disloyal films like it deserve more than Lott's "no-no."

Wolf Like Me

> Can it be, I thought, can it actually be? And I knew that it was. I had heard of it before but I'd never come so close. Still, could he be all of them: Rine the runner and Rine the gambler and Rine the briber and Rine the lover and Rinehart the Reverend? Could he himself be both rind and heart? What is real anyway? But how could I doubt it? He was a broad man, a man of parts who got around. Rinehart the rounder. It was true as I was true. His world was possibility and he knew it. . . . The world in which we lived was without boundaries. A vast seething, hot world of fluidity, and Rine the rascal was at home. . . . It was unbelievable, but perhaps only the unbelievable could be believed. Perhaps the truth was always a lie.

—RALPH ELLISON, *INVISIBLE MAN*

Derived from the never seen performer in *Invisible Man*, Ellison's phrasing of Rinehartism alludes to what he characterized as a distinctly American modality: "Rinehart is my name for the personification of chaos. He is also intended to represent America and change. He has lived so long with chaos that he knows how to manipulate it."[78] Kin to Herman Melville's Confidence Man, Rinehart is a master chronotope in the sense of one capable of dictating the spatiotemporality of any and all settings. Street's adroit refusal to be named and quantified rests on the plasticity of racial taxonomies of being in much the same way as Rinehart's.[79] His "notorious negro" affect is a concentrated abundance, a plenitude of being that, like Rinehart, "embodies multiplicity in ceaseless motion, undermining every certitude, destabilizing every authority, *concealing* the 'truth' of his character *by performing* its proliferation in public."[80] Thus the skilled racings or stagings of race by Street as a black cipher of "myth and dash, being and non-being,"[81] exceed allegiances or determinacy. *Chameleon Street* executes Rinehartism in a cinematic key as it is crucially guided by an immaculate abandon and liquidity exemplified by Street's exploits.[82]

The final sequence of *Chameleon Street* begins with Street in his law office at the Detroit Human Rights Commission on 12 September 1985. A coworker comes in as Street begins a monologue that recaps his own folklore: "William Douglas Street Jr. Born in a log cabin in the backwoods of Kentucky, young

FIG 2.7 Captured. *Chameleon Street* (Wendell B. Harris Jr., 1989).

Douglas soon elevated himself from field hand to Tiger, from Tiger to reporter, from reporter to doctor, from doctor to co-ed, from co-ed to attorney, from attorney to congressman, from congressman to president. I could play president." The shot/reverse shot rally between Street and his coworker provides a survey of Street's office, decorated with posters of America's most precious ideal: various ratifications of the Constitution. The coworker nervously interrupts Street's Honest Abe fabling with news that U.S. marshals and thirty armed policemen wait outside the office door. The coworker whispers, "The fire escape." Rather than run, however, Street raises his hand to his throat and motions a slash across his neck; the jig is up. The authorities enter his office, and while they arrest him, he discovers that his wife turned him in.

Led outside in handcuffs, flanked by marshals, Street walks in slow motion through a gauntlet of officers to a waiting car (fig. 2.7). The final shot of the film is from Street's side. The spectacle of his punishment, his perp walk, is magnified by the temporal elongation and winding down of the slow-motion effect. Before exiting the frame altogether, he looks directly at the camera and smiles (fig. 2.8). Cheeky until the end, Street raises his shoulders ("I yam what I yam") as the shot becomes a freeze frame. While he was once a figure of performative fluidity and improvisational momentum, one with a limitless repertoire of poses, the motionless image of Street now indicates a fixed and secured body.

The end credits scroll alongside a montage of actors from the film. Their voices and visages are spliced together in a collective reciting of "The Scorpion

FIG 2.8 "I yam what I yam." *Chameleon Street* (Wendell B. Harris Jr., 1989).

FIG 2.9 "It's my character." *Chameleon Street* (Wendell B. Harris Jr., 1989).

and the Frog." Caught in a storm, the Scorpion rides across a rising river on the Frog's back after convincing the Frog he will not sting him. The Frog works his way through the swelling water and suddenly feels the Scorpion's sting on his back. Succumbing to the poison and sinking beneath the water, the Frog asks why the Scorpion would sting him, condemning them both to die. The montage recitation closes on a shot of Street in his prison cell as he indifferently offers the closing explanation from within a cloud of cigarette smoke: "Well, because it's my character" (fig. 2.9). *Character* connotes personality, portrayal, and, in the case of *Chameleon Street*, a black performative prerogative. A self-critique, an intertextual nod to auteurist designs, and a psychoanalytic and philosophic rendering of the black existential condition, the collision of meanings attributable to the significance of the tale's place in the film evinces the contradictions and intricacies of an extraordinary performer.[83]

In this final shot Street delivers the "character" line with his back to the barred window of his prison cell. Strongly backlit by the light pouring through and cloaked in smoke, Street appears completely blown out and obscured, an indecipherable spot, a black hole. Then again he has always been that way. In the end the immaterial, if not ectoplasmic, Street is a black space. Rather than concluding with epistemic capture or limit, the film closes with Street's incarcerated body as a dematerialized one. His literal and metaphorical imperceptibility and unfinalizability are all that remain of him. A vision of pure horror, the film's black hole summation delivers an anchored Street veiled in a churning fog of improvisational chaos. As the real Douglas Street reflected on his impersonation impulse in the 1985 interview that inspired Harris to make *Chameleon Street*, "The nightmare part of it is there is no me, no Doug Street in the picture. I'm the sum of my parts, but all my parts are somebody else. Where's me, man?"[84] Clever and rigorous, *Chameleon Street* compels an understanding of film blackness that details the narrative indexing of race's affective quality. The history of its formal experimentation and the challenges it endured demands more recognition than as a film lost or too odd to be of value. By enlivening the racial passing tradition with the force of racial performativity, *Chameleon Street* accounts for the art of film blackness in challenging yet necessary ways.[85]

THREE

VOICES INSIDE (EVERYTHING IS EVERYTHING)
Deep Cover and Modalities of Noir Blackness

Only in the multi-era imaginary world of a Jurassic Park do the categories of a previous evolutionary state continue to exist. In the genre world, however, every day is Jurassic Park. Not only are all genres interfertile, they may at any time be crossed with any genre that ever existed. The "evolution" of genres is thus far broader in scope than the evolution of species. Unencumbered by the limitations of the flesh, the process of genre creation offers us not a single synchronic chart but an always incomplete series of superimposed generic maps. Every time our eyes concentrate on the map, we find that a new map, currently in the process of being drafted, is just coming into view. Never is the map completed, because it is the record not of the past, but of a living geography, of an ongoing process.

—RICK ALTMAN, "REUSABLE PACKAGING: GENERIC PRODUCTS AND THE RECYCLING PROCESS"

Rick Altman details the inability of film genres to effectively resemble the evolutionary sciences, as some criticism tacitly alleges. Any attempt to compose an equivalent species log or map is fundamentally thwarted by the absence of a fully corporealized object or synchronic integrity. If genre, as Altman claims, represents a "living geography" that cannot be reconciled by a strict adherence to the rules of biology, then a renewed focus on discursivity ("an ongoing process") might offer a different investment in genre. With this in mind, this chapter builds upon the previous visual historiography and black performativity inquiries to examine film blackness in the key of film noir. I am interested in the critical function of genre, noir in particular, and the consequential ways that blackness as the animating force of noir refines our understanding of genre.

A common feature of classical film noir is its consistency as a racialized mode of white masculinities in crisis. Often this normative focus on whiteness, masculinity, and racial privilege codes difference as aberrant, a potential threat, or a mark of hierarchal contrast. This measure of difference as deviation from and threat to the standard manifests in figures such as the strong-willed woman, the homosexual, the Hispanic, the Greek, the Italian, and the African American. Issues of narrative authority, racialization, and power deeply inform noir beyond its aesthetic profile as a high-contrast play of light and shadow. As James Snead acutely notes, "'Whiteness' and 'Blackness' lie perpetually at the intersection of power and metaphor."[1] In this chapter I consider how the noir register, with its connotative chromatics and the fissured contrast of blackness and whiteness along with its narrative predisposition to effectuate issues related to the social contract, the law, and racial privilege, can be transgressed and redeployed.

The generic status of noir remains as much a subject of debate as the generic classification of black film. The shared rupture of the two ideas, the way each mutually informs the other with unsettled expectations and delimitations, acts as the guiding principle of this chapter. Thus the idea of black film in the context of a discussion of genre practice deliberately provokes the problematic collusion between the historical legacies of racial classification and genre. Film blackness mediates this dialectic overdeterminacy, the specious motivations of race as a category of being that becomes the exacting foundations for a genre ideal loosely organized around industrial history, form, subject matter, or style. This chapter engages American cinema in terms that will complicate the categorical imperatives of national cinema, raced cinema, genre, and the cinematic apparatus itself. I consider the diacritical distinctness of modalities of noir blackness in order to recuperate the unvoiced and racialized structuring of the noir idea while attending to the distinctness of film blackness. *Mode* and *modality* refabulate genre with hints of texture, relationality, improvisational scales, procedure, and manner.

Beginning with a framing of noir as a discursive phenomenon, I shift to a focus on the place of blackness in these considerations. Additionally I stage Chester Himes and his engagement with the black absurd as the central component of noir blackness. The remainder of the chapter focuses on Bill Duke's *Deep Cover* (1992) to illustrate and elaborate on the discrepant engagement of this manner of film blackness. In my analysis of *Deep Cover* I argue that the film's noir practice represents a difference that reaccentuates the hidden polemics of the genre. My reading of noir through the conceptual frame of film blackness looks at how *Deep Center* renders elements of black visual and expressive culture in a way that richly demonstrates the critical capacity of the idea of black film.[2]

Darker Than Blue

Much criticism that seeks to detail the attributes that substantiate a claim for the generic status of noir addresses concerns such as narrative structure and disposition, formal qualities, noir as allegorical inquiry of post–World War II America, and noir's prehistory. In *More Than Night: Film Noir in Its Contexts*, James Naremore addresses the lack of a satisfactory or definitive consensus about noir's origins and status as genre and the missing link of a shared critical and cultural concern for its value. He suggests that the ultimate indeterminacy of film noir's status as an inert, generic category represents a need to reconceive the terms by which noir has been critically addressed and the idea of genre more broadly: "If we want to understand it [film noir], or make sense of genres or art-historical categories in general, we need to recognize that film noir belongs to the history of ideas as much as to the history of cinema; it has less to do with a group or artifacts than with a discourse—a loose, evolving system of arguments and readings, helping to shape commercial strategies and aesthetic ideologies. . . . Film noir is both an important cinematic legacy and an idea we have projected onto the past."[3] With this stipulation Naremore recuperates the idea of noir by proposing that it represents the cinematic legacy of a discursive phenomenon, the history of an idea. In doing so he proposes that the engineering of noir as a critical object entails an institutional legacy and multiaccentual system that has framed noir as allegory, nostalgia, and social critique. This suspension of the noir categorical coherence question is supplemented by another line of inquiry.

Naremore addresses film noir's intercultural and transnational character as a negotiation between popular culture and high modernism. He does so by way of an initial consideration of how the genre function of the noir sensibility arises out of the existentialist and surrealist communities of Paris and their respective exposures to hard-boiled literature, exposure that would subsequently inform their perceptions of the large number of American productions of "murder melodramas" that flooded the European markets just after World War II. As a result these existentialist and surrealist spectators applied their critical and aesthetic literary affinities to the cinematic, especially to themes of crime, abstracted and evocative mise-en-scènes, narratives predisposed toward elliptical flashbacks, first-person narration with the use of voice-over, and an ambiguous and conflicted sense of an ethical good and evil. For the surrealists of the 1920s noir attested to their organizing principle of the absurd. For the existentialists noir represented the cruel ambiguity and irrationality of the universe. Together the readings of hard-boiled fiction generated by each group provided the categorical imperative for the idea of film noir.

What is unsatisfying about Naremore's "history of an idea" thesis is the absence of a critical follow-through attentive to noir's emplotment of blackness. In his chapter "Other Side of the Street," Naremore suspends his thesis to avoid what he claims is speculation. He explains that the chapter will emphasize those "racial, ethnic, and national issues" that are rarely addressed by noir criticism. Yet the terms of engagement with these neglected concerns pose a problem. He writes, "I try to give a fairly comprehensive treatment of the topics I discuss, but I avoid theoretical speculation about the political or racial 'unconscious' of noir. I merely want to observe recurring patterns or themes, chart relatively obvious social changes, and offer a glancing commentary on the ways in which America's dark cinema has both repressed and openly confronted the most profound tensions in the society at large."[4] If speculation connotes arbitrary and unfounded reasoning, how would his observation, analysis, and "glancing commentary" warrant concern if it is indeed grounded in the analytic of the history of an idea? The chapter tacitly suggests that in spite of a thesis devoted to how noir is discursively conceived, race remains fixed. Unfortunately this fixing evokes a colonial encounter of "contact zones" and the colonialist imperative to classify the Other with Naremore's use of the continental categories of Africa, Asia, and Latin America as subheadings.[5] With geography and thus cartographies of power acting as the mediating trope for a journey to the other side of the street or another country, he neglects that the history of the idea is very much about the crossing of manufactured borders, gender trouble, and racial ambiguity.[6] Geography as the structure of this continental and formalist design is not an appropriate investment of complexity in regard to the question of film blackness. Stained by an unintended irony, Naremore's work raises the specter of the Middle Passage and the Black Atlantic with connotations of cartography and the geopolitics of racialization. Consider it in cartographic terms: after the sum assemblage of the continental parts, what of the remainder? Is this unvoiced and invisible land the home of whiteness?

For the noir idea whiteness and blackness operate as intercultural or intra-cultural markers and aesthetic phenomena. Naremore's analysis suffers from a significant inconsistency: a conflation of the craft (black visual and expressive culture) with the sociological (the social category of race and the black lifeworld itself)—or, to put it another way, the distinction between the black and "the black." Therefore his chapter bears out the consequences of a social constructionist sense of race. It is not an uncommon critical occurrence but a testament to the critical struggle with framing blackness that informs the writing of film history and much of cinema studies more broadly. Naremore's subsequent analysis is more about a history of race and less about the discursivity of race and American cinema, the dialogics of blackness, and the history of an idea. In response I offer a reading of the inscription of race and film practice that bears out the richness of Naremore's thesis. If the idea of noir entails "an imaginary entity whose meaning resides in a set of shifting signifiers," then why must the shifting signification capacity of noir discursivity be fixed and concretized by the sociological when the question of blackness arises?[7] "You played it for her. You can play it for me."

We Real Cool

Invested in the function status of blackness and its enfolding in the noir record, Manthia Diawara executes a contrapuntal intervention of film noir. In "*Noir* by *Noirs*: Towards a New Realism in Black Cinema," he suggests that the imprint of film noir bears out blackness as latently "a fall from whiteness." Extrapolating from Raymond Borde and Etienne Chaumeton's seminal work, *Panorama du Film Noir Américain* (1955), Diawara writes, "Film noir is black because the characters have lost the privilege of whiteness by pursuing lifestyles that are misogynistic, cowardly, duplicitous, that exhibit themselves in an eroticization of violence."[8]

Eric Lott suggests a similar accounting of noir as the performative abjection of whiteness. He examines how the noir idea is constitutively structured by cultural, ethnic, and racial differences: "The 'dark' energy of many of these films is villainized precisely through the associations with race that generated some of that energy in the first place. Film noir is in this sense a sort of white-face dream-work of social anxieties with explicitly racial sources, condensed on film into the criminal undertakings of abjected whites."[9] Lott argues that the "indispensable" utility of race by noir represents the genre's fundamental dependency on racial difference to such an extent that the genre operates as an exercise in "white pathology" that parallels the antiblack rendering of black bodies as socially invisible.[10] With their respective approaches, Diawara and Lott identify the stakes of race and this chapter's consideration of a noir practice focalized around blackness.

Modalities of noir blackness cast a distinct light on noir's most precious preoccupation, "America," and the social contract around which noir has always orbited. With the noir unconscious metastasized, Diawara surmises, "In a paradoxical sense, the redeployment of the noir style by black film-makers redeems blackness from its genre definition by recasting the relation between light and dark on the screen as a metaphor for making black people and their cultures visible. In a broader sense, black film noir is a light (as in daylight) cast on black people."[11] Therefore "noir by noirs" organizes the "play in the light" of dark ruptures long disavowed by the classical textual processes of categorization. Diawara argues that noir by noirs, with their distinct chronotopes, mise-en-scènes, and narrative topoi, are not "poor imitations of their white counterparts" but films that reaccentuate the racialized tendencies and privileges of this particular generic mode.

Diawara vitally insists on the paradigmatic function of Himes for noir by noirs. Then he sets out to identify the key and constitutive elements of this manner of noir as being black rage, class critique, and the emplotment of black expressive culture. Yet a complication becomes evident in the absence of a satisfying account of the classification of the body of films he considers (e.g., *Rage in Harlem* [Bill Duke, 1991], *Deep Cover* [Bill Duke, 1992], *Boyz n the Hood* [John Singleton, 1991], *Straight out of Brooklyn* [Matty Rich, 1991], *New Jack City* [Marion Van Peebles, 1991], *One False Move* [Carl Franklin, 1992]). In spite of his significant contextualizing of noir by noirs in the Reagan-Bush era (1980–92), the social realism and cultural nationalism categories he employs do not adequately quantify these noir films because the categories do not account for the crossing equivalences of style and politics. In other words, it is not clear how social realism and cultural nationalism function as discrete categories that ultimately forestall the possibility of a film diacritically demonstrating features of both categories. Moreover his accounting for the critical role of Himes at times appears too quick to fix the irreconcilable force of Himes's transgressiveness as Diawara's circumscription of noir by noirs does not fully exploit the complexity of Himes for the sake of categorization. So then, just as with Naremore's "history of an idea" thesis, this chapter extends the inspiration of Diawara's work as an intervention I am identifying in terms of modalities of noir blackness.

> Why rebel if there is nothing permanent in oneself worth preserving?
>
> —ALBERT CAMUS, *THE REBEL*

> Albert Camus once said that racism is absurd. Racism introduces absurdity into the human condition. Not only does racism express the absurdity of the racists, but it generates absurdity in the victims. And the absurdity of the victims intensifies the absurdity of the racists, ad infinitum. If one lives in a country where racism is held valid and practiced in all ways of life, eventually, no matter whether one is a racist or a victim, one comes to feel the absurdity of life.
>
> —CHESTER HIMES, *MY LIFE OF ABSURDITY*

The rich difficulty of Chester Himes lies in his abandonment of the literary limits of political efficacy in the terms of what Jonathan Eburne calls "vernacular surrealism." Eburne writes, "For Himes, the question of a surrealist affinity or a surrealist method did not hinge upon his cultural access to French ideas or his contact with the actual movement. Rather, for him, hard-boiled crime fiction already exceeded, even exploited, the limits of literary naturalism in ways that resonated with surrealist ideas of representation"[12] Thus Himes's Harlem detective fiction thrives in some measure by a conjunction of creative traditions: surrealism and hard-boiled fiction. Using the hard-boiled conceit of "telling it like it is," Himes posits Harlem as the hard-boiled and noir "love object" in the place of America.[13] This staging directs a sense of the absurd as black existential trope and as narrative device. For Himes, Harlem was a place he readily admitted never really knowing or perhaps a place that he never really wanted to know by the available standards of social protest literature or strictly in terms of antiblackness. As he wrote, "The Harlem of my books was never meant to be real; I never called it real; I just wanted to take it away from the white man if only in my books."[14]

While distinctly different from the surrealist ideal of the absurd, the *black absurd* derives inspiration from a supplementarity that compels noir with another priority. Devoted to a deeply maintained distrust of the philosophical traditions of the West, this supplementarity, or Himes's sense of urgency, illustrates the shared motivations of "two absurds": surrealism and the antiblack everyday.[15] Himes's Harlem detective novels represent a protracted and complex dispute with the ideological underpinnings of the hard-boiled tradition. Himes became a part of this tradition when the editor Marcel Duhamel asked him to write for the Gallimard series *La Serie Noire* in 1957. One of the central concerns of hard-boiled fiction through the 1930s and 1950s concerned the social contract and the ideological conception of the citizen-subject. Through what Sean McCann calls a "political fabling," hard-boiled fiction retroactively speculates on the political and cultural changes undergone by the American citizen-subject as a result of the New Deal. In *Gumshoe America*, McCann writes:

> Hard-boiled fiction became as it developed between the wars, not just a style of popular entertainment, but a kind of literary critique—a metaphorical account of the possibilities of public life in a society newly acquainted with the power of mass media and with the preeminence of a national professional elite. By the same token, it amounted to a telling political fable for an era in the midst of profound transformation. . . . The various methods they [hard-boiled writers] chose to pursue or to depict that effort mirrored particular strains of the New Deal thinking, and the frustrations they inevitably encountered in their pursuit of a utopian, democratic culture dramatized the conflicts and contradictions that would dog New Deal liberalism as it evolved from the 1930s through the 1950s and beyond. A pop genre, a cultural complaint, a political myth, hard-boiled crime fiction thus became a symbolic theatre where the dilemma of New Deal liberalism could be staged.[16]

The classic noir protagonist, a New Deal citizen, is forced, if not thrust, by an event, an act, a circumstance, or some pretext that precipitates a struggle with the revelation of the dangerous and maiming contradictions of the law of the state.

Himes's Harlem novels represent the sum and surplus of a prison or ex-con writer, a social protest writer, and a disaffected expatriate composing cruel sorrow songs. After all, what distinguishes his sense of dread from that of the existentialists was not an abstraction on one's lot but very much a historically and culturally precise sense of angst. In the register of the black absurd, these novels execute the surrealist ideal of the absurd, with its instantiation of irrationality, disorientating skepticism toward convention, and "humour noir" in Himes's vernacular key.[17]

His emplotment of antiblack racism and white supremacy disputes the New Deal inflection of hard-boiled fiction by tracking and cycling through the "unattractiveness" of America.[18] If modern noir writers such as Dashiell Hammett, Raymond Chandler, James M. Cain, and Graham Greene were taking to task the puzzle-solvers like Edgar Allan Poe and Conan Doyle, then the work of Himes takes to task the extent of this New Deal rebelliousness, with its rugged manliness and its noble, fair and square detectives. "For Himes the genre *is* the message."[19] Himes's Gravedigger Jones and Coffin Ed Harlem novels feature a pair of detectives not privy to the hard-boiled tone of (white) antediluvian nostalgia for the better days before the war.[20] Blackness as the organizational principle of the Harlem novels cannot be contained or recuperated by a safe and familiar past as this Harlem is where "you try hard and you die hard / Down and out in New York City."[21]

Himes's Harlem novels operate with an awareness of a procedural ruse, a game of misdirection that bypasses the genre's core misrecognition of crime as a matter of science and a clear delineation of the asocial in contradistinction to the social. There is consistently the a priori offense of the Racial Contract that informs the Harlem novels. Himes's subversion is radical for the way it fulfills noir's critical engineering as a meditation on America. His proposition of a Harlem operates in the parodic register of the vernacular as the "calling out of one's name."[22] Dennis Porter writes, "In representing crime and its punishment, whether evoked or merely anticipated, detective novels invariably project the image of a given social order and the implied value system that helps sustain it. The dimension that is missing from formulaic works in the detective genre is, in fact, any recognition that the law itself, with its definitions of crimes and its agencies of law enforcement and punishment, is problematic."[23] In the cut of the gutbucket, Himes's assessment of noir fiction, the function of the detective, and crime insists that while the novels document transgression and investigation, and although his detectives may solve crimes and thus reestablish the social order, the systemic crime of white supremacy and antiblackness remains intact.

In these chilling comedies of violent irrationality, men and women are set ablaze, bludgeoned, run down by all manner of conveyance, and have their limbs amputated and their throats slit like hogs. In this Uptown people do not die from gunshots as much as their corporeal beings are itemized in a haphazard toss into the air of brain, blood, and teeth with a healthy dose of bone and random tissue; people are disintegrated. In this Harlem mother-rapers trump motherfuckers every time. Here black people stir in hard, dark places, sweating and banging themselves while drinking smoke. Christopher Breu notes of this shattering oppositionality, "Himes novels are designed to shock or disturb, producing narratives that not only resist categorization but also flaunt conventional morality and eschew easy recuperation by any single ethical or political position."[24] Himes's disobedient reformulation and restaging of noir conventions becomes a discrepant engagement with America through the hard-boiled form.

Who'll Pay Reparations on My Soul?

Bill Duke's *Deep Cover* posits a dispute with the idea of black film and the idea of film noir closer to the absurd spirit of Himes than any of the film adaptations of his Harlem detective work.[25] The film follows a police officer, Russell Stevens (Laurence Fishburne), recruited for an undercover operation by the Drug Enforcement Agency (DEA) to infiltrate a drug-trafficking organization comprising the major distributors and suppliers of cocaine on the West Coast. Becoming "John Hull," Stevens moves up the infrastructural pyramid of the drug trade as his assignment grows increasingly complicated by his success as a drug dealer and the shifting priorities of his function as a government agent. The film renders black visual and expressive culture in a heteroglossic manner that illustrates a nuanced sense of the absurd.

Deep Cover began as a collaboration between the screenwriter Henry Bean and the producer Pierre David after the success of their previous project, *Internal Affairs* (Mike Figgis, 1990). The film was written with a white character as the lead, but studio heads aware of the emerging crossover profits of black film suggested changing the character to a black man. As an article in the *Los Angeles Times* recounts, "It was former Paramount production executive Gary Lucchesi at Paramount, said Bean, who suggested that they revise the role to accommodate an African-American actor. At that time, the studio, impressed with the successes of Spike Lee, was looking for a film that they first could 'niche-market' to blacks. Back at the drawing board for a script revision, Bean said he was intrigued by the idea. 'The details of blackness gave the character a particularity and resonance that it otherwise didn't have,' he said. 'The dilemmas that were stock in an abstract form became less stock.'"[26] Paramount passed on the revised screenplay, and no other film studio wanted the project until the following year, after the strong box office returns for *Boyz n the Hood* and *New Jack City* reassured studio heads skeptical about whether a black lead could guarantee a profitable film.[27]

Bill Duke sought to avoid "the John Singleton thing," his description for the way the pervasiveness of the hood film after 1991 began to signify all black film. Tracing the thematic origins of the hood film from blaxploitation and the beginnings of "new black cinema" in the 1980s, Keith Harris argues that the hood film represented an emergent form of black crossover cinema that in addition to an allegiance to hip-hop culture consistently rendered the world through a binary opposition of crime or community: "The narrative and anti-hero characterization unfolded around socially overdetermined choices or responsibilities within the black lifeworld: the choice between a gangsta life or responsibility to the black community, which would necessitate refusal of the gangsta life."[28] Moreover the hood film cycle had a narrative predilection reminiscent of the social problem film or message film.[29] With a repurposing of the noir ideal, *Deep Cover* forestalls the potentialities of an advisory or moral tone.

The film's opening scene begins with a crane shot tracking at a downward angle to screen right from behind a tree strung with Christmas lights. Over the strings and choral hums of "Silent Night" the shot reveals a snowy street with a jalopy pulling off the main street into a parking spot. The car slows to a stop as the camera dollies forward toward it and an insert title appears: "Cleveland, 1972." This spatiotemporal marker signals the start of the voice-over narration by a man as a meditation on the past, a flashback: "So gather 'round as I run it down and unravel my pedigree." There is a cut to the interior of the car and the reveal of a man and a child as the voice-over resumes: "My father was a junkie." Taking a bump of cocaine, the father looks at the son and says, "Don't you never do this shit. You hear me? Don't you never do this shit. This some bad shit." The boy rolls his eyes, looks away, and mutters, "Yeah, okay." The incensed father begins pummeling the boy with his hat as he viciously repeats, "'Yeah, okay'? Don't you hear me talking to you? Don't you ever be like me! Don't be like me! Don't do it! Dammit!" His lashing out becomes tempered with tenderness as he asks, "Whatcha want for Christmas?" This is not *A Wonderful Life*. The boy replies, "I don't know," and the bemused father retorts, "You don't know? Boy, how you expect to getting anything in this world if you don't know?" The father reaches across the boy for a gun in the glove compartment, and as he turns to leave the car the boy reaches out to him, protesting, "Daddy, don't go!," only to recoil for fear of a backhand now suspended. As the boy cries the father embraces him ("Come on, you my main little nigger"), while the camera cuts to the father's POV of casing the liquor store over the boy's shoulder.

The father exits and the son watches from inside the car as his father holds up the store. Suddenly a drunken Santa Claus presses his face against the car window, blocking the boy's view, and screams, "Hey, Merry Goddamn Christmas, kid. You been a good boy?" In the background the father shoots the liquor store clerk and stumbles out, warding off Claus: "Get down, you

FIG 3.1 "The money." *Deep Cover* (Bill Duke, 1992).

red devil. Don't be teaching my boy that fairytale elf shit." Still in the son's
POV through the car window, the father pauses triumphant in armed rob-
bery and the vanquishing of Santa with his frenzied junkie nationalist rant.
Holding the ill-gotten gains, a few crumpled bills in either hand, he pleads
with his son, "Do ya see? Do ya see?" Suddenly his innards are slathered on
the window from the shotgun blast to his back from the wounded clerk from
the liquor store. The son jumps from the car crying, "Daddy." The father apol-
ogizes ("Sorry") and in a final gesture hands the son the bloodstained bills,
whispering, "The money" (fig. 3.1). With a close-up on the face of the child,
the voice-over closes the scene: "My father when I saw him die like that, saw
him find his grave in the snow, I only had one thought. It wasn't gonna happen to me."[30]

Cross-fading on the shot of the weeping son cradling his dead father,
there is a flash-forward within the flashback with a cut to city skyline and another insert title: "Cincinnati. 20 years later." Gerald Carver (Charles Martin
Smith), an administrative-looking white man behind a desk, reads papers in a
file, thumbing a Polaroid paper-clipped to it. Looking up he matter-of-factly
asks, "Tell me, do you know the difference between a black man and a nigger?" (fig. 3.2). The reaction shot reveals a nervously stammering black police
officer sitting on the other side of the desk, who replies, "No, I, uh, don't."
Carver continues, "Most niggers don't. Thanks for coming in. Next." There
is a matching shot of Carver posing the question as a second reaction shot
reveals another black officer, who quickly rises, grabs Carver by the lapels,

FIG 3.2 "Tell me, do you know the difference between a black man and a nigger?" Gerald Carver (Charles Martin Smith) in *Deep Cover* (Bill Duke, 1992).

FIG 3.3 "The nigger is the one who would even answer that question." Russell Stevens (Laurence Fishburne) in *Deep Cover* (Bill Duke, 1992).

and lifts him out of his seat: "Do you know who the fuck you're talking to?" To this the nonplussed Carver responds, "Thank you. Next." Finally there is a cut to a third black officer sitting in front of the desk, identified as Officer Stevens. Again Carver asks, "Tell me, do you know the difference between a black man and a nigger?" Neither stunned nor belligerent, Stevens responds, "The nigger is the one who would even answer that question" (fig. 3.3). The rejoinder impresses Carver, who pitches an assignment: to go undercover and infiltrate a drug cartel.

The necessity for the question and, more precisely, how Stevens's response to it proves his appropriateness for the assignment are not immediately clear. The Goldilocks responses by the three candidates (too hot, too cold, just right) are assessed as responses to hypothetical "nigger naming," the justification for which rests on the patent assumption that for the sake of argument, *nigger* can be deployed as mere hypothesis without antiblack intent. Meant to absolve the questioner of culpability, this hypothetical framing nonetheless remains dependently credible on the very real affairs of white supremacy and antiblackness, not merely conjecture. The available categories of *nigger* and *black man* are fashioned as opposing and accounting poles of acceptable and unacceptable blackness. Like *Chameleon Street*, the question expresses an entitlement to know and label the black through a debilitating logic that Charles Johnson summarizes thus: "To perceive a content is to conceive that content."[31] For Johnson the "black as body" condition represents the processing of a black embodiment index. *Deep Cover* as a narrative processing of black embodiment summons a sense of what Johnson considers the non–mutually exclusive strategies of signification and black existential survival, the demonstration of racial exceptionalism, and the radical break of cultural nationalism.[32] The film's extensive braiding of blackness and noir, a thematic sweep of "passing, dissembling, and double consciousness," fixates on race and personhood.[33] The interview sequence crystallizes the film's leitmotif of power, privilege, and speculations on black personhood—a tenacious contest over the meaning of black being.[34]

Stevens's answer to the question temporarily suspends the rhetorical trapping act of racialization and pathology baiting. His response diffuses the negation behind the question and the presumed authority of antiblackness to categorize and know the black. His response, a vernacular redirection, predates the Althusserian interpellative hailing scenario with a tone reminiscent of the expression "It's not what they call you; it's what you answer to." However, one cannot assume syllogistically that the black man is the one who would not answer and sidestep the negation intention. In this instance the black man is as hypothetical and compromised as "the nigger." Together these terms do not demonstrate dialectics; they constitute a confidence game.

As the pitch scene continues, a skeptical Stevens becomes mortified by the prospect of being a snitch for the DEA. He insists that he has always avoided narcotics assignments, even drinking, but Carver silences him by wondering aloud whether the avoidance might have something to do with Stevens's father when he says, "I'm God." Carver asks the now silent Stevens why he became a cop. Stevens responds, "Because I wanted to be of use. Because I wanted to make a difference somehow." To this Carver replies, "You ever taken a look at your psychological profile? You know you score almost exactly like a criminal? Look at this. 'Resents authority.' 'Rigid moral code, but with no underlying system of values.' 'Insufficiently developed sense of self.' Look at this, look at these scores. Look at all the rage. Look at all the repressed violence. I'm telling you, undercover all your faults will become virtues. You'll be a star there, John. You'll do a lot more good there than you ever would have in uniform. You will be of use. You will make a difference."

Carver's pitch to convince Stevens of his untapped potential as "a scumbag for the right side" signals the possibility that if he takes the assignment he might fulfill his destiny and productively channel his lack and degeneracy, a decision that might make him a dutiful "vendor of information," a native informant with the border-crossing imperative of the detective.[35] The innate deficiencies of blackness are framed along an axial hypothesis that the "nigger/black man" scenario depends on a connotative substitution under the auspices of denotative authority. Carver's character assessment is predicated on the empirical objectivity of personality testing and social behaviorism, yet the objectivity of the testing is clearly compromised by the normative tone of whiteness and the antiblack marking of pathology and criminality. Stevens is exhibited by empirical data as existential truth, a black pathology showcase. The psychological profile marks his (black) rage as pathological and unfounded in spite of the fact that his test results could be those of a latent rebel or a sociopath.[36] Rather statistical degeneracy must be managed and channeled toward the capable degeneracy of government service; thus Stevens's black rage must be directed to a proper use (the assignment). A black avenger employed by the Man?[37]

While Stevens avoids the initial interpellative ploy of the distinction, he bites on the social pathology ploy of destiny. Therefore the film is less about the difference between a black man and a "nigger" than about the untenable and narrativized, antiblack epistemological foundations of the question. Stevens will make a good undercover operative because his blackness is convincingly criminal. He remains a "nigger," but more precisely one of use, so long as he is simply his true self, thus echoing Fanon's sense of antiblack precognition: "And so it is not I who make a meaning for myself, but it is the meaning that was already there, pre-existing, waiting for me."[38] The pitch does not hinge on a scripted performance but on an antiblack belief in the "social instrumentality" of Stevens's natural/stereotypical being.[39] If Carver is God, as he claims, then he casts Stevens as an ebony archangel, chosen to carry out the necessary and noble, dirty work.

Notably there is a continuity error in the scene of the assignment pitch when Carver calls Stevens, whose first name is Russell, "John," the name of his cover. At this point Stevens has not accepted the mission and there is no explanation for who John is. As such the error highlights the premeditating dynamics surrounding Russell/John and cues the purposeful scenes to come.

Crossfading to LA several weeks later with the compounded construction of criminal, victim, and avenger, the voice-over narration comments, "I didn't want the assignment. I sat there the whole interview thinking that if I took it, it would be the biggest mistake of my life . . . and I was right." The film extensively employs wipes as transitions from scene to scene. Tonally the wipes suggest a turning, if not tearing. As opposed to a linear narrative chain along a strictly horizontal axis, the deliberate reflexivity of the wipe suggests a peeling back or reveal of the *underneath* of the shot. These indications of levels and opacities, shadows and acts, are concretized in the first shot of Stevens's arrival in Los Angeles, undercover as John Hull—a canted shot of the Hollywood sign. Welcome to the dream factory, player.

Will the Circle Be Unbroken

The voice-over in *Deep Cover* complicates the classical function of the noir voice-over due to the extent that the voice acts as a sign of black interiority and narrative authority. The film's use of first-person voice-over narration fulfills the structuring purpose of a diegetic presence or "implied author" who provides for a film's "moral/ideological agency."[40] Furthermore the noir voice-over is distinguished by its "male narrational perspective" that utilizes either a "confessional" or "investigative" mode. As Karen Hollinger notes, the noir voice-over often operates as a voice of fragmentation and crisis within the narrative: "Voice-over creates this fragmenting effect by establishing within the film a fight for narrative power as the narrator struggles to gain control of the narrative events recounted. This battle between the narrator and the film's flashback visuals leads to an extreme tension between word and image."[41] In the absence of a voice that signifies a unifying authority, the disembodiment crisis of the noir protagonist hovers over the question of a "complete persona," what Kelly Oliver and Benigno Trigo recognize as a central conceit of noir: "The noir convention is that the separation between the voice and body gradually disappears as the film comes to the end, when we are gradually brought to the present of the narrative and to the reunion of the voice and the body of the detective, whose complete persona we see end the film."[42] If the disconnection between the voice and the body of the noir protagonist operates as a battle for authority that propels and structures the narrative toward resolution and unification, then the distinctness of the voice-over in *Deep Cover* disputes the narrational arc of noir closure.

The *Deep Cover* voice refabulates the disconnection conceit with the accented difference of blackness. As a noir narrative preoccupied with embodiment, authenticity, and blackness, *Deep Cover* pivots between presence and absence as the voice-over operates as a vital element of the black scripting narrative. In the film the assurances of a rejoined mind and body proffer a distinctness that augments the generalized sense of the noir voice-over as interiority, or an unconscious where "desire and repression interact and seek formulation" with black consciousness at the crux.[43] The voice of *Deep Cover* engages with agency and critical performativity in much the same way as the strategic in/visibility of *Chameleon Street* recasts Du Boisian double consciousness.

The voice-over's claim to a subject and a body was established in the "blackened primal scene" that opened the film: "So gather 'round as I run it down and unravel my pedigree."[44] In particular the voice signals a genesis with a black grain yet does not claim to be an everyman or universal black subject. Instead the voice avoids the relativizing truth of anonymity while navigating the narrative's guiding cue of loss.[45] Moreover the voice-over bears out the distinction between a speaking subject and a spoken-for object.[46]

Upon Hull's arrival in Los Angeles and a review of the DEA reconnaissance of the pyramid structure of the drug network (with its levels of import suppliers, distributors, managers, and dealers), he begins procuring from street-level dealers. A few weeks into the mission, Hull meets two important characters: an LAPD detective named Taft (Clarence Williams III) and a lawyer and drug trafficker named David Jason (Jeff Goldblum).

The film introduces Detective Taft during Hull's arrest in the middle of purchasing a kilogram of cocaine, later discovered to be baby laxative. As Hull tries to dispose of what he thinks is cocaine and escape, he runs right into the detective and a punch to his gut. Hull drops to his knees as Taft kneels down into a close-up and whispers, "How ya' doin', Judas?" The crossfade to the next scene opens on an interrogation room with Taft and his partner in the middle of questioning and Hull claiming complete ignorance of circumstances and associates. The partner leaves and Taft calmly asks, "Are you a Christian?" before moving on to further assess Hull. He doubts Hull's cover story, surmising that he comes from back east and not Oakland, as he claims. He continues:

> Let me ask you something. You got kids? [He pulls out his wallet and shows a photo of two little girls.] Well, these are my African American beautiful babies. If somebody put a gun to your baby's head, would you try and kill them if you could? [Pause. He closes the wallet and returns it to his pocket.] Me too. And by selling that stuff you're putting a gun to my baby's head. Let me warn you. I'm like a mad dog after a bone. I'd be all over you like stink on doo-doo. Trust me. Here, you read this. It gives me a lot of pleasure.

Taft tosses a prayer book across the table. Picking it up, Hull responds, "Check this out, Reverend. God bless you." He crosses himself while laughing and throws the book across the room at the departing Taft.

Historically the offer of the Bible (Talking Book, or the Word) to the black is the offer of literacy to the slave and the subsequent equating of literacy to freedom. Hull's refusal of the prayer book represents the rejection of the ethical veracity of the Judeo-Christian sense of a sanctified blackness and the cultural nationalist hermeneutics of a black embodiment index. As Henry Louis Gates Jr. argues, the Talking Book is the interstitial and intertextual trope of the African American literary tradition: "[The Talking Book] also reveals, rather surprisingly, that the tension between the black vernacular and the literate white text, between the spoken and the written word, between the oral and printed forms of literary discourse, has been represented and thematicized in black letters at least since slaves and ex-slaves met the challenge of the Enlightenment to their humanity by literally writing themselves into being through carefully crafted representations in language of the black self."[47] In this way the offer of the prayer book to Hull resonates as the offer of the Word and a script.

Throughout the film Taft encourages Hull to feel remorse for his sins as a drug dealer.[48] But this is a doubled sense of sin as it at once refers to missionary piousness and a violation of the black community. Taft is both a stand-in for the black patriarch lost in the snow and a Christian crusader who attempts to impress upon Hull how the sins he commits impact his soul. Thus he epitomizes a compulsory sense of respectable black masculinity. Devoted to his little girls, cleaning up the streets, and circulating the Gospel, he exhibits the cross-purposes of a cultural nationalist patriarch and a missionary. Thus he measures Hull's blackness as a traitorous slight of the Christ with the conditional rider of traitor to the race, a meeting of religiosity and black nationalism.[49]

Carver parallels Taft with an ideological concern for the function status of

Hull's blackness. Early in the undercover operation, Hull sees a young street dealer shot dead and begins to express doubts about his assignment:

HULL: What am I doing here, man?

CARVER: Have you ever seen a crack baby? A newborn crack baby, six hours old, screaming its heart out because it's going through withdrawal? Over the course of the next year it doesn't learn to crawl or walk or talk on time because it's got deformities. Physical deformities. Mental deformities. It's got brain damage, lowered IQ, dyslexia—god only knows what else. Maybe it goes to school but it can't learn. And it's violent, so it gets in trouble with the law. It's unable to form any close emotional ties so it's faced with the prospect of going through this hideous, miserable life completely alone. There are millions of these babies, John. There's a whole generation of your people who are being destroyed before they are even born because these guys are bringing that shit into this country. Now do you remember what you're doing here?

The rhetorical close to this review of purpose completes the conjoined saving of the beautiful black princesses, "your people," and the Jesus children of America. Marked by canonical sociology and the rhetoric of cultural nationalism, Hull's embodiment entails a multiple servicing of his blackness: a black apostle, a black panther, a black avenger of the state. In other words, he must be a saint and not another "bad nigger."[50]

Mighty Mighty, Spade and Whitey

David Jason is a lawyer whose job with the drug cartel is to manage the street-level distributors and provide legal services. The partnering of Hull and Jason distends the buddy film trope of interracial male coupling.[51] Building on Fredric Jameson's notion of "strategies of containment" as an analytic tool, Ed Guerrero recognizes the distinct containment measure of "protective custody" that directs the interracial buddy film and prevents the possibility of a systemic critique of antiblackness and white supremacy: "The buddy formula is able to attract the demographically broadest possible audience while negotiating, containing, and fantastically resolving the tangled and socially charged issue of race relations on the screen."[52] These dalliances in interracial brotherhood often rely on distinctions of racial typologies whereby the balm of black simple truths assuages the white man's burden of analytic reasoning.[53] These ebony-and-ivory brotherhood escapades often build on banalities like

"Our blood is red" and "We are both men." For *Deep Cover* the protective custody measure strikingly fails as the coupling builds on a magnification of differences that disproves egalitarian designs of the coupling.

Deep Cover deviates from and viciously signifies on the foundational motive for interracial coupling in cinema: the social problem film. The social problem tendency of American films entails an address of the black as a problem, but a problem removed from any potentially systemic indictments. This means that the tacit collusion of the academy and the trade press with the film industry perpetuates an idea of America that often means that staged eruptions of racial conflict should by the film's close be resolved and contained in such a way as to frame film spectatorship as an analyst-analysand dynamic and enacted cures. Michael Rogin notes, "Hollywood, inheriting and universalizing blackface in the blackface musical, celebrated itself as the institutional locus of American identity. In the social problem film it allied itself with the therapeutic society. Generic overlap suggests institutional overlap; Hollywood was not just Hortense Powdermaker's dream factory, but also the American interpreter of dreams, employing roleplaying as national mass therapy."[54] In the precise terms of genre, Frank Krutnik hints at the execution of this kind of American prerogative by noir's composite interest in social issues: "The crime narrative provides a generically recognisable structure for the handling of [social problem issues], allowing both an elaboration of the problem and its containment within familiar narrative and narrational parameters. Because they incorporate elements of crime, violence, and psychological and sexual disturbance . . . [it] is not uncommon for some of these films to be included within the '*film noir* corpus.'"[55] Ultimately *Deep Cover* bypasses the expectation that cinema regulate or diagnose with a quantifiable narrative cure.

Ultimately the social problem narrative equates exhibition and spectatorship to public policy. These films are founded on addressing the black (never blackness) in ways that absolve the spectator from complicity or a revelation that the issues at play are more systemic than they appear on the screen. Predicated on the narrativizing of color-blind liberalism, whereby resolving the narrative conflict lies in overcoming the difference of race as the fundamental problem, the primary feature of interracial male coupling appeals to utopian homogeneity. Through the assured flattening of differences to a universal humanist and homogeneous core of shared values racialized difference must be disavowed for the sake of the normative standards of whiteness. The resultant couplings are thus saddled with the extradiegetic responsibility of reconciliation between the races.

FIG 3.4 "I don't know, maybe you feel like you're fucking a slave." David Jason (Jeff Goldblum) and John Hull (Laurence Fishburne) in *Deep Cover* (Bill Duke, 1992).

The film's enactment of a noir devoutly fashions discomforting proposals about national consciousness. One exchange in particular between Hull and Jason illustrates how the film consequentially deviates from the ideological censure of interracial male coupling. The scene opens with Hull in a hotel hallway growing impatient with Jason's lateness for a meeting. Jason appears in the doorway attempting to finish getting dressed and part from his lingerie-clad black mistress, Jacqueline ("With a J"), with postcoital farewells ("Oh, it won't go down baby") before finally making it into the hallway (fig. 3.4):

HULL: David, we got to go man.
JASON: How come I like balling black chicks so much?
HULL: I don't know, maybe you feel like you're fucking a slave.
JASON: What do you mean, like a bondage thing?
HULL: No, like a racist thing.
JASON: You ever been with two women at once?
HULL: Yeah, your mother and your father.
JASON: Yeah? Did my mama get buck wild on you?

This exchange irretrievably shatters the social problem-solving objective of interracial male coupling. As opposed to being a non sequitur, Hull's reading reflects on the dynamics of power and racialization that shadow Jason's desire. The disrupting candor of "fucking a slave" sharply accounts for Jason's jungle fever with a contextual account of slavery. "Brown sugar, how come you taste you good?" A cruelly parodic observation of desire, spectacle, and fetishistic consumption, the livid retort "fucking a slave" ruins the utopian designs that have historically guided the interracial male coupling tendency.

Robyn Wiegman's sharp assessment of the 1980s interracial male coupling phenomenon centers on how the representational reckoning of these couplings entices with the transcendental assurance of America, a presumably shared and interpellative ideal of the nation. But in fact these couplings thrive due to a regulatory function pitched as a cultural or national palliative. Wiegman explains:

> It is at the site of interracial male bonds that popular culture in the 1980s most repetitively struggled to rehabilitate "America" from its segregationist as well as its imperialist past. In the bond's quest for a self-enclosed, racially undifferentiated masculine space, cultural production casts its net around a reconfiguration of "America," providing narrative trajectories that pivot on the confrontation with difference and its ultimate shimmering transcendence. . . . The interracial male bonding narrative embodies the oscillation of "America," constructing on the one hand the ideological dream of cohesion, of an essential, uniform masculine identity, while forging, on the other, discriminations that qualify and specify the boundaries of that identity.[56]

The interracial coupling of *Deep Cover* holds a cheeky disregard for this transcendental ideal. The resulting stipulation of America that this Jason-Hull coupling is thought to embody signifies a difference-driving capacity to insolently alter the resolute conditions on which traditional noir stands.

Jason's Jewishness impacts the film's coupling dynamic in crucial ways. Wahneema Lubiano suggests he "represents the graying boundary between whiteness and blackness, between Jewish ethnicity and black racialism, between 'real' and 'false' masculinity and patriarchy."[57] This graying frames Jason as a liminal figure whose shifting capacity marks his inability to fulfill the allegorical promise of interracial male coupling as reconciliation as, over the course of the film, Jason and Hull experience an accordant crisis of masculinity. As Hull's transformation is an extended contest of embodiment and black subjectivity, for Jason this transformation is tempered by his fetishistic designs of black expressivity and masculinity in contradistinction to Jewishness. Thus Jason's liminal subject position between racialized other and white man shadows the film's focus on black masculinity in flux.

Marked as a Jew enmeshed in WASP trappings (a blue-eyed, blonde shiksa wife), Jason routinely becomes the subject of ethnic infantilization (called a "bar mitzvah boy"), feminine lack, or pejorative homosexual: "It's a good thing he never went to jail, because if he came out, he'd have an asshole big enough to swallow a watermelon." He is even framed in a decidedly nonphallic way between the spread legs of a stripper dressed as a nun. And there is Felix Barbosa (Gregory Sierra), the supplier of product for Hull and Jason and the person primarily responsible for the escalating humiliation of Jason. At one point in the film Barbosa admonishes Jason with a statement that foreshadows Jason's eventual evolution: "You ought to kill a man someday, Jason. It's . . . it's liberating." Yet Jason possesses a transtextual quality in the sense of a coterminous act of intertextuality and translation.[58] As a Jewish character enlisted in an interracial coupling under the shadow of racial performativity, he touches on the shared legacy of the social problem film and blackface musicals. In *Blackface, White Noise: Jewish Immigrants in the Hollywood Melting Pot*, Michael Rogin argues that the social problem film and the blackface musical converged and separated over the course of the New Deal. Rogin focuses on *The Jazz Singer* (Alan Crosland, 1927) as a significant moment of convergence that demonstrates how the presumed opposition between these two generic modes in fact represents the "split halves of a single Ur-film." Rogin notes, "Moving back and forth between silence and sound, blackface and whiteface, Jew and gentile, street and stage, *Jazz Singer*'s genre liminality is part of its generic liminality. The first talking picture unties the subgenre of the social-problem film that it climaxed, the generational-conflict/intermarriage/passing motion picture, with the genre it originated, the musical, more particularly, the self reflexive movie musical about making musicals or making music, which encompasses at its foundation the blackface musical."[59] Jason complicates this history for he is not the progeny of Jack Robin (né Jakie Rabinowitz) alone. One way that the character's rendering as a Jew exceeds the blackface musical machinations requires a consideration of racechange and Jason's circulation as ideological kin of "the white negro."[60]

I'm Waiting for My Man

In "The White Negro," Norman Mailer extolled the birth of a new man, a figure with the cool pose of a flaneur and performer-participant in New York City: "In such places as Greenwich Village, a ménage à trois was completed— the bohemian and the juvenile delinquent came face-to-face with the Negro, and the hipster was a fact in American life. If marijuana was the wedding ring, the child was the language of Hip for its argot gave expression to abstract states of feeling which all could share, at least all who were hip. And in this wedding of the white and the black it was the Negro who brought the cultural dowry."[61] Mailer ordains the protean Beat a vessel of "racechange," with black expressivity as the creative and compositional conduit.[62] At the core of Mailer's heart of darkness resides an existentialist hipster who insists that the black, to paraphrase Fanon, be black in relation to the white negro as an abstracted vessel for the hipster's entitled racechange and negrophilia. For Mailer the negro must be a negro in relation to the white negro's fears of totalitarianism, genocide, nuclear Armageddon, the homosexual, the vagina dentata, and the Jewish eunuch.[63]

In a conspiring language of consent and white dada, a dual purposing of blackness resulted in distinctly different yet tendential cruising subcultures of whiteness (the juvenile delinquent and the bohemian). Driven by the suggestion that the black offers a dowry in this jumping of the broom, the premise of equal exchange signals not a random trafficking in expressive assets but the historical exchange of people.[64]

"The White Negro" signals the way the Beats came to represent a creative legacy and elitist transgression dependent on a masculinity project intricately dependent on blackness as more than merely a muse accelerant for whiteness and modernism. Extending Mailer's oft-cited matrimonial delirium, the proposition becomes that the written vows for this performative consent of coupling have a hard-boiled trace. The noir conceit provides the terms of this encounter and exchange, which parallel the occupational conversation that so often facilitates the noir figure's ability to maneuver and circulate through the shadows and colored milieu as one capably versed in the lingo of another's tongue, another country. The concurrent strains of Mailer's essay as an autobiography of negrophilia, white masculinity, and the noir detection of otherness inform the blended complication of Jason as a social problem and racechange model.

The scene immediately following the "fucking a slave" exchange is their late arrival for the meeting at a downtown Los Angeles art gallery. The gallery owner, Betty (Victoria Dillard), facilitates the money-laundering operation for the drug cartel through a finance scheme that involves an unnamed African bank. Foreshadowing the romance to come, Hull and Betty begin an antagonistic courting ritual of double entendre and lingering glances as they sit on opposite sides of the desk. Much of their banter occurs while Hull wears a *wanara* (monkey) mask, which Betty claims he could never afford (fig. 3.5).[65]

FIG 3.5 The mask and the masked. Russell Stevens/John Hull (Laurence Fishburne) in *Deep Cover* (Bill Duke, 1992).

In the midst of the building antagonism between Betty and Hull, Hull re-moves the mask and places it back on the desk. Jason picks it up and begins to dance with the mask over his face. High on cocaine, he eventually sits at the desk next to Hull and begins regaling Betty with a recounting of Hull's showdown with a rival drug dealer:

> JASON: Lighten up, Betty. What's the vibe here? You should have seen this guy on the street the other night. He's the shit. I didn't tell you. [Turning to address John he continues.] You were so like some beautiful panther or . . . or . . . or . . . jungle storm. This is not my condescending infatua-tion with just everything black. Those politically conservative negroes can kiss my ass and these anti-Semitic pricks can kiss my ass but you have the gift of fury. You're like a . . . a . . . dangerous, magnificent beast.
> HULL: Watch your mouth, David.
> JASON: Watch my mouth? I can say anything I want.
> HULL: You can say anything you want?
> JASON: What? You didn't hear me? I can say anything I fucking want to say! [They both stand and step toward each other (fig. 3.6).]
> BETTY: Boys. Is this some type of male-bonding thing? Because you can take it outside. You're blowing my high.
> JASON: She wants us bad. She wants us both. Mmm! But we got to go. We got to go.

FIG 3.6 "Boys. Is this some type of male-bonding thing?" Jason and Hull in *Deep Cover* (Bill Duke, 1992).

Conjoined by traces of ethnographic surrealism and the noir phenomenology of detection, Jason's observations on magnificence and danger expose the fundamental tendencies of the stereotype as object of desire and repudiation.[66] All one has to do is remove "beautiful" and "dangerous, magnificent" to appreciate the point. In a room devoted to artifice and masks (if not mirrors), all Jason perceives or conceives is an authenticity, a salacious noting of a black essence. The way multicultural value and international finance are at play in the art gallery reeks of a colonial prerogative of collection and ownership. With these themes of consumption and finance capital at hand, the gallery sequence intones the trafficking and the economics of the Middle Passage.[67]

The masks also allude to questions of identity and performativity. In particular they allude to the tropology of the veil, the caul, and the cloak that has circulated throughout the tradition of black existential philosophy. Michelle M. Wright specifies that when evoked in "the Western discourse on the Negro," the mask serves several distinct functions, two of which are especially pertinent: "First, the African mask is part of a chain of signifiers in the Western imagination in which savages dance around in a jungle wearing terrifyingly oversized masks. Although the mask is ostensibly *not* a body part, quite often the 'savages' are only shown with masks on, suggesting that the mask is in fact their face. This leads to the second link: even without a mask, the African is not seen as actually possessing a face."[68] The mask, the performing face or masquerade, evokes the leitmotif of the double bind of the drug dealer/cop and the nigger/black man.

One of Betty's functions in the narrative appears to be a variation on the beard for Hull and Jason while simultaneously fulfilling the role of love interest for Hull. She is absent from any significant role in the narrative beyond exposition as she lacks any interiority. Clearly the film's primary preoccupation with standards of masculinity continues the historical persistence of inadequately accounting for the place of women in the social problem or interracial male coupling deliberations.[69]

Hull draws closer to the top of the drug pyramid and defies direct orders to not go to a meeting that was meant to result in the arrest of Betty and the murder of Jason. Carver declares that the undercover operation is being shut down and announces his reassignment to the Washington office. He offers the explanation of a change in State Department policy regarding sympathetic leadership in Latin America. When told this, Hull responds, "This whole fucking time, I'm a cop pretending to be a drug dealer. I ain't nothing but a drug dealer pretending to be a cop. I ain't gonna pretend no more, Gerry. I quit." As Hull drives away, the voice-over begins, "So, the whole game had been a joke, a joke on me. I was a fool. I'd been turned out like a two-dollar ho. Used. Abused. But, with no towel and no kiss." Hull takes his first drink of alcohol, a swig from Carver's flask, as he walks away, appearing well on his way to being that apple that never falls far from the tree, a father's son after all.

While Hull is seated in his car in an empty alleyway and in the throes of the caffeinated flu of a cocaine high, the voice-over continues, "You know the jungle creed says that the strongest feed on any prey it can, and I was branded beast at any feast before I ever became a man" (fig. 3.7). This is a supreme moment of self-abjection in the register of underground and invisible men. The beat poetics of the verse suggests a vernacular toast, hip-hop spoken word, or even the poetry of the Black Arts Movement. Ego-tripping with a brick of cocaine in the center console?[70]

The Long Goodbye

In possession of over half a billion dollars in drug profits, Jason and Hull arrange a meeting on a docked cargo ship with the top figure of Carver's drug triangle, Hector Guzman (René Assa). Guzman is a Latin American ambassador whose diplomatic immunity was used for the unrestricted import of

FIG 3.7 "I was branded beast at any feast before I ever became a man." Hull in *Deep Cover* (Bill Duke, 1992).

cocaine to his nephew, now dead. Jason begins pitching the dream scheme of designer drugs by presenting Guzman and his people with a prospectus, and explains how the manufacturing of a legal designer drug eliminates the expenses related to cultivation, refinement, importing, and labor costs. Guzman replies, "You racist Americans. You just want to cut us poor Hispanics completely out of the market." To this Jason responds, "No, Mr. Guzman. I think you know it. There is no such thing as an American anymore. No Hispanics, no Japanese, no blacks, no whites, no nothing. It's just rich people and poor people. The three of us are all rich, so we're all on the same side." Postracial solidarity meets the ways of capital in the new global village as gated community.

Guzman samples the product and agrees to the terms in the prospectus, but just as the deal is being closed, Detective Taft arrives alone to make an arrest. Guzman quickly exits the ship, Jason leaves to get the van filled with the money, and Hull and Taft face each other, guns drawn. Taft pleads with Hull to drop his gun; Hull eventually fires into the air as the returning Jason shoots Taft. Hull rushes to the fallen Taft, who convulses while spitting blood and exclaims, "I know you're a cop." Hull becomes Stevens again as he grabs Taft's radio and frantically speaks in procedural code over the police radio, alerting the dispatcher that there is an officer down. When Jason asks what he is doing he simply says, "Jason, I'm a cop." Jason kneels over the dying Taft and looks closely at Stevens:

JASON: Five hundred million dollars and no more nigger. Forget this Judeo-Christian bullshit. The same people who taught us virtue are the very ones who enslaved us, baby. We've had fun and I know your dick gets hard for money, power, and women. And it doesn't matter that you're a cop, so get in the van. Is this what's standing between us and destiny? Is this what stands between us and greatness? Is this it?! [Jason puts the gun to Stevens's head.] Is this it?! [Jason lowers the gun from Stevens's head and shoots Taft dead.][71]

STEVENS: You shouldn't have done that, David.[72]

JASON: But I did, so get in the fucking van. Wake up, my brother. Wake up. There's not much time. Wake up! Wake up![73]

Jason slaps Stevens, stirring him from his trance-like mantra of "You shouldn't have done that, David," and Stevens begins to recite the Miranda rights. As Jason rises and walks away to leave with the van, Stevens calls out, "David, you're under arrest." Jason turns and somberly asks, "John, what's the weirdest thing you did sexually?" Stevens replies, "Nothing seems that weird anymore." Jason quietly says, "We were almost there." They raise their guns and fire at one another as Jason is fatally hit and slides to the ground dead. The scene ends with a shot of Stevens standing in tears looking at the dead Jason with the sounds of ship horns and approaching police sirens.

Lubiano suggests that the shootout confirms the latent patriarchal inscription of the film. As she surmises, with the killing of Taft the film is caught in a moment of ideological revelation as Taft's death seemingly provides safe passage for Hull/Stevens back to the patriarchal fold: "The death of that good father [Taft] brings Hull back into the black family as well as back into the law-and-order family."[74] Yet strictly reading Taft as "good black father" disavows the ambivalence surrounding his function in the film. He is, after all, just another narrative trope of black containment. Ultimately *Deep Cover* is about raising children, not killing fathers. While Taft's death is a necessary trigger in the reemergence of Stevens, it does not wholly signal consent to the patriarchal authority of cultural nationalism. Rather the sequence compels a critique of this authority.

Notably the aftermath of the showdown occurs in the absence of an interracial *pietà*, a variation on Mary cradling the dying Jesus in the context of the social problem tendency as a sign of racial tolerance. Rogin identifies the World War II drama *Home of the Brave* (Mark Robson, 1949) as the first staging of the interracial pietà in the scene where Moss (James Edwards) cradles the dying Finch (Lloyd Bridges) as a feminine or maternal nurturer.[75] The ideological force of the pietà resides in its "translating [of] racially coded actants into gender-coded ones."[76] Thus the possibility of crossracial identification is mediated by the heteronormative and a gender binary dependent on a "rejection of mutability."[77] *Deep Cover* disavows the interracial pietà and its heteronormative prerogative to manage the threat of equivalence and desire.

To illustrate the distinctness of the *Deep Cover* showdown, consider the following two closing scenes that make use of the interracial pietà in more compulsory ways than *Deep Cover*. In *The Defiant Ones* (Stanley Kramer, 1958), Noah (Sidney Poitier) sits with John (Tony Curtis) lying in his lap following their attempt to escape by hopping a train. Noah has chosen to stay with John rather than escape and leave him behind. With the sounds of dogs approaching, Noah lights two cigarettes and places one in John's mouth—the closest thing to a kiss that the sequence can allow:

> NOAH: How you doing, Joker?
> JOHN: Okay.
> NOAH: You hurt bad?
> JOHN: I feel fine.
> NOAH: Sure you do.
> JOHN: You're gonna make someone a fine old lady someday.
> NOAH: Ain't it the truth.

The second scene occurs in *Lethal Weapon 2* (Richard Donner, 1989) and follows the climactic showdown of Roger (Danny Glover) and Riggs (Mel Gibson) on a cargo ship. With the South African diplomatic corps responsible for drug smuggling vanquished, Riggs has seemingly been fatally shot. Roger kills the final villain, then rushes to cradle Riggs in his lap over strains of Bob Dylan's "Knocking on Heaven's Door" (1973). Roger pleads, "Don't die. You're not dead until I tell you. Breathe. Breathe." Riggs regains consciousness and says, "Hey, Rog, did anyone ever tell you, you really are a beautiful man? Give us a kiss before they come." As the camera pans upward, leaving the couple off-screen, the closing song plays over the sound of police cars arriving at the docks. Muted beneath the nondiegetic and diegetic is the continued exchange between Riggs and Roger:

> ROGER: Hey, where did that bullet hit you anyway?
> RIGGS: Oh God. Oh God. Don't make me laugh.

Thus the film closes on phallic dispossession by crudely suggesting that Riggs has had his penis shot off.

The interracial male coupling in *Deep Cover* operates in contradistinction to the pietà scenes of *The Defiant Ones* and *Lethal Weapon 2*. In place of liberal piety *Deep Cover* substitutes Stevens standing still. He does not rush to, or rather *consent* to the place usually made available for his kind in these couplings. His immobility is a refusal to legitimize the noir idea's social problem-solving intention. He does not go to Jason and whisper sweet nothings into his ear to help him cross over. As Jason says, "Forget this Judeo-Christian bullshit. The same people who taught us virtue are the very ones who have enslaved us, baby." No magical negro, Stevens does not inhabit his prescribed pietà role as nurturer.

The showdown between performativities, racechange, and mimicry softly registers as a breakup between two men. Jason is no longer the bar mitzvah boy but a man who kills with ease, a man always dressed in black, more Ice-T than Johnny Cash. The division and ambivalence between the two is imprinted on both as, in the midst of this oscillation, the two men become each other's doppelganger.[78]

The traditionally heteronormative design of the interracial male coupling conceit becomes homosocial desire in *Deep Cover*. In addition to the absence of the pietà image, the other significant refusal that occurs in this scene involves Stevens's deflection of Jason's joke. In *The Defiant Ones* and *Lethal Weapon 2*, the joke serves the purpose of defusing male desire by framing the coupling in terms of the wounded masculine (whiteness) and the colluding codes of the weak and selfless feminine (blackness).[79] In this way the wit of the joke seeks to bar a "touch" that might provide an opportunity for what Eve Sedgwick qualifies as "homo/heterosexual definitional panic."[80] In his consideration of the narrative aversions of *The Defiant Ones*, James Baldwin writes of the connotative capacity of touch, "I doubt that Americans will ever be able to face the fact that the word, homosexual, is not a noun. The root of this word, as Americans use it—or, as the word uses Americans—simply involves a term of any human touch, since any human touch can change you."[81] Stevens stands still and weeps for Jason (not Taft). His stillness demonstrates an ambivalence that dissuades the possible suspension or redirection of a look of desire between the two. Instead their dissolution allows for the mutuality and change that Baldwin describes. The showdown points to a stake in the transgressive touch to court loss and desire in the place of triumph.[82]

Haldeman, Ehrlichman, Mitchell, and Dean
It follows a pattern if you dig what I mean.

—GIL SCOTT-HERON AND BRIAN JACKSON, "H₂OGATE BLUES"

It is undeniable that a wildly successful conspiracy to import cocaine existed for many years, and the innumerable American citizens—most of them poor and black—paid an enormous price as a result. This book was written for them, so that they may know upon what altars their communities were sacrificed.

—GARY WEBB, *DARK ALLIANCE*

Crossfading from the docks, the next scene opens a month later in Washington, DC, with Stevens preparing to speak to a congressional committee that is evaluating the success of the undercover operation. With the threat of money-laundering charges against Betty, Stevens agrees in writing to speak favorably of the DEA, the operation, and Carver. While Carver and his boss sit in the gallery behind him, Stevens performs as agreed. Yet as the hearing draws to a close a congresswoman asks him directly whether the operation was a success. He replies, "Almost." Stevens retrieves a videotape from a companion and proceeds to play it on one of the monitors in the room. He continues, "What you're about to see is a videotape of Hector Guzman, a diplomat to this country, a very powerful and important Latin American politician and a friend of our president. Here you can see him meeting with drug dealers, including myself, late last month in Los Angeles. For years Mr. Guzman has been a conduit for his nephew Anton Gallegos, a major drug importer." The videotape features the failed negotiation with Guzman on the docks. With this revelation pandemonium erupts, and the chairman of the committee calls for the videotape to be seized, to which Stevens replies, "I'm sorry. Copies have already been distributed to the press." It is video as evidentiary truth in a post–Marion Barry, pre–Rodney King world. As reporters rush to the dais to question committee members, Stevens tries to leave and Carver pulls him aside:

> CARVER: You and Jason took a hell of a lot of money out of that van before you gave it to Guzman. How much was that exactly?
> STEVENS: [pulls Carver close to him] Gerry, what's the difference between a black man and a nigger?

CARVER: What? [Stevens punches Carver in the stomach, dropping him to the ground.]

STEVENS: The nigger is the one that would even think about telling you.

The twist of this hypothetical "nigger naming" comes with a violent reprisal. The rebel is complete, no longer the native informant that the government hoped for but a native performer turned whistleblower.

The scene at the congressional hearing is the only solution of the crime that the film offers. The closer Stevens came to completing his ascension of the triangle, the closer he came to the revelation of the conspiratorial involvement of the U.S. government and the more dangerous he became. As such Stevens refines the efficiency of the triangle by implicating the government. Jacquie Jones writes, "By linking conspiracy theory to domestic issues of particular interest to African Americans, the film validates a Black nationalist agenda... while calling for a reformulation of 'the law,' a shading of criminality, a hybridization of cinematic traditions."[83] The hybrid resolution of *Deep Cover* refabulates the drug culture of the hood film and new black cinema with the plotting of a conspiracy film and an indictment of the U.S. government.

The film's scripting of conspiratorial claims involves a precedent-probability event, a historical precedent that supports the truth of a claim. For example, the second Tuskegee experiment devoted to monitoring the effects of syphilis was the precedent-probability event for conspiracies involving the engineering and spread of pathogens for the deliberate purpose of black genocide. And, at the very least, the COINTELPRO (Counter Intelligence Program) actions by the FBI against the Black Panthers and the American Indian Movement were the precedent-probability event for conspiracies surrounding the persecution or assassination of revolutionary activists of color.[84]

The extradiegetic innuendo of the film entails drug trafficking, Latin America, and a U.S. government policy that prioritizes foreign interests over domestic affairs, as the film is set in the 1980s (e.g., references to "Just Say No" and fishing with the president). The Iran-Contra Affair and the Reagan-Bush years thus function as the film's precedent-probability event. What was once explained away as urban legend became something far more complicated than the causality deliberations that organize conspiracies. Perhaps conspiracy and paranoia are not appropriate designations for *Deep Cover*, where the inquiries of *why* and *how* are ruthlessly preempted by a question of *what people will not do*. The film suggests that a desire for Latin American leadership receptive to the policies of the U.S. government allowed for and tolerated the substantial importation of cocaine. Nevertheless the film's conspiratorial prop-osition ended five years after its release on 18 August 1996, the day the *San Jose Mercury* ran the first of Gary Webb's three-part investigative series, "Dark Alliance."

With the heading "America's 'Crack' Plague Has Roots in Nicaragua War," Webb's article opened simply enough: "For the better part of a decade, a San Francisco Bay Area drug ring sold tons of cocaine to the Crips and Bloods street gangs of Los Angeles and funneled millions in drug profits to a Latin American guerrilla army run by the CIA."[85] Alexander Cockburn and Jeffrey St. Clair summarize: "Webb stuck closely to a single story line: how a group of Nicaraguan exiles set up a cocaine ring in California, establishing ties with the black street gangs of South Central Los Angeles who manufactured crack cocaine out of shipments of powder cocaine. Webb then charted how much of the profits made by Nicaraguan exiles had been funneled back to the Contra army—created in the late 1970s by the Central Intelligence Agency, with the mission of sabotaging the Sandinista revolution that had evicted Anastasio Somoza and his corrupt clique in 1979."[86]

Webb's series exposed how cocaine trafficking was a more consistent and lucrative channel for funding the Contras than the profits of arms deals with Iran. The legislative caps in place through 1987 barred the Reagan administra-tion from directly funding paramilitary operations and resulted in collusion with figures who would become the largest importers and suppliers of cocaine in the country. With the cheap manufacturing of crack cocaine and efficient distribution across the United States established by the Los Angeles gangs, the profits made by these Nicaraguan émigrés and Somoza sympathizers be-yond their own personal coffers went toward the funding of the CIA-backed Contras. Furthermore substantial evidence points to the diversion to under-ground domestic channels of military arms earmarked for the Contras.

The DEA, FBI, and Department of Justice were discouraged or thwarted in their investigations of key figures; the first major drug indictment did not occur until 1989. Reagan, the CIA, and the secret counterinsurgency funding by any means necessary did not deliberately set out to spark the crack cocaine epidemic of the 1980s. Yet the end does justify the means when the spread of communism in Latin America dictated the endorsement of a foreign policy on the offensive against agitator dominoes.

In the wake of the "Dark Alliance" series, the profilmic staging of *Deep Cover* retroactively becomes historical fiction.[87] The conspiratorial capacity of the film's staging of noir modality corresponds to those strains of black

FIG 3.8 "What would you do?" Stevens/Hull in *Deep Cover* (Bill Duke, 1992).

expressive culture that conceive of revolutionary probabilities (e.g., the King Alfred Plan, Chitterlings Inc., Dr. Crookmore's "black no more" treatments, Captain Blackman's coup d'état, the *Imperium*, and Dan Freeman).[88]

Entroducing

The ellipsis of the flashback that opened the film closes on Belinda Chacon's grave, the woman whose child (James) joins Betty to become the new family unit. Chacon's death from an overdose was a sin on Hull's eternal soul, according to Taft, a death for which he would have to atone. The film opens on a grave in the snow and closes on a more conventional site of repose, with the child and Stevens kneeling side by side at the grave, each a drug orphan. Stevens places the final gift from his dying father, the blood-stained bills, on the headstone, and they blow away in the company of rambling leaves. He walks away neither a drug dealer nor a cop nor even a rogue cop (fig. 3.8). The film closes with the reflexivity of the voice-over's direct address: "We took eleven million in drug profits from the van. The money doesn't know where it comes from, but I do. If I keep it, I'm a criminal. If I give it to the government I'm a fool. If I try and do some good with it maybe it just makes things worse. Either way I'll probably just wind up getting myself in more trouble. It's an impossible choice. But in a way we all have to make it. What would you do?"

The voice of he who was once Stevens, then Hull, and is now Stevens again pivots on a shift in tense. Whereas the voice-over throughout *Deep Cover* was in the past tense, the voice at the end occupies the future. This final gesture complicates the voice and body reunification that the noir idea is expected to fulfill at the close. The reconstitution of the character's blackness suggests ambiguity and discursivity as the film provides no answers and summons a closural deficiency.[89] Undetectable and unbound, he who at this point may not be Stevens or Hull moves through the graveyard as a provenance marked X. In the end the narrative cycles out of ritualized loss with the tossing away of the fetish objects—the father's blood-stained bills—and the keeping of the laundered drug profits.[90]

"What would you do?" There is a more obvious point to be made about this moment of closure and reunification: the noir protagonist lives. This reconstituted character is revealed to be neither dead (*Sunset Boulevard*) nor dying (*Double Indemnity* or *D.O.A.*). Also, in contrast to the hood film (e.g., *Jason's Lyric* and *Menace II Society*), the black protagonist survives in the end.[91] Will he be a black avenger charged with saving a crack-addled generation of the unborn? Will he become *Superfly*, a missionary man or crusader? Can he be the cultural nationalist ethos of an organic intellectual met with the Talented Tenth? "I'm a blackstar / I'm not a gangster."[92]

Deep Cover confirms the critical import of Himes's work as the film shares the aesthetic and political plotting of a critique engendered by Himes and, subsequently, the reprioritized force of noir blackness. The film's noncompliance with a singular representational mode of blackness is not a problem but a rewarding complication that resonates with the aesthetic and political engagement of Himes and the black absurd.[93] I have insisted on the formal innovation, reanimation, and augmentation of the noir tradition with the conjoining of two questions: What is noir? and What is black film? How these questions modify and enliven one another has directed my conception of a noir and film blackness nexus as modalities of noir blackness. *Deep Cover* began with a question and closed with yet another. The distance between the two, the space between the black man / nigger query and the direct address of "What would you do?," illustrates the vast archive of cultural, aesthetic, and political possibilities that is black visual and expressive culture.

FOUR

BLACK MAYBE
Medicine for Melancholy, Place, and Quiet Becoming

A focus on the city, the cinema, and African American representation . . .
tells us much about the mythology of transformation that is so integral to
American life. In their often conflicted attitudes toward the city as either
promised land or dystopian hell, African American texts (film, literature,
music, painting) explore themes of hope, mobility, and escape.

—PAULA MASSOOD, *BLACK CITY CINEMA: AFRICAN AMERICAN URBAN EXPERIENCES IN FILM*

To walk is to lack a place. It is the indefinite process of being absent and
in search of a proper. The moving about that the city multiplies and
concentrates makes the city itself an immense social experience of lacking
a place—an experience that is, to be sure, broken up into countless tiny de-
portations (displacements and walks), compensated for by the relationships
and intersections of these exoduses that intertwine and create an urban
fabric, and placed under the sign of what ought to be, ultimately, the place
but is only a name, the City.

—MICHEL DE CERTEAU, "WALKING IN THE CITY," IN *THE PRACTICE OF EVERYDAY LIFE*

I have argued that film blackness entails a conceptual reframing, a critical re-
investment in the idea of black film. This chapter builds on my previous discussions of visual historiography, performativity, and modalities by focusing
on the consequential ways that *Medicine for Melancholy* (Barry Jenkins, 2008)
and its narrative conceit of a serendipitous romance critically contends with
blackness, genre, and place. Shot in fifteen days for around $13,000, the film
is propelled by the story of a black man and a black woman in San Francisco

who couple for a day after a one-night stand.[1] Micah (Wyatt Cenac) identifies as born and raised in the city, a native son who claims to be the second best designer of custom home aquariums in the city. A transplant to the Bay, Joanne Hardwicke, or Jo (Tracey Heggins), is a self-employed designer of T-shirts that feature the last name of women film directors (e.g., Alice Guy-Blaché, Barbara Loden). She lives with her white curator boyfriend in his townhouse. Together they imbue bohemia in a black indie key. At the start of the film the characters are strangers on a walk of shame for two. Yet the narrative grows more significant with their increasing attachment and maneuverings through the city, an extended courting stroll.

De Certeau's regard for the unstable and textual nature of the city coupled with his focus on mobility and rhythms of place and placelessness influences my consideration of *Medicine for Melancholy*. Just as de Certeau concludes that movement through the city bonds a subject, the movement of Micah and Jo through the city produces encounters with the rhythmic traces of histories and cultures of San Francisco. In the film the couple cross active intersections of these traces that produce the city as an affective phenomenon. Not simply a finite mass, the city is structured by shifting states of materiality and immateriality, resonances and concentrations. Thus, as Paula Massood contends, the city as profilmic phenomenon poses an urban state and process that particularly stirs with African American cultural histories.

With an achingly slow pace, the film has little in the way of effusive drama as ambient sounds are a major feature. I argue that the film's quiet tonality resonates with Kevin Quashie's contention that quiet can act as a mode of black resistance that is distinguishable from silence and connotations of something repressed. In *The Sovereignty of Quiet* Quashie argues that quiet represents a nonpublic expressivity, a sense of interiority not as apolitical but as agential in the sense that "anything we do is shaped by the range of desires and capacities of our inner life."[2] As an enactment of film blackness, *Medicine for Melancholy* organizes quiet as interiority force, an affective arrangement of the film's pulsing speculation on black capacities. After all, there is no explicit explanation for the escalating desire between the two black characters. In the absence of an unequivocal epiphany or illumination about their coupling, I consider how the film's quiet conjures the politics of black becoming, fantasy, and the cultural geography of San Francisco.

According to Stuart Hall, cultural identity represents a nonlinearity as culture produces subjects in and across time in a way that defies a strictly synchronic measure of identity. Instead, as Hall insists, there is a ceaseless oscillation between being and becoming, a cycling of subjectivity that is perpetually driven by culture, history, and power:

> Cultural identity . . . is a matter of "becoming" as well as of "being." It belongs to the future as much as to the past. It is not something which already exists, transcending place, time, history and culture. . . . Far from being eternally fixed in some essentialised past, they [cultural identities] are subject to the continuous "play" of history, culture and power. Far from being grounded in mere "recovery" of the past, which is waiting to be found, and which when found, will secure our sense of ourselves into eternity, identities are the names we give to the different ways we are positioned by, and position ourselves within, the narratives of the past.[3]

It is this temporal contingency of blackness that particularly resonates with the way the couple in *Medicine for Melancholy* amble ungrounded as a black potentiality. The generative nature of their black becoming and coupling across multiple temporalities is bounded by the film's extended mediation on blended losses, material (urbanism) and immaterial (black love).

The attachment adventure plot of coupling black strangers traffics in "racial sincerity." John Jackson notes that sincerity is distinguishable from authenticity: sincerity operates as a finite categorical determination of racial being, while authenticity implies negotiation and discursivity. Thus "sincerity presumes a liaison *between subjects*—not some external adjudicator and a lifeless scroll. Questions of sincerity imply social interlocutors who presume one another's humanity, interiority, and subjectivity. It is a subject-subject interaction, not the subject-object model that authenticity assumes—and to which critiques of authenticity implicitly reduce every racial exchange."[4] In this dialogic spirit of gradations and intracultural calibrations, the film's aesthetic palette depicts a mutely textured San Francisco through a variable abstraction of color. Shot oversaturated and then desaturated in postproduction, the film is constantly animated by the variant expressivity of color within its sepia and black-and-white base. Thus the film's timbre, or tone, results in a mutability of hues that, more than digital excess or color psychology, produces an active tableau, an unstable spectacle. In particular this chromatic system sporadically becomes more animated during scenes of rising intimacy between Micah and Jo. This unfixed filtering obliges the film's sustained speculation on racial scripts and connotes the design of a fantasy.[5]

The title comprises remedy and diagnosis and evokes Ray Bradbury's short story of the same name (1959) and the general connotative lore of the power of love and melancholia cures; the narrative of *Medicine for Melancholy* is driven by fantasy.[6] As Lauren Berlant elaborates, fantasy as a psychoanalytic principle has an organizational function in the structuring of unconscious wishes. *Medicine for Melancholy* ultimately details a spontaneous propensity of two complementary wishes that converge and flourish for a time even if neither Micah nor Jo explicitly articulates his or her desiring motivations. Significantly Berlant notes, "If we think of romance as a genre of action film, in which an intensity of the need to survive is played out by a series of dramatic pursuits, actions, and pacifications, then the romance plot's setting for fantasy can be seen as less merely conventional and more about the plotting of intensities that hold up a world that the unconscious deems worth living in."[7] The film's plotting of intensities evinces a cinematographic escapade that concentrates around a romance conceit and blackness, examining the stakes and ransoms of black love.

If desire entails the misrecognition of an object choice thought to restore or recuperate a conceived hole in one's self, then, as Berlant notes, "your object . . . does not express transparently who you 'are' but says something about what it takes for you to anchor yourself in space and time."[8] The anchoring mechanism of *Medicine for Melancholy*, the film's effort to abide the romance conceit and racial calibrations, is bound to a precise space and time: San Francisco in the early twenty-first century. This profilmic city significantly informs the couple's circulation with the material and immaterial traces that structure the everyday San Francisco.[9] The texture of the city and its cultural geography left a distinct mark on the screenplay. When asked about the initial considerations of other settings for the film, Jenkins commented, "San Francisco was not the original location of the film. Originally, . . . the movie was to take place in New York City or Chicago. In that version of the film, the characters were different, *quite* different. . . . Once I decided the film *would* be set in San Francisco . . . it was impossible to not allow the film to push beyond the simplicity of the premise and include the cultural geography of the place."[10] In *Medicine for Melancholy* the cinematic geography concerns a place impacted by redlining, urban redevelopment, gentrification, displacement, and a dwindling African American population.[11] A web of policies and cultures, this San Francisco incites multiple spatiotemporal encounters but not as diametrically opposed forces. Instead incompatibilities, material and symbolic, actuate the city as a heterotopic force that mirrors the film's staging of blackness as a cycling of juxtapositions and ambivalences, but never a singularity.[12]

Shadowed by cultural, historical, and spatial tensions, Micah and Jo's attachment escapade glides with an air of Walter Benjamin's time of emergency. "To articulate the past historically," Benjamin writes, "means to seize hold of a memory as it flashes up at a moment of danger . . . to retain that image of the past which unexpectedly appears to man singled out by history at a moment of danger."[13] The coupling voyage of Micah and Jo occurs with the stressed inflection of shifts between the diegetic and nondiegetic historical past and present under an eclipse of black futurity dilemmas. Thus the emergency and memory flashes of *Medicine* involve ceaseless historical and cultural processes related to blackness, desire, and the city. In a quiet key the film intones a braiding of becoming, the cultural and cinematic geography of San Francisco, and a politics of desire. With these keywords, composites, and critical filters in mind, this chapter tracks *Medicine for Melancholy* as an enactment of film blackness.

Walk Among Us

The film opens in a bathroom, with Micah splashing water on his face, then cuts to Jo waking in the bed nearby. They eventually dress in silence, with an occasional awkward meeting of looks. This is the morning after a one-night stand. A brief series of shots details the debris from the party the night before as they make their way downstairs and leave the house (figs. 4.1 and 4.2). Hung over in the sun, they reintroduce themselves, although Jo says her name is Angela. Micah suggests walking to a café nearby in the Noe Valley section of the city and she agrees. Once seated there, a markedly enthusiastic Micah attempts to spark a conversation, while Jo appears aloof and annoyed about the prospect of "getting to know you" banter as her responses to his questions are curt. When he inquires whether she has a job and discovers she does not, he asks her how she pays her rent. Mildly defensive, Jo remarks, "Who said I pay rent?" Later she says vaguely, "I'm figuring it out." Their shared cab ride occurs in complete silence as Jo looks forward, oblivious to Micah's occasional side glances, his thirsty attempts to catch her eye and spark some kind of chat. After abruptly asking the driver to stop at the curb, she steps out and walks away, ignoring Micah calling her false name. He discovers that Jo has left her wallet in the taxi, so he uses social media (MySpace) and a telephone operator to track her down. Arriving at her townhouse in the Marina District he remarks that her home is nice and then revisits his previous query about rent:

MICAH: So, you don't pay rent here?
JO: [Shakes head.]

FIG 4.1 Micah (Wyatt Cenac) in *Medicine for Melancholy* (Barry Jenkins, 2008).

FIG 4.2 Jo (Tracey Heggins) in *Medicine for Melancholy* (Barry Jenkins, 2008).

MICAH: Who does pay rent here?
JO: No one.
MICAH: Okay, who pays the mortgage here?
JO: My boyfriend.
MICAH: Your boyfriend?
JO: My boyfriend.
MICAH: And where is he?
JO: London.
MICAH: London?

JO: Yes, London. Would you stop repeating me?

MICAH: All right. So, what does he do?

JO: He's a curator?

MICAH: Curator? Sorry. It just seems weird that as a curator he didn't really have any art on the walls. Like, none. I mean it just seems that they probably have an extra painting or sculpture lying around that he could have brought home. Sorry. Is he white?

JO: Does it matter?

MICAH: Yes and no.

JO: Well, what if I told you he is white and we met in a volunteer program in Bayview. Would that matter?

MICAH: Yes and no.

JO: Oh. Okay. I see now. You're one of those people.

MICAH: Those people?

JO: Yes, those people that think that Black History Month is in February because it's the shortest month of the year.

MICAH: It is.

JO: Black History Month is in February because Carter G. Woodson wanted Negro History Week to coincide with the births of Frederick Douglass and Lincoln, both in the same week in February. Okay, well thank you for returning my wallet. You have to go.

MICAH: Whoa, we're just getting started.

JO: You need to leave.

MICAH: What did I say?

Throughout their exchange, Jo exhibits the same disinterest from earlier that morning. When she asks him to leave, Micah implores her to reconsider, picking up a nearby guitar and playing "Won't You Be My Neighbor" ("Hey there, one-night-stand neighbor"). Though she does not ask him to stay, she smiles and does not repeat her request that he go. She goes upstairs to shower, and when she returns, they agree to start over and reintroduce themselves; this time she tells him her proper name. Their escalating exchange illustrates how racial sincerity moderates the tenor of an address between raced subjects. Their exchange in the foyer suggests calibrating acts of recognition. Beyond chemistry and attraction, Micah's interest in Jo also functions as an assessment of her. His question about her luxurious digs in spite of being unemployed rises to a judgment about her object choice before culminating with the Black History Month contention. Overall their conversation involves two distinct

FIG 4.3 Coupling. Jo and Micah in *Medicine for Melancholy* (Barry Jenkins, 2008).

FIG 4.4 Coupling. Jo and Micah in *Medicine for Melancholy* (Barry Jenkins, 2008).

racial scripts or epistemological purviews (urban legend and institutional knowledge), two distinct politics of pleasure and becoming.[14]

When Jo receives a phone call from her boyfriend, Micah gestures to the wall and the stick figure drawing he has placed there. Finally there is some art on the walls. Jo leaves on her bicycle to run an errand for her curator partner and Micah cycles with her (figs. 4.3 and 4.4). When they arrive at the building, she asks him to wait downstairs until she returns from the gallery upstairs: "You have to wait right here." Micah asks why, and Jo replies, "Just think about it," as he returns her wallet.[15] When she returns, Jo suggests a trip to the Museum of Modern Art. He retorts that going to a museum is not what black people do on a Sunday:

> JO: Okay, black man. So what do two black folks do on a Sunday afternoon?
> MICAH: Go to church. Eat fried chicken. What do two black folks not do on a Sunday afternoon?
> JO: What?
> MICAH: Go to a museum.
> JO: That's not funny.
> MICAH: It's funny because it's not funny.

Sunday: the quiet fantasy of the film offers the first verbal marking of time. The unfunny moment cuts to a tracking shot of the pair walking their bikes down the sidewalk as Micah instructs Jo on hip-hop sampling. The expressive culture instruction then cuts to a shot of two faces: the windowed façade of a building and the large image of a black girl hanging inside on a wall. As the camera tilts down from the building into the ambient sounds of the city Micah quips, "MoAD, mama, not MoMA" (fig. 4.5). This is the Museum of the African Diaspora, an altogether different archiving of the modern. The glass-paned face of the building showcases a two-story-tall portrait of a young black girl. Yet the singularity of the girl's image is actually a pixilated mosaic made up of hundreds of photographs. The symbolic import of the whole (the image of the black girl) and its parts (photographs of the black diaspora) bears out what Brandi Catanese identifies as MoAD's foundational ideal of the "universal diasporic subject." She writes:

> Instead of a traditional, single photograph, the image of the girl is a photomosaic, made up of what we might call thousands of micro-identifications with the symbolic import of the girl's picture, known within the museum as "The Face of the African Diaspora" and based on Chester Higgins's photo of a young Ghanaian girl in the 1970s.... The pictures are from the past and the present, and span the globe, their performative unity making legible MoAD's claims of the Universal Diasporic Subject.[16]

The identificatory solicitation of "The Face of the African Diaspora," an invitation to the parts from a whole, proffers an embodying prompt of diasporic subjectivity. This narrativization cue of universal diasporic subjectivity intersects with the unvoiced anchoring between Jo and Micah as their affection escalates from a one-night stand and begins to slide across symbolic scripts of

FIG 4.5 "MoAD, mama, not MoMA." *Medicine for Melancholy* (Barry Jenkins, 2008).

blackness. Their coupling drifts from serendipitous desire to a shared history made legible by the museological frame. Yet this frame cannot arrest the tensions provoked by the pairing of "heritage (as an essentially territorializing process) and diaspora (as a formation that always encompasses a deterritorialisation of identities and memories)."[17]

As Micah purchases admission tickets, Jo peruses the museum store and picks up a greeting card from a rack. The card has a photograph of two black children playing soccer with a quote below: "Whatever you can do or dream you can do, begin it! Boldness has genius, power, and magic in it. Begin it now!" Ironically the quote is incorrectly attributed to Goethe, but it sounds like something he would say and has circulated as a Goethe saying since W. H. Murray misremembered a passage in his *The Scottish Himalaya Expedition* (1951). This gesture of equivalence in the spirit of Goethe demonstrates a transliterative impulse and not something patently false. This approximation or substitution signals the institutional claims on which MoAD exists.

Micah and Jo mount the stairs to the second floor while inspecting the snapshots that make up "The Face of the African Diaspora" (fig. 4.6). Following various shots of their movement in the museum space, this shot sequence closes with Micah and Jo at the "Music of the Diaspora" listening stations. There is a cut to a point-of-view shot of a photograph on the wall farther down the corridor: "The Door of No Return." A passageway cut through the stone wall of a former slave fort on Gorée Island off the coast of Senegal, "The Door of No Return" overlooks the shore and the sea. This opening has

FIG 4.6 The parts of "The Face of the African Diaspora." Jo and Micah in *Medicine for Melancholy* (Barry Jenkins, 2008).

come to represent the exit of the abducted Africans to the slave ships near the shore and the start of the Middle Passage as part of the transatlantic slave trade. Thus the passage symbolizes the trauma of a shift from personhood to thing and property, a crossing over from home to diaspora. "The Door of No Return," as Dionne Brand contends, "signifies the historical moment which colours all moments in the Diaspora. It accounts for the ways we observe and are observed as people, whether it's through the lens of social injustice or the lens of human accomplishments."[18] The photograph is an empty portal with a severe threshold that signifies movement and the inception of the diaspora.[19]

In the context of MoAD "The Door of No Return" photograph occupies a place on the sign for the "Slavery Passages" exhibit. A cut from the photograph reveals a detail of the caption: "Choosing to resist or escape slavery has often been punishable by whipping, maiming, branding, and crueler forms of torture, including mutilation and amputation. Still, tens of thousands of people have risked such treatment to be free, and many succeeded."[20] Micah and Jo enter the exhibit through a sound curtain; the nearly pitch-black room with benches features recorded testimonials, accounts of what the sign at the entrance labels tales of resistance to and escape from slavery. Inside, dark to themselves, they listen to an excerpt from Olaudah Equiano's *The Interesting Narrative of the Life of Olaudah Equiano, or Gustavus Vassa, the African* (1789), the chapter "Boarding a Slave Ship," in which he recounts his life in

Eboe (Nigeria), his and his sister's kidnapping, and his arrival on the African coast after being sold to slave traders: "The first objects which saluted my eyes when I arrived on the coast were the sea and a slave ship. As well as the multitude of black people of every description chained together, every one of their countenances expressing dejection and sorrow. No, I no longer doubted of my fate but I was not long suffered to indulge my grief for I was soon put down under the decks. There I received such a salutation that I had never experienced in my life." Notably the "Slavery Passages" exhibit commutes the meaning of "salutations." In the original text the passage is "I was not long suffered to indulge my grief; I was soon put down under the decks, and there I received such a salutation in my nostrils as I had never experienced in my life: so that, with the loathsomeness of the stench, and crying together, I became so sick and low that I was not able to eat, nor had I the least desire to taste any thing."[21] The stench greeting Equiano's nose becomes the greeting from a collectivity and solidarity in the hold. More symbolic than egregious, the abridgment of the passage infers the ethos of adaptation that circulates through MoAD.[22]

Billed as a space of contemplation, the room—its sensory deprivation coupled with the sonic adaptation of the Equiano text—compels an immersion in and through black time. Frank Wilderson proposes, "The most coherent temporality ever deemed as Black time is the 'moment' of no time at all on the map of no place at all: the ship hold of the Middle Passage."[23] In the context of the room's staging of the hold, the coupling of Micah and Jo operates in contradistinction to Equiano's record of dispossession. In this way their coupling in the hold suggests an act of fugitivity as well as an affective discontinuity and replotting of Middle Passage epistemology.[24] "Slavery Passages" is a chamber of black time travel that also exhibits the performative force of museums to engineer "the narratives and ontologies that they purport merely to commemorate."[25] Thus the space obliges a meeting between an institutional conceit, a black spatiotemporality, and the affective force of an autobiography.

The universal diasporic subjectivity imperative is meant to produce an audience through its hailing mission as much as it might appeal to a preconstituted one. This point touches on the complication of categorizing and producing a diasporic community. Michelle Wright contends, "Any truly accurate definition of an African diasporic identity . . . must somehow simultaneously incorporate the diversity of black identities in the diaspora yet also link all those identities to show that they indeed constitute a diaspora rather than an unconnected aggregate of different peoples linked only in name."[26] The

"Slavery Passages" immersing frame of black time emanates as a providential fixing, an attempt to quantifiably bind the signifying function of diasporic aggregation. Yet, as Catanese notes, MoAD must manage the local and global dynamics of diasporic identity in very particular ways:

> The global rather than local orientation of MoAD seems to anticipate and tactically respond to the persistent diminution of the local black population. In the most pragmatic way, shifting from a focus on African Americans to a wider examination of African cultures allows MoAD to acknowledge black San Franciscans without being inextricably bound to them — or to their gradual disappearance from the city. Technically beholden to a local black population but unable to rely upon this locality as its sole audience or subject matter, MoAD relocates African Americanness within a larger transnational map of connections.[27]

The museum's accounting for the diaspora in global terms ("When did you discover you are African?") cannot fully oblige the demands of an increasingly displaced locality ("When did you discover that black people are disappearing from San Francisco?"). This rhetorical distinction between two not altogether complimentary black futurity poses inflects the stakes of the attachment between Jo and Micah. In *Medicine for Melancholy*, the function of MoAD in the attachment affair is not merely about the transparency of their sameness; it also suggests difficult differences.

After over four minutes of no dialogue, Micah and Jo leave MoAD and its grounding of displacement, dispersal, and the global. Their silence echoes the chapter's opening consideration of the ponderous potentiality of black quiet. Outside the museum, instead of retrieving their bicycles Jo asks that they walk a bit. Through continuity editing they walk down Mission Street and arrive at the Yerba Buena Center for the Arts, the city arts center. As they enter the complex and move toward the Yerba Buena Gardens, the camera pans and tracks their movement to the Martin Luther King Jr. Memorial. Entitled *Revelation*, the memorial features a large waterfall with a walkway beneath. A cut to the interior details the walls of the walkway that are lined with photographs and Dr. King quotes etched in granite and glass. The camera hovers behind them in the chamber beneath the falls before turning to the wall and lingering on the following quote: "I believe that a day will come when all God's children from bass black to treble white will be significant on the constitution's keyboard. San Francisco, CA, 1956." Micah and Jo move together down the corridor as they continue to read passages under the falls (fig. 4.7). Their

Under the waterfall. Jo and Micah in *Medicine for Melancholy* (Barry Jenkins, 2008).

movement through the memorial space highlights the jeopardy of negotiating between the social function of memorialization and the architectural imperative to adapt over time and remain significant to future generations.[28]

Guided in speechlessness, their walk from the museum to the memorial occurs as a soundwalk that exhibits the immateriality of quiet contemplation and interiority while also being attuned to the city environment and its swirling rhythms. Like the acoustical design of the "Slavery Passages" exhibit, the water masks sound in the walkway. Water links the baptismal contemplation of the walkway and Equiano's account of a journey across the sea as their walk down Mission Street invokes an arc from slavery to freedom, the Middle Passage to the civil rights movement. The walk from the hold to the mountaintop, a spatiotemporal bridge and a historiographic passage, moves between two distinct institutional historiographies and memorialization strategies. Yet the conjoining of these two sites does not suggest a linear or progressive reading of African American history as a heroic narrative arc of struggle to progress.[29] More than strictly historical determinism, Micah and Jo are still drafting their attachment chronicle.

From a shot of the characters drawing closer under the waterfall there is a cut from the MLK memorial to Micah and Jo walking side by side toward a bridge as the score emits the rising sound of an organ and a pizzicato string ensemble. Piano and drums join the piece as Micah and Jo slowly draw closer with each step. Micah reaches for her hand and pulls her to the side of the bridge (fig. 4.8).[30]

FIG 4.8 "Le Rallye." Jo and Micah in *Medicine for Melancholy* (Barry Jenkins, 2008).

> MICAH: It looks like LA.
> JO: Never been.
> MICAH: Yeah. Like the view from the hills. It's like the hills in LA.
> JO: This is a one-night stand.
> MICAH: It's only been one night, can't do nothing about that. I mean, it
> is what it is.

Jo's non sequitur is the first address and evasion of their coupling; an attempt to break away from the Cupid vibe and set a limit. In spite of the ethereal convenience of their coupling, its fantastical timelessness, Jo briefly breaks the spell with a moment of truth-telling. The scene then cuts to Jo playfully dashing to a nearby carousel (the Children's Creativity Carousel) with Micah following.[31] The sequence ends with shots of them laughing while riding the carousel steeds with the full swell of the music.

While the narrative premise of intimate strangers might allude to several films, this plot coupled with the sound signature of Dickon Hinchliffe's "Le Rallye" precisely signals Barry Jenkins's inspiration for *Medicine for Melancholy*: Claire Denis's *Friday Night* (2003). Set in Paris, *Friday Night* tracks the coupling of strangers, a man and woman who cross paths one evening during a public transit strike due to a citywide ride-sharing initiative. Laure has just packed up her apartment in preparation for moving in with her boyfriend, and Jean is a man who needs a ride. The spatiotemporal quality of the film narrativizes a Paris of relentless estrangement and intimacy in the time of now. Denis insisted that *Friday Night* "could not be 'once upon a time,' it has to be now."[32] Thus the use of "Le Rallye" in *Medicine* acts as a temporal and intertextual animator. Like *Friday Night*, *Medicine for Melancholy* occurs in what George Clinton called "once upon a time called right now" with an equivalent affective sense of acceleration.

Writing on *Friday Night*, Elena Del Rio draws on Gilles Deleuze and Félix Guattari's proposition of rhizomatic intensity and examines the couple's perpetual state of "betweenness": "The film shows that the possibility of moving does not depend on one's own individual will or control, but, more precisely, on the willingness to let oneself be carried away by the inevitable flow of movement (of perception and affection) taking place everywhere in and around our bodies." The coupling of Micah and Jo parallels Del Rio's assessment of Jean and Laure as a pair whose alliance of desire "relies on its own unmotivated force/desire as it traces a wholly unforeseen trajectory."[33] In the context of *Medicine*, the MoAD–Yerba Buena sequence alludes to constitutive rhythms that compel Jo and Micah's "unmotivated force/desire." *Medicine for Melancholy* enlivens the Denis incentive with black time and becoming. In place of a traffic jam, *Medicine* substitutes another kind of congestion trigger with the incremental clustering of temporalities, discourses, and attachments in the MoAD–Yerba Buena sequence: diasporic museology, civil rights memorialization, an intertextual gesture toward the now.[34] Their trajectory, loaded and random, through spatiotemporalities ultimately boosts the film's staging of romance, but this sense of romance effectuates something other than the lore of lost souls and soul mates. *Medicine* problematizes the politics of pleasure that inform the literary tradition of the black romance.

Yogita Goyal argues that while the idea of romance is often framed in the ahistorical and apolitical terms of the eternal or the ontological, the black romance's ideological nature evidenced in twentieth-century African diasporic literature renarrativizes the compulsory sense of romance with attention to issues such as racial uplift, nation building, redemption, and recuperation. In *Romance, Diaspora, and Black Atlantic Literature*, she writes, "Impure at its very origin, romance inevitably implies a repatterning and rebeginning, rather than the birth of something wholly original, as the writers of diasporic romance compose narratives that function both as recovery and as an imaginative projection. In this respect, romance allows these writers to collapse time and space to give us a whole, or to shine a beam of light onto one moment, or even to give us a progressive history read backwards from a future point of redemption." Goyal refabulates Benjamin's designation of temporality with regard to "ruptures" and "simultaneities" to what she identifies as "diaspora time": "While nation time links past, present, and future in a march towards progress, diaspora time emphasizes the breaks and discontinuities in such a movement, recalling the trauma of the Middle Passage and looking forward to the Jubilee."[35] In the case of *Medicine for Melancholy*, diaspora time portends the film's accented distinction of diasporic love time. Micah and Jo shift away from the one-night stand regimen and hanging out to something yet to be quantified. But the historiographic and agential capacity of the black romance with the gathering of spatiotemporalities during their MoAD–Yerba Buena stroll indeed concur with Micah's reply to Jo's dismissal of what has been growing between them: "It's only been one night."[36]

Destroy This Memory

The carousel cycles down and "Le Rallye" fades from the score as the film cuts to the pair arriving at Micah's studio apartment in the Tenderloin. While Micah is in the bathroom, Jo looks at a framed poster on the wall; it features an excerpt from a city planning survey with "LIES" stenciled or "tagged" across it (fig. 4.9). It demonstrates a core principle of protest art, a graphic rebuttal to specious policy:

> SAN FRANCISCO is now developing programs to correct blighted and congested conditions and to deal with an accumulation of housing that is continuously aging and deteriorating faster than it is being rehabilitated or replaced. The study area contains an estimated 1008 residential structures, many of which are in various degrees of deterioration and in need of rebuilding or replacement. More than 50 percent of the structures are past middle age with an estimated average of sixty-seven years. It is this condition which results in neighborhood blight and calls for both major public improvement and private rehabilitation and reconstruction.
>
> Leonard S. Mosias for the San Francisco Redevelopment Agency, "Residential Rehabilitation Survey Western Addition Area 2" July 1962

Micah returns to the room and sees Jo reading the poster.

MICAH: You familiar with that?
JO: Um, kind of. I'm a transplant.

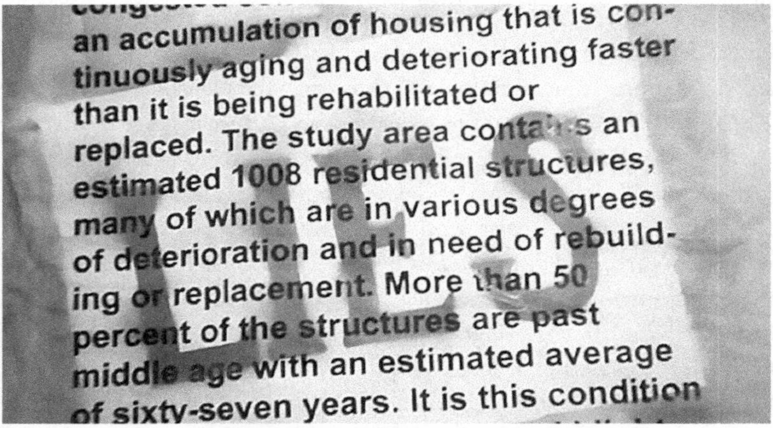

FIG 4.9 "LIES." *Medicine for Melancholy* (Barry Jenkins, 2008).

MICAH: Born and raised. My folks lived out there. Imagine the Lower Haight with nothing but black folks and white artists.

JO: Hum. But why would you put it on your wall? I know you're not supposed to forget, but it's not like you would forget without seeing it every day.

MICAH: It's not like that. You know people just walk around this city like everything is so perfect and it's all good and everything. This just reminds me, you know. Poor folks still got it hard. Like, if you look at Mission Bay, and this poster is still relevant. I'm just saying. [Pause.] You want some tea or something?

JO: [She nods.]

The conversation circles around the value of memory. For Jo the poster is a superfluous reminder of an absence of which Micah is always aware ("It's not like you would forget without seeing it every day"). He responds with a series of allusions and hesitant declarations before trailing off to a dejected close. Who are the people that walk around San Francisco basking in all things good? What do these people who believe in the perfect city have to do with the poor folks who are still struggling? What is the connection between Mission Bay, the Western Addition, and the declaration that public policy is a lie? "I don't know, I'm just saying." Forgetting is a luxury that Micah can neither afford nor condone. Born and raised, a native son, he tries to articulate a history and a memory, but the poster speechlessly offers the only clear tell.

Micah's comments intimate an everyday survival, the way his melancholizing and critical black memory direct his constitutive knowledge of the city's affective flows and his grounded perception of loss and erasure.[37]

The poster continues to critique redevelopment plans in San Francisco, then and now. Following World War II public and private sectors sought to position San Francisco as the capital of the emergent global flows of the Pacific Rim. Formed in 1948, the San Francisco Redevelopment Agency cited in the poster was created as a result of congressional legislation in the 1940s and 1950s that gave cities more authority over redevelopment financing. By the 1960s this measure had generated a significant collusion between the private and public sectors. The poster refers to a history of urbanism and city initiatives that disproportionately impacted working-class neighborhoods and communities of color under the auspices of renewal and redevelopment.[38] Dated July 1962, the poster refers to the second phase of the Western Addition project, whose first phase began in 1953. Once known as the "Harlem of the West," the Fillmore (a part of the larger Western Addition area) was subjected to urban renewal that began after the war and would for decades contribute to the erosion of the community's economic and cultural base.[39] Micah remembers that *improvement*, *rehabilitation*, and *redevelopment* operated as code words for displacement and erasure. Of course one of the key things that enabled these top-down urban planning frenzies was a disavowal of the material ways antiblack racism informed poor housing conditions, low employment rates, and wealth disparity. The statistical accounting took precedence over a concerted policy of social justice.[40] Hanging the poster on his wall is not about never forgetting; it is about remembering that many communities in San Francisco, now and then, have not been the intended beneficiaries of the city's future. These communities have not even warranted being classified as collateral damage.

The poster articulates San Francisco's new diaspora, those who could be or have been displaced by city initiatives that prioritize economic growth over sustaining local communities and histories. "A vicious circle is created in which the poor are continuously under pressure of displacement," Peter Marcuse writes, as "the wealthy continuously seek to wall themselves within gentrified neighbourhoods. Far from a cure for abandonment, gentrification worsens the process."[41] The poster records a time of struggle against how gentrification acts as an edict of temporal sovereignty, a manufactured sense of the new and the old as the demarcation of the past and the future becomes directed by market forces. Sandhya Shukla notes, "That unrelenting focus on the future is of course prescriptive rather than analytical. Its teleology of coherence and efficiency relies on conceptions of the past as full of unmanageable chaos. As this is applied to the modern metropolis, future dreams of greater global community rest on constructed pasts of dislocated peoples and incompetent economies. The past in neoliberal narratives of what is possible in the city is either residual or nostalgic (and therefore irrational). Neoliberalism provides the logic and the alibi for the form of 'urban renewal' that is gentrification."[42] The history of redevelopment in San Francisco is littered with premature autopsies that have been coupled to this refabulating rhetoric of progress and premeditated inevitability. In fact these intimations of erasure and progress are serendipitously evident in the MoAD–Yerba Buena sequence that precedes the visit to Micah's apartment.

The San Francisco of *Medicine for Melancholy* does not subscribe to the classical function of place in cinema. The film suggests another option for cinematic place, neither strictly extradiegetic nor idle backdrop nor merely profilmic. This other possibility entails how the couple's trajectory through the city encounters several cartographies of urban history.[43] The city thickens the stakes of fantasy for these desiring black subjects. This is vitally evident as they walk through MoAD and the Yerba Buena Center complex, a significant site of urban renewal, gentrification, community activism, and displacement. Once considered the skid row section of San Francisco, the south of Market Street area (SoMa) had been targeted by the San Francisco Redevelopment Agency (SFRA) after the success of the Western Addition plan. SoMa was part of a development plan devoted to a new city center that included what would eventually become the Moscone Convention Center and the Yerba Buena Cultural Center. After acquiring almost half of the land, SFRA faced opposition from the Tenants and Owners in Opposition to Redevelopment (TOOR), a community organization formed in 1969 that primarily comprised poor, working-class, and senior residents. The central concern for the TOOR was SFRA's promise of low-income housing for the displaced residents.

The issue came to a head when the TOOR filed a restraining order in federal court against SFRA that would stop all demolition and relocation action until a binding agreement could be reached between the two parties. In April 1970 the court ruled in favor of the TOOR and issued an injunction that cut federal funding of the redevelopment project until an acceptable relocation plan was in place. In spite of the ruling SFRA colluded with the San Francisco Housing Authority to fast-track those residents in the planned Yerba Buena area as the majority of SoMa residents along with those displaced residents from the Western Addition still on the long waiting list were never relocated to affordable and acceptable housing.[44]

The transvaluation of the diaspora in the couple's stroll sustains a multi-accentual sense of capital: slave trafficking and the displacing force of the real estate market. Their movement in the MoAD–Yerba Buena Center sequence moreover entails a navigation of dispirited spaces, reclaimed land that still abounds with reified histories of race and class.[45] The unvoiced consequence posed by Micah is whether cultural memories can be redeveloped. Immediately after the discussion of the poster he elaborates on these politics of place. While he gets water for them from the kitchen, Jo asks from the other room, "Do you even like it here?"

MICAH: What?

JO: It seems like the city just pisses you off.

MICAH: Nah, I love this city. I hate this city, but I love this city. In the hills, the fog, any man who can find a street corner has got himself a view. San Francisco's beautiful and it's got nothing to do with privilege. It's got nothing to do with beatniks or hippies or Yuppies. It just is, and you shouldn't have to be upper middle class to be a part of that.

During Micah's love-hate monologue on his ambivalence about life in the Bay Area a brief montage of five high-saturated color images of the city is shown. Together these images illustrate a part of the San Francisco tourist imaginary: hills, fog, Victorian houses, pride flags, and a beach. These postcard abbreviations of the city are stock approximations of an everyday "Wish you were here" San Francisco, a place of vacation marketing and real estate brochures. Micah's reproach that access to the view is an inalienable right that cannot be purchased resonates with the sense that access to the experience of the city has become tied to an elite or upper-class privilege. When experiencing the view becomes a matter of class and social hierarchy, then your quotidian space or everyday geography is in the process of being merchandised into a lifestyle you may no longer be able to afford. The rising cost of sightlines leads to the feeling of trespassing in one's own neighborhood, a neighborhood that has become a "location, location, location" affair with greater surveillance, policing, and other material and psychic costs of everyday life. Micah despises gentrification because he recognizes that it has a tendency to operate as the exclusivity of a branded everyday for an upwardly mobile and consuming class of people. This new class partakes in the accrued cool of spaces and cultures whose histories are refabulated in the revisionist terms of capitalism and obsolescence. Ultimately locals are revised and coded as outsiders and space invaders in a public attuned to newly arriving and ordained insiders.[46]

The redevelopment projects by the city planners treated the city as an untapped resource to be refined and cultivated. The historical and cultural traces are evident only to the extent that these residues in plain sight contribute to a branding, a marketing of an exclusive future, the trafficking of local flavor for new market value and the lure of "new city users" who exercise what Saskia Sassen describes as a "claim" to the city: "The new city users have made an often immense claim on the city and have reconstituted strategic spaces of the city in their image: their claim is rarely examined or challenged. . . . The new city of these users is a fragile one, whose survival and successes are centered on an economy of high productivity, advanced technologies, and intensified exchanges."[47] In this way the semiotics of the city, its system of histories and cultures, are repurposed as anecdotal enablers of a renaissance and a subsequent erasure to come. Micah argues that these new users are guided by a measure of manifest destiny and the core values of privilege that thrive on arrogating the everyday.

When Micah leaves the room to shower, Jo searches his MySpace page, where she sees a torn photo booth strip of Micah and a (white) woman embracing. The image has been photoshopped and captioned, "I want my fuckin' heart sewn back together" (fig. 4.10). The native son has wounds as pressing as neoliberalism and the flows of global capital. When Micah returns, he and Jo eventually make their way to a cuddle that accelerates. The foreplay resembles a shipwreck, with the handheld camera jaggedly rocking to their motion. The awkward tonality of their framed movements is matched by the opening swirl of strings from Gypsophile's "The One I Dream Of" (2012) on the soundtrack. The song and the camera abruptly decelerate to an acoustic guitar and the vocalist's entrance: "You are a sun / You are a sea."

They awake from a postcoital nap and go grocery shopping for dinner. As they walk back to Micah's apartment from the Rainbow Grocery in the Mission District, an urban history of San Francisco, working-class communities, bohemianism, venture capital, and a dotcom boom trails them. The camera's handheld observations from an obstructed distance tracks them from across the street as they move down the sidewalk. The sound of a group talking begins to rise over the ambient sounds of the city as they draw near the open door of a storefront. They stop at the doorway and look in as the film cuts to the interior. Micah and Jo are at the AIDS Housing Alliance and become outside observers of a Housing Rights Committee meeting (fig. 4.11).

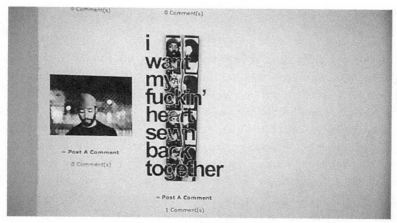

FIG 4.10 "I want my fuckin' heart sewn back together." *Medicine for Melancholy* (Barry Jenkins, 2008).

FIG 4.11 Housing Rights Committee. *Medicine for Melancholy* (Barry Jenkins, 2008).

Tightly framed on the faces of individual speakers, the series of shots features a range of people and opinions. The first speaker notes:

> Property values mean more than human lives . . . I think that's what happened in the Castro. As the upscale people moved in, the attitudes became, you know, more of the attitudes of the upper class. There is this sense in this town that we are becoming a city of the very rich and the very poor. We all know people have been pushed out at an alarming rate. I mean, I would say thousands and thousands of people have been pushed out in

the last twelve years from mainly the eastern side of the city where all the renters are.

A collectivity gathered and articulating a time of crisis, the choral montage addresses how rent control went unmentioned in the previous mayoral campaign. They display frustration and skepticism with redevelopment claims of market-rate condominium projects coexisting alongside what is left of the once majority black population of Bayview, a historically segregated and marginalized section of San Francisco near the former Hunters Point Naval Shipyard: "You know what's gonna go, and it ain't gonna be the market-rate condos. We're already seeing that Bayview is gonna go the way that Fillmore did and they're gonna gentrify the neighborhood and push out the people who are living there now and bring in more upscale people."

The exchange points to how the escalating loss of affordable housing in San Francisco has forced people out of the city to the East Bay and beyond (e.g., Richmond, Oakland, Vallejo). This trend creates a forced exodus of East Bay residents as more people escape the unsustainability of life in San Francisco. The closing comment of the sequence sums up the distressing nature of the crisis: "There's a ballot initiative that supposedly is about eminent domain issues but actually will repeal rent control throughout the state. So San Francisco could lose rent control next June. Think of over 350,000 apartments suddenly losing rent control in San Francisco and all the people that could get displaced potentially by something like that. As far as I'm concerned, it's the end of the whole East Side of San Francisco. The whole East Side will just gentrify overnight, and all of the great things we love about San Francisco would be gone overnight."[48] The conceit of Micah and Jo bearing witness to the unscripted vérité of the community meeting contextualizes and amends the urgency of their coupling with the crisis of impending displacement. Yet while the camera crosses the threshold to the assembly, the couple remains outside. The sequence ends with a cut to Micah and Jo on a high plain looking out at City Hall in the distance, out of earshot of the community meeting yet inhabiting the conversation. They stand quietly on a hilltop watching an emergency unfold below them.

Gentrification urges discussion of how urban renewal displaced ethnic, working-class, and poor communities for the sake of luring a new consumer citizen to the city with signals of revitalization and new channels of consumption.[49] But these revitalized zones of capital are no longer dependent on a new middle class, as was the gentrification model of the late twentieth century.

Instead the targets are a more lucrative consumer-citizen: the upper class, if not the 1 percent. As has always been the case, frontier rhetoric abounds as the authorization for how capital enacts deterritorialization measures. In the collateral context of the gentrification of the Lower East Side in New York City Neil Smith notes, "Whereas the myth of the frontier is an invention that rationalizes the violence of gentrification and displacement, the everyday frontier on which the myth is hung is the stark product of entrepreneurial exploitation."[50] With growing frequency, redevelopment initiatives generate unequal access to new circuits of capital and rationalize the displacement of established communities.

The grievances of the group inform, and to some extent guide, Micah's lifeworld view and his romantic overtures. Anne Cheng queries, "How does an individual go from being a subject of grief to being a subject of grievance? What political and psychical gains or losses transpire in the process?"[51] Might his pursuit of Jo in the shadow of melancholy distend the strict sense of loss as the infinite revisiting loss as a quantifiable cure?[52] Cheng deduces that melancholy acts as regulation and prescription: "We might then say that melancholia does not simply denote a *condition* of grief but is rather, a *legislation* of grief."[53] Micah's measure of loss concerns the city in manifold ways and trails his overtures to Jo. In this way, the film recounts grievance with an arcing urgency that is particularly mobilized around spatial and black cultural measures of loss and residuals.

All Tomorrow's Parties

As Micah and Jo close in on twenty-four hours together, the film has focused on a place of urban development and erasure while following the calibrating between raced subjects and a courting of black love. Returning to the apartment and easing into a mellow domesticity, they cook dinner, drink wine, smoke weed, laugh, and continue to endear themselves to one another. In splashes throughout the film, Micah has articulated the history of San Francisco and *his* San Francisco, a city of memory and experience. Yet the film's provocation of love and crisis shifts from an elusive sense of loss to the exact terms of a dwindling black population in San Francisco. This shift begins innocently enough with Micah fixing the brakes on Jo's bike. As he encourages her to switch to a fixed-gear cycle the conversation and a dialectical tension of history, memory, desire, and place trails in such a way to suggest that he intends to fix more than just her bike (fig. 4.12).

FIG 4.12 "Seven percent." Micah in *Medicine for Melancholy* (Barry Jenkins, 2008).

MICAH: You'll be like Mae Jamison, first black woman to ride a fixed-gear bike through the Marina. . . . Hell, you're probably the first black woman in the Marina. Hey, you ever think about how black folks are only seven percent of the city?[54]

JO: You have a real issue with race. You know that?

MICAH: Obviously, but I'm serious and this ain't the weed talking. You ever think about how we're only seven percent of the city?

JO: You're not seven percent, you're Micah.

MICAH: You know what I mean. Like if black folks are seven percent of the city, and then you take, whatever, one or two percent consider itself like punk or indie or folk and, you know, not what you see on BET. Like you ever realize just how few of us there really are?

JO: No.

MICAH: I mean, check it. You might go to a show and for every like three hundred people there's probably one black person, and they're damn near guaranteed to have their arm around somebody white. [Pause.] I'm just saying. All right, check it. How do you define yourself?

JO: Excuse me?

MICAH: Like, how do you define yourself? Like, if you had to describe, you know, your idea of how you see the world. Like, how would you do it in one word?

JO: That makes no sense. People aren't that simple. How can you define yourself in one word?

MICAH: Easy. Me, I'm a black man. That's how I see the world and that's how the world sees me. But if I had to choose one, then I'm black before I'm a man. So therefore I am black.

JO: I don't see it that way.

MICAH: Why not?

JO: That's your problem. You feel you have to define everybody. You limit them to the point that they're just a definition and not people.

MICAH: How you figure?

JO: You just said it. You went from "I am Micah" to "I am black."

MICAH: I'm not?

JO: Yes, but you're everything else too.

MICAH: That's not how society sees it.

JO: Well, who gives a shit about what society thinks. [Pause.] I don't want to talk anymore. Let's do something.

MICAH: What you want to do?

JO: I want to dance.

MICAH: All right. White folks or black folks?

JO: [An unamused glare.]

MICAH: My bad.

Like their difference of opinion about Black History Month, their discussion of the poster announcing the Western Addition project, Micah's love-hate soliloquy, and, to a lesser extent, his instruction on sampling and hip-hop, the "seven percent" conversation reveals the irresolvable paradox of their differing black epistemological poses. Again they do not wholly agree about blackness and a politics of black personhood, but they do share a finite sense of compatibility. This exchange makes plain all that was unspoken by Micah: "This is who I am. Are you down? Do you understand? I'm just saying." Micah's furious arithmetic on the diminished possibilities of a black presence in the music scene, be it punk or indie or folk, finds that the majority of this minor key would rather settle for Black Entertainment Television and black bourgeois respectability. This steady disappearance of African Americans from the city reinforces his calculation of the decreasing possibilities for a black subcultural remainder.

In 2007, the year before the premiere of *Medicine for Melancholy* at the South by Southwest Film Festival, numbers like 7 percent had received a great deal of attention in the Bay area. In July of that year the Task Force on African American Out-Migration held their first meeting; this was an initiative proposed by the mayor of San Francisco, Gavin Newsom, and City Supervisor Sophie Maxwell to address the disproportionate decline in the city's African American population. While the African American population in the city peaked in 1970 at 13.4 percent (approximately 96,700 people), by 2010 that rate was a mere 6.1 percent (approximately 48,700 people). Thus from 1970 to 2010 the African American population shrank by more than half. According to the census data, while there was a 20 percent decline in the African American population between 1970 and 1990, from 1990 to 2010 the rate of decline increased to 40 percent.[55]

Through the Mayor's Office of Community Development (MOCD), the task force worked with the Ethnic Studies and Africana Studies Departments at San Francisco State University and the Public Research Institute to identify factors contributing to African American out-migration. The task force would propose "action recommendations" to maintain and increase San Francisco's African American population. According to the mission statement, the MOCD "are investing political and economic resources to mitigating the out-migration of African Americans as well as to develop a comprehensive strategy for making San Francisco an attractive location for African Americans looking to relocate."[56] Composed of city officials, community organizers, civil rights activists, professors, and other professionals, the task force submitted its report in 2009.

The cover of the report is an image from Jacob Lawrence's *The Migration Series* (1940–41), a collection of sixty paintings that documents the movement of over 6 million African Americans from the South to urban areas in the Northeast, Midwest, and West that began in the 1900s. The painting featured on the report cover is entitled *Panel 3: From Every Southern Town Migrants Left by the Hundreds to Travel North* and depicts a huddled mass of black figures burdened with all manner of baggage and moving northward in unison with the parallel progress of birds above them. In place of the painting's title are the words "IN MOTION" along the bottom border.[57] In this way the report ambitiously suggests the possibility of another Great Migration, specifically to San Francisco. Yet, this co-optation of African American history ironically makes light of reverse migration, a phenomenon first identified in the 1970s, in which African Americans are moving to the South as African American populations outside of the South have steadily declined. Evoking the Great Migration as a conditional equivalent for the goals of the task force also alludes to the factors of antiblack racism and segregation that triggered both the Great Migration and reverse migration.

The task force identified a number of factors related to African American out-migration: compared to the rest of the city's population, African Americans had a higher rate of unemployment, higher level of poverty, lower rate of homeownership, lower rate of high school graduation, and higher rate of felony arrest. In addition there had been a drastic decline in black-owned businesses and black business receipts. The task force's recommendations were organized into five clusters: housing, education, jobs and economic development, cultural and social life, and public safety and quality of life. Time will reveal the effectiveness of the task force's proposed remedies, but it is clear that at the current rate of decline, San Francisco, perennially ranked as one of the best American cities, will continue to have the lowest African American population of any major American city by the middle of the twenty-first century. The effectiveness of the task force's recommendations might be inferred to the extent that the report never identified the vast American history of systematic collusion by local and federal institutions that has continued to disenfranchise African American communities. The report makes no claim as to how antiblack racism as an institutional policy might have informed their findings.

Micah's "seven percent" self-definition is supported by the statistical data and the findings of the task force, as well as his experiential memory. Jo, however, would rather dance this mess around; she cannot be *just black* for Micah or indulge his black criteria. They leave the apartment for a club and an indie scene of drink, dance, and jouissance. The frenetic handheld camera coverage and the editing distend the spatiotemporal resonance of the club through jump cuts that counterpose acceleration and deceleration, a cutting through time. Micah and Jo carouse in and through an indie scene and the archival whims of the deejay to keep the crowd up and moving. The playback music on set during the shooting of the club scene was 1960s soul music, but because the licensing was too expensive to use that music in the film, postproduction supplanted soul with a less expensive option: indie music. The consequence of this budgetary concern is borne out by the positioning of Jo and Micah as deliriously lost in a moment that is figuratively and literally post-soul.[58]

Mark Anthony Neal defines the post-soul generation as those born between the March on Washington (1963) and the *Regents of the University of California v. Bakke* Supreme Court ruling (1978) that upheld affirmative action but ruled that racial quotas were unconstitutional. In *Soul Babies: Black Popular Culture and the Post-Soul Aesthetic,* Neal identifies a generation of African Americans as beneficiaries of the social and political advances of the civil rights era who also have experienced the retrenchment of those advances. As he elaborates, these are "folks born between the 1963 March on Washington and the *Bakke* case, children of soul, if you will, who came to maturity in the age of Reaganomics and experienced the change from urban industrialism to deindustrialism, from segregation to desegregation, from essential notions of blackness to metanarratives on blackness, without any nostalgic allegiance to past . . . but firmly in the grasp of the existential concerns of this brave new world."[59] *Medicine for Melancholy* enacts the historical specificity and ethos of post-soul by implying a crucial refusal of a distinct brand of strategic essentialism that would only frame the contemporary by the tenets of the civil rights platform. Post-soul represents a "radical reimagining of the contemporary African American experience, attempting to liberate contemporary interpretations of that experience from sensibilities that were formalized and institutionalized during earlier social paradigms."[60] With this post-soul particularity in mind, the exchanges between Micah and Jo exhibit two distinct impressions of historicity and black being.[61] They are post-soul beneficiaries and pragmatists, but not Jack and Jill dream warriors.[62]

During the club sequence, their distinct positions conjoin and bind around a pleasure that is ultimately in contradistinction to the cultural politics that divides them. The soundtrack up to this point has featured a range of modes and styles. Rather than the deadening homogeneity of mainstream pop, the songs are distinct and hint at the elusive mythology of the perfect mix tape, the perfect narrative arc of songs.[63] An important change in the film's theme of placelessness occurs in the club; it is the first sequence that features Micah and Jo as a couple actively inhabiting and interacting with a public. Not invisible in plain sight, they dance, drink, laugh, and move with a crowd.

At this point in the film the nondiegetic score gives way to the diegetic conceit of Micah and Jo listening. The scene redirects them, a black couple in a majority-white crowd, from their racial sincerity trail to a paradoxical pleasure. The indie scene refracts Micah's crucial focus on authenticity and black erasure. A coupled difference among majority peoples, they are imbricated in the music and its politics of pleasure that are antithetical to Micah's internal fury. Yet this scene remains significantly marked by the tension of subcultural ambiguity, the general way that all indie-identified music scenes can elicit allegiance from a broad range of people. But this allegiance also at times entails a refusal to recognize the multiple codes of difference that mark the scene's followers, for these codes are not universal or transcendental. To concretize these engendering codes of authenticity would result in a scene indistinguishable from the others, a standard that pithily hinges on "we all like this music."[64]

Micah and Jo are black bodies in a club, a space that neither rebuffs nor wholly engenders their difference. The club sequence compounds a contradiction that has inflected the film's overall navigation of blackness: Is there an ethics of blackness that can account for the irresolvable nature of pleasure?[65] Micah's love of indie music and the scene does not represent an act of deracination or self-denial, but it does allude to the individual complicated pulls and soothing drags of a pleasure that resists being strictly dictated or recuperated by essential black subjectivity, wish fulfillment, or psychic survival.[66] Their pleasure in this time and space cannot be formalized and equivocated as the mutual exclusivity of politics and pleasure.

During the club sequence, Micah and Jo enter a photo booth for a keepsake of intimate play behind the curtains (figs. 4.13 and 4.14). But does this photograph redress or re-edit the "I want my fuckin' heart sewn back together" of the other photograph and the other woman? Is it okay for Micah to be brokenhearted over his white girlfriend and judge Jo for having a white boyfriend? Regardless, they are happy in the moving crowd with life agitating around them while passing strange in the bohemian cool.

I doubt whether the term *hipster* can ever be productively recuperated from its current pejorative meaning. Yet the hipster's relationship to blackness suggests something more than just a late capitalist, hip, consumer culture. Anatole Broyard contemptuously assessed the hipster of the 1940s Greenwich Village scene as someone who talked about rebellion but was just another dirty formalist:

> The hipster promptly became, in his own eyes, a poet, a seer, a hero. He laid claims to apocalyptic visions and heuristic discoveries when he *picked up*; he was Lazarus, come back from the dead, come back to tell them all, he would tell them all. He conspicuously consumed himself in a high flame. He cared nothing for catabolic consequences; he was so prodigal as to be invulnerable. . . . The hipster—once an unregenerate individualist, an underground poet, a guerilla—had become a pretentious poet laureate. His old subversiveness, his ferocity was now so manifestly rhetorical as to be obviously harmless. He was bought and placed in the zoo. He was *somewhere* at last—comfortably ensconced in the 52nd Street clip joints, in Carnegie Hall, and *Life*. He was *in-there*. . . . He was back in the American womb. And it was just as unhygienic as ever.[67]

FIGS 4.13 and **4.14** Post-soul. Jo and Micah in *Medicine for Melancholy* (Barry Jenkins, 2008).

Broyard's judgment—perhaps a matter of "game recognize game"—pivots on a reading of the hipster as performative heretic, one who fundamentally lacks authenticity. This question of the hipster's rebel sincerity tacitly informs every countercultural movement.

Yet the brand of hipsterism that Micah and Jo seemingly subscribe to negates the assumption that all hipsters are white poseurs or aesthetes, and they are certainly greater than the pithy overtones of "blipster." Cool and hip, their style praxis might wrestle with enduring veracity critiques, but it remains an indisputable source of nonprescriptive pleasure. Regardless, as Rebecca Solnit comments, "Bohemia is not so much a population as a condition, a condition of urbanism where the young go to invent themselves and from which cultural innovation and insurrection arise. As that cultural space contracts, the poor and individual artists will go elsewhere, but bohemia may well go altogether, here and in cities across the country."[68] The innovation culture that animates this club sequence and enfolds Micah and Jo always operates in a state of precarity, as this state of innovation is slowly and increasingly leveraged by the rebranding intent of gentrification and redevelopment plans devoted to the precious natural resource of real estate. Perhaps not all contemporary hipsters truly warrant the contemptuous suggestion that they profit from gentrification if they are to some extent kin to the bohemian and not just trust-fund brood.[69]

As Sunday spills into Monday, Micah and Jo leave the club for a taco truck and meet a criminalization-gentrification joke in the form of two black men dealing in illicit wares: kombucha and Arizona Tea. Market forces have refabulated the politics of racial profiling. Micah drunkenly strolls with his arm around Jo's neck, but the intimacy ends when Jo receives a phone call and Micah assumes the caller is her white curator boyfriend.

> MICAH: Who is that?
>
> JO: Huh?
>
> MICAH: Is it any surprise? I mean, is it any surprise that folks of color in the scene date outside their race?
>
> JO: Okay.
>
> MICAH: I mean, think about it. Like, everything—
>
> JO: No.
>
> MICAH: Think about it? Every—
>
> JO: It's not.
>
> MICAH: Everything, everything about being indie is all tied to not being black.
>
> JO: I don't want to talk about this.
>
> MICAH: Like, everything about being indie is all tied to not being black. Like, friends who are indie? White. Bands who are indie? Like, okay, you got TV on the Radio. But the rest of them are white.[70]
>
> JO: Okay.
>
> MICAH: No, it's not okay. It's not. Like, everything. I mean, people call it interracial dating, but there's nothing interracial about it. Nine out of ten times, it's somebody of color hanging on to a white person. You never, you never—[He slips on the sidewalk's edge.]
>
> JO: Watch your step.

FIG 4.15 Dreams deferred. Jo and Micah in *Medicine for Melancholy* (Barry Jenkins, 2008).

MICAH: Fuck my step. You never see, like, a—you never see a fucking, like a black girl and an Asian dude. You never see an Indian guy and a Latino girl. It's always one of us clinging on to one of them. I mean, look at you. Why the fuck you got to date some white guy?

JO: Why are you doing this? What do you want from me? You think just because I'm black and you're black, that we should just be together? We're just one, right? We fucked and I didn't even know you. I've been spending the last twenty-four hours cheating on my boyfriend. And you think because I'm black and you're black that we should be together. You're so fucking crazy.

What had been a tremulous pull, a "we are black, cool, and want" fascination shatters with "You're so fucking crazy." What has been said cannot be unsaid as the "once upon a time called now," their temporal state of desire and black becoming, takes an irremediable turn (fig. 4.15). Their fortuitous circumstance collapses and gives way to the realization that this was just a thing, a terminable yet consequential thing, but not a fairy tale. The narrative arc does not gently close by fulfilling the promise of black love as redemption. Instead, the fantasy quickly unravels. Micah and Jo are neither model minorities nor full subscribers to black exceptionalism or respectability. What has occurred is the grinding down of a fantasy to a precise and unfortunate point: "Why the fuck you got to date some white guy?"

And When the Groove Is Dead and Gone

> I'm always drunk in San Francisco.
> I'm never feeling any pain.
> But tell me, why does San Francisco,
> Just like a lover's kiss, go straight to my brain?
> I guess it's just the mood I'm in
> That acts like al-co-hol.
> Because, I'm drunk in San Francisco
> And I don't drink at all.
>
> —CARMEN MCRAE, "I'M ALWAYS DRUNK IN SAN FRANCISCO"

> And so we stay with them until they understand why they've been brought to-gether. The longer they're together, the more curious of the other each becomes. This entire film could simply span from when they wake up together knowing nothing of each other until they fall asleep together again the next night, love-lorn and lost in conversation. Open for interpretation at that point.
>
> —BARRY JENKINS, EXCERPT FROM ORIGINAL IDEA FOR *MEDICINE FOR MELANCHOLY*

Micah's rant may very well be the futile philosophizing of the black lonely, but there is something other than the weed or the alcohol at play. As Carmen McRae croons, perhaps the city itself is to blame for his crocked high, his painful stew. Yes, perhaps the city and the film's tracking of its quiet collisions of cultures and histories might explain how, like a lover's kiss, this damn place does go straight to his brain.[71] In the end this thing that was stained by rumors of love or a feeling that might rectify the brokenheartedness of diasporic exile became a case of incompatible measures of historical consciousness and cosmopolitanism. Something strange that then was not strange, a film that at the start provided only a thin explanation for the black courting does incrementally allude to grounding clues for its attachment shenanigans. In spite of the risks of displacement and statelessness, Micah and Jo are two black chronotopic beings caught in something that code-switched between a fantasy of raced desire and a cautionary tale about unbecoming. The film's mapping of their ambling encounter ends as an unsustainable object-choice affair. As Langston Hughes wrote, dreams deferred dry, fester, sag, and explode. And as *Medicine for Melancholy* makes plain, they sometimes become drunken assholes in the street who think they know you.

Micah's compulsion to judge and remake Jo suggests a belief that she must be brought up to speed, acculturated, and versed in his cultural nostalgia and lifeworld view. His courting of her at times appears to operate as instruction. He is not merely a sensitive jester; there is a pitch and indeed the thinking of a master plan. Crazy? A survivor? One attuned to the evidence of things not seen? With the urgency of a dying language, he appears to be pushed to court her for what he wants her to be but not for who she is. Crucially his nostalgia does not recognize that the past that preoccupies and drives him also represents a self that no longer exists.[72] Yet he is afraid of becoming a ghost or one of those things that might cause people to say in hushed tones, "I see black people."

Jo's motivation to spend the day coupling with Micah is more enigmatic, though between the two of them she appears to be the character that experiences the most significant arc of transformation. She does not equivocate about black becoming as vigorously as Micah does: "You think just because I'm black and you're black, that we should just be together?" She wants something altogether different from and collateral to Micah's fantasy. While her motivation is slippery and she ultimately disagrees with his black personhood politics, does that mean she is postracial or pejoratively postblack? Her disagreement with him cannot be assumed to be a sign that she is a sepia Candide or, worse, a universal humanist. Furthermore, to insist that Jo be deracinated or lost, a Nubian princess in need of an ebony knight to save her from the white curator's undecorated tower, says more about the critic than the film. Overall, concluding that she does not think enough about race or that he thinks too much disavows the unfinalizable spirit of the film.[73] He is an open wound and she is a willing participant as their encounter points to distinct politics between them, an alliance and disunion.[74] Two random black folk hook up, synchronize, accelerate, and disintegrate. Micah fails in his pitch not because black love is a frivolous thing but because the political designs of his memory do not produce the love he craves. Instead of a black romantic, perhaps he is a black romantic saboteur. He fails because Jo refuses to believe in shame. She crushes his read with "We just fucked." She won't apologize for a white boyfriend and "figuring it out." She does not submit to a remedial script or disavow her choices as not black enough.

They began as intimate strangers and end as estranged familiars. Maybe their attachment is merely a game of false diasporic cures.[75] His insistence on romantically coupling with her is mediated by a native son's despair as a watcher and embedded chronicler of the cultural geography of San Francisco.

His memory is a tally of disabling losses. The film is not an indictment of desire but a meditation on how desire as a structuring principle of black love can and perhaps must fail. Lamentations represent rituals as much as they signify devotion, yet when might a regimen of "never forget" give way to "make room to grow"?[76] Their extended ramble leads to the discovery of some of the ransoms that result from being raced and desiring in this particular time and place. As Sharon Van Etten sings, "You're the reason why I'll move to the city / You're why I'll need to leave."[77]

No more real talk; the wounded words are done. Following a silent cab ride to his apartment, they kiss in the doorway before Jo crosses the threshold and begins to gather her things. Micah weakly feigns surprise by asking "Why?," and she raises her head and holds a stare. With that look he says, "Just stay here tonight. You can go back to your life tomorrow. Stay. Stay. Stay." Standing and leaning forward with their heads touching, they rock together in an embrace as the film fades to black. This chronicle of a weekend was an attachment happenstance, a cycling of affections, but also a scripting exercise. It was never free love. The final scene fades to the most stable color shot of the film, revealing a sleeping Micah while slowly tracking to a halt at the window ledge and a view of the fire escape and the street. In the end the Doppler hum of black love fades out and fades in to Monday and the sight of Jo on her bicycle in the street below. The early riser is disentangled and uncoupled as she glides away, perhaps to continue to explore and negotiate with other urban histories and racial scripts. Nevertheless there is no definitive answer for Jo. Maybe this was her story all along. As for Micah, perhaps this was not the first time he put his pain on a stranger, nor will it be the last. Maybe they will meet again in Oscar Grant Plaza? They are two diasporic states of consciousness: his one of erosion and displacement, and hers one of roving adaptation. In all its quiet glory and pace, *Medicine for Melancholy* advances a poignant sense of film blackness as a meditation on romance, place, and ruin.

CODA

DESTINATION OUT

Blackness functions . . . as both a free-floating trace unmoored from individual subjects and as a concrete index of power relations that reveals the deep structure of modernity's modes of visualization, the despotism on which they rely, and the ways that they might be contested in the present.

—HUEY COPELAND, *BOUND TO APPEAR: ART, SLAVERY, AND THE SITE OF BLACKNESS IN MULTICULTURAL AMERICA*

What if black film could be something other than embodied? What if black film was immaterial and bodiless? What if black film could be speculative or just ambivalent? What if film is ultimately the worst window imaginable and an even poorer mirror? What if black film is art and not the visual transcription of the black lifeworld? These are some of the questions I posed in the beginning of this book, questions that ultimately inferred potentialities and stipulations regarding the idea of black film. As Huey Copeland vitally notes in the epigraph, the differential forces and textures of blackness compel its multivalence as aesthetic practice, cultural coherence, existential state, and praxis. Copeland's consideration of the immateriality and materiality of blackness—a free-floating trace and a concrete index of power—parallels my commitment to considering the intricacies of black film. *Film Blackness* foregrounds the creative and critical capacities of cinema with black visual and expressive culture as its signifying core. In place of a strict taxonomic or social reflectionist approach, film blackness entails considering other prerogatives that concentrate on discourse, sedimentations, and modalities. In this book I have questioned what a film does rather than what a film must do, and thus I have focused on the way blackness is cinematically figured and staged.

With an interdisciplinary and multidisciplinary investment in cinema studies, I have reconciled the *black* of black film through a consideration of the idea of black film in relation to the other arts and fields of study as a way of bridging collateral questions about blackness and the arts. Film blackness puts emphasis on generative assemblages and suspends the determinism of black film as a diagnostic category. Race matters, and this book has not suggested otherwise. Instead I have produced readings that dissuade the rule of realism or a hermeneutics steeped in social category denotation and aggressive prescription. The principle of film blackness enlivens as an epistemological corrective of the idea of black film with an interest in cinema's capacity to generate creative theorizations about visuality, blackness, and the arts. The racial grotesque, black performativity, modalities of noir blackness, and a narrative matrix of the city, desire, and black becoming have been my rhetorical and thematic concerns. With attention to film blackness, I have ascribed new values to the idea of black film. By deploying new rules of engagement with greater allegiance to black visual and expressive culture, I have argued how each film enacts blackness with a specific confluence of aesthetics, politics, history, and culture.

Coonskin skewers the history of American popular culture and antiblack visual culture with attention to cultural producers and propagators. In place of innocuous pleasures, the film offers deeply discomforting acts of reanimation. By stipulating the passing tradition in the terms of performativity, *Chameleon Street* accounts for the fluidity of blackness as an aesthetic and cultural strategy. With regard to the film's circulation and reception, the erasure and condescension that Harris and the film endured serve as a caution against delimiting expectations that prove to be ruinous for the idea of black film. The critical challenge of *Deep Cover* results from the way the film dynamically cuts through the shadows of noir with the differentiation of blackness as its signifying core. The visual, historiographic, affective, and narrative force of *Medicine for Melancholy* quietly paces the attachment affair of blackness, love, and urban history. Each chapter expands on the one before it with movements across visual historiography, performativity, genre, and affect. Moreover the book has defended a politics of pleasure derived from the inventive and emboldened possibility of cinema to titillate and confound. The methodological interventions of *Film Blackness* offer instruction for how to critically assess and appreciate cinematic works in the twenty-first century ever more distant from the paradigmatic crush of an essential blackness. This means even more possibilities for thinking through the modalities of film blackness. For this reason I conclude by briefly addressing some commonalities and emergent trends of this growing body of work that has exercised different aesthetic values and impressions about social fact and art practice. In this way, *Film Blackness* and its concentration on visuality, textuality, and sociality might inform the critical tactics to come.

Still Raining, Still Dreaming

Enactments of film blackness in the early twenty-first century moment have reanimated cultural history as visual historiographies and remediations (Margaret Brown's *The Order of Myths* [2008], Tanya Hamilton's *Night Catches Us* [2010], Christine Acham and Cliff Ward's *Infiltrating Hollywood: The Rise and Fall of The Spook Who Sat by the Door* [2011], Steve McQueen's *12 Years a Slave* [2013], Yoruba Richen's *The New Black* [2013], and Stephen Winter's *Jason and Shirley* [2015]), actualized new diasporic aesthetics (Andrew Dosunmu's *Restless City* [2011] and *Mother of George* [2013]), and offered strikingly alternative narratives of black performativity and becoming (Cheryl Dunye's *Stranger Inside* [2001], Spike Lee's *Passing Strange: The Movie* [2009], Lee Daniels's *Precious* [2009], Tina Mabry's *Mississippi Damned* [2009], Dee Rees's *Pariah* [2011], Keith Miller's *Welcome to Pine Hill* [2012], Ryan Coogler's *Fruitvale Station* [2013], Josh Locy's *Hunter Gatherer* [2015], and Rick Famuyiwa's *Dope* [2015]). Furthermore, in the same vein as the poignant diegetic accounting of place in *Medicine for Melancholy*, David Gordon Green's *George Washington* (2000), Lance Hammer's *Ballast* (2008), and Benh Zeitlin's *Beasts of the Southern Wild* (2012) are part of a cluster of films that share a complimentary attention to blackness, melancholy, and the cinematic South that signals further possibilities for thinking about film blackness with attention to the material and symbolic traces that constitute cinematic place.[1]

Additionally there has been significant formal experimentation with black quiet and temporality in work that includes the elliptical structure and exquisite animation of Terence Nance's *An Oversimplification of Her Beauty* (2013); Kahlil Joseph's nonclassical music videos / short films for Shabazz Palaces, Flying Lotus, and Kendrick Lamar; and Ava DuVernay's *Middle of Nowhere* (2012). *Middle of Nowhere* centers on Ruby (Emayatzy Corinealdi), a nurse whose husband, Derek (Omari Hardwick), is incarcerated. She exists in a state of waiting for her husband's release, his collect calls, his parole hearing, and the ritual cycle of her bus visits to the prison. Her paused life becomes roused by a new relationship. The film details how Ruby quietly persists and moves with the memories of the past, the everyday diffusion of New Jim Crow and carceral time, and the advancing desire of this new attachment.[2] Thus the film delicately tracks a black woman who endures as an affective vessel of temporalities; she abides black love as grief and absolution.

Finally there is Kevin Jerome Everson. His work represents a distinct film and video processing of materials, craft, and blackness. While he has worked in various mediums (e.g., photography, printmaking, sculpture, painting), since the late 1990s his work has shifted to primarily film and video and has been shown at film festivals, museums, galleries, and other exhibition sites throughout Europe and America. His growing catalogue, which includes over 130 shorts and eight feature films to date, makes him one of the most prolific black filmmakers. His art practice deftly defies abating categorical claims. His work includes documentaries with deliberately fabricated elements, found footage, and time-thickening one-shots. All his work is mediated by experimental or avant-garde gestures, and yet there is a refined insistence on form, the everyday, black people, history, performativity, labor, and repetition. Yet his work never proffers anything resembling an essence or definitive answer to the questions of blackness but demonstrates a devotion to quotidian occurrences and the varied tasks of everyday life. As he declares, "It's my responsibility to make art. I have a responsibility to my family, my hometown of Mansfield[, Ohio], close friends, and a history of former students to keep making that art. I'm not a doctor so I don't heal and I'm not a lawyer so I don't advocate. I'm an artist so I have to keep cranking out cultural artifacts. I tell my students I am an artist and a teacher, but mostly an artist. I want them to believe that. So, I prove it every day, week, month, season, and year. Art has got to be made."[3] Everson's acute justification of his artistic practice bears keeping in mind for critics and artists invested in the idea of black film. Opening an aperture illuminates, and stopping down or closing one does not. To repeat, this book is founded on the belief that the idea of black film is always a question, never an answer. Throughout I have put critical stress on narrative, visuality, the experimental nature of blackness, black visual and expressive culture, and my own black cinephilia. *Film Blackness* models an urgency and a hope that the idea of black film will carry on as an irreconcilable discourse that will continue to defy, challenge, and enliven our sense of art, history, and culture.

NOTES

INTRODUCTION

1. Isaac Julien and Kobena Mercer write that this sense of tension is "the tension be-tween representation as a practice of depiction and representation as a practice of delegation" ("Introduction: De Margin and de Centre," 4).

2. As Valerie Smith writes, "Directors, studios, and their marketing experts collude in shrinking the distance between referent and representation in films . . . , thereby delimiting what counts, or sells, as black film" ("The Documentary Impulse in Con-temporary African-American Film," 58).

3. Harry Allen, "Telling Time: On Spike, Strike and the 'Reality' of *Clockers*," *Village Voice*, 3 October 1995, 84. See Kobena Mercer, "Black Art and the Burden of Repre-sentation," in *Welcome to the Jungle*, 233–58.

4. For more elaboration on the distinction of the adaptation from its source, see Mas-sood, *Black City Cinema*; Harris, "*Clockers*: Adaptations in Black."

5. After some experimentation, Malik Sayeed, the cinematographer, convinced Spike Lee to use Kodak 5239 stock for *Clockers*. A special 35mm version of the stock had to be created, as there was only a 16mm version used by news reporters before the industrial switch to video, and by NASA and the U.S. Air Force for surveillance op-erations. See "Between 'Rock' and a Hard Place," *American Cinematographer*, Sep-tember 1995.

6. For a reading of the realism issues surrounding the reception of *Clockers* in contra-distinction to *Hoop Dreams* and the rhetoric of "America," see Cole and King, "The New Politics of Urban Consumption."

7. As Judith Butler notes, "To question a form of activity or a conceptual terrain is not to banish or censor it; it is, for the duration, to suspend its ordinary play in order to ask after its constitution" ("Competing Universalities," 264).

8. Thanks to Dana Seitler for thinking through this line of inquiry.

9. Ralph Ellison, "Change the Joke and Slip the Yoke," in *Shadow and Act*, 59.

10. Benston, *Performing Blackness*, 6. The vital import of the black arts movement and those artists who engineered a shift in the hermeneutics of black art as an irremedi-

able break from the biological to an emphasis on political engagement with socio-cultural practice informs film blackness. Granted, elements of the movement prob-lematically insisted on directives of compulsory blackness, but I am less interested in the consequences of the Black Arts Movement and more invested in how this break provided for a new articulation of art practice and conception of being and the relationship between the two. This shift to the political and sociocultural features of race and away from the denotative and static interpretations of birthright exposes crucial tensions. These tensions represent the Black Art Movement's resolutely ex-perimental tendencies. As Benston writes, "At one moment, blackness may signify a reified essence posited as the end of a revolutionary 'metalanguage' projecting the community towards 'something not included here'; at another moment, blackness may indicate a self-interpreting process which simultaneously 'makes and unmakes' black identity in the ceaseless flux of historical change" (3–4).

11. Lubiano, "'But Compared to What,'" 175.

12. My use of "raced" is derived from Kendall Thomas's consideration of the discursiv-ity of race: "I have suggested in some of my work in critical race theory that 'race' is a verb, that we are 'raced' through a constellation of practices that construct and control racial subjectivities" ("The Eclipse of Reason," 1806–7).

13. Coco Fusco notes, "A serious discussion of the meaning of our desire to see race in visual representation is impeded by the difficulties we have in distinguishing be-tween racialisation as visual process, and racism as an ethical and political dilemma" ("Racial Time, Racial Marks, Racial Metaphors," 23).

14. "There is no guarantee, in reaching for an essentialized racial identity of which we think we can be certain, that it will always turn out to be mutually liberating and progressive on all the other dimensions. It *can* be won. There *is* a politics there to be struggled for. But the invocation of a guaranteed black experience behind it will not produce that politics" (Stuart Hall, "What Is This 'Black' in Black Popular Cul-ture?," in *Stuart Hall: Critical Dialogues in Cultural Studies*, 474).

15. Stuart Hall, "New Ethnicities," in *Stuart Hall: Critical Dialogues in Cultural Stud-ies*, 443.

16. Kobena Mercer's use of Mikhail Bakhtin toward his conception of critical dialo-gism significantly informs my sense of film blackness: "Critical dialogism has the potential to overrun the binaristic relations of hegemonic boundary maintenance by multiplying critical dialogues *within* particular communities and *between* the various constituencies that make up the 'imagined communities' of the nation.... Moreover, critical dialogism questions the monologic exclusivity on which domi-nant versions of national identity and collective belonging are based" ("Diaspora Culture and the Dialogic Imagination: The Aesthetics of Black Independent Film in Britain," in *Welcome to the Jungle*, 64–65).

17. For Nathaniel Mackey, the term *discrepant engagement* accounts for his dispute with the reality claims projected on the work of black writers. Drawing from the creaking of the Dogon weaving block, he augments his critique with this aural component

as sounding against the (in)coherence of social applicability readings of black literature. He writes, "Discrepant engagement, rather than suppressing resonance, dissonance, noise, seeks to remain open to them. Its admission of resonances contends with resolution. It worries resolute boundary lines, resolute definitions, obeying a vibrational rather than a corpuscular sense of being. It is to be at odds with taxonomies and categorizations that obscure the fact of heterogeneity and mix" (*Discrepant Engagement*, 20).

18. "Marginality," Charles Gaines writes, "is not a simple theory, but a complex construction of overlapping social, philosophical, biological, and historical ideas. Much writing on the subject is reductionist and essentialist because the politics of the subject almost requires simplification. It almost begs for a simpler form, a diagram, perhaps, that will give shape to an impossibly complex machine, a coding that will make the difficult choices for us, to relieve us of the annoying spectacle of its insurmountability" ("The Theatre of Refusal," 20).

19. Thanks to Cathy Davidson for this early and crucial assessment of film blackness.

20. Fleetwood, *Troubling Vision*, 6.

21. Wiegman, *American Anatomies*, 5–6.

22. Reid, *Redefining Black Film*, 2–3.

23. Reid, *Redefining Black Film*, 135.

24. English, *How to See a Work of Art in Total Darkness*, 29, 27.

25. Moten, *In the Break*, 255n1.

26. *Dreams Are Colder Than Death* was commissioned by ZDF and ARTE, the German and Franco-German television broadcasters, as part of their programming devoted to the fiftieth anniversary of the March on Washington. The day-long program aired on the exact date of the anniversary, 28 August 2013, beginning with a broadcast of Dr. King's "I Have a Dream" speech in its entirety. Other films included *Killer of Sheep* (Charles Burnett, 1977) and *Do the Right Thing* (Spike Lee, 1989) and documentaries on Oprah Winfrey, David Adjaye, gospel music, and the civil rights songbook.

27. For further elaboration on Hortense Spillers's thoughts on black culture, see Spillers, "The Idea of Black Culture."

28. I highly recommend viewing Jafa's *Slowly This* (1995) as a vital precedent for understanding his practice of experimental temporality.

29. Jafa has spoken about this nonsynchronicity strategy as related to a concern for the inherent power of the camera with its equivalence to the white gaze: "The camera functions as surrogate for the white gaze and we put on these survivor modalities. . . . So I just decided, okay, we weren't going to film anybody, not while we were talking to them at least" (in Diana Buendia, "A Groundbreaking Approach to Storytelling: The Essay Film," Film Independent blog, 17 July 2014, http://www.filmindependent.org/blogs/a-groundbreaking-approach-to-storytelling-the-essay-film/#.Vqp3v_HVnxt). Also see Jafa's public conversation with bell hooks at The New School (10 October 2015): "bell hooks and Arthur Jafa Discuss Trans-

gression in Public Spaces at The New School," YouTube, 16 October 2014, https://www.youtube.com/watch?v=fe-7ILSKS0g&index=97&list=PLB703F4F24EDo BBAA.

30. For an elaboration on visual historiography with a comparable distinction between historiography and "historiophoty," see White, "Historiography and Historiophoty."

31. See Moten, "Blackness and Nothingness," for a further elaboration on his blackness and love query.

32. Writing elsewhere, Moten identifies a form of study that signals noninstitutional or alternate forms of knowledge production and research. Formally, *Dreams* cinematically enacts this sense of study. As Moten notes, "When I think about the way we use the term 'study,' I think we are committed to the idea that study is what you do with other people. It's talking and walking around with other people, working, dancing, suffering, some irreducible convergence of all three, held under the name of speculative practice. The notion of a rehearsal—being in a kind of workshop, playing in a band, in a jam session, or old men sitting on a porch, or people working together in a factory—there are these various modes of activity. The point of calling it 'study' is to mark that the incessant and irreversible intellectuality of these activities is already present. . . . To do these things is to be involved in a kind of common intellectual practice. What's important is to recognize that that has been the case—because that recognition allows you to access a whole, varied, alternative history of thought" (Harney and Moten, *The Undercommons*, 110).

33. See Kelley, *Freedom Dreams*.

ONE. Reckless Eyeballing

1. The names correspond to characters Crothers played in the following films: Mr. Bones, *Yes, Sir, Mr. Bones* (1951); Smiley, *Walking My Baby Back Home* (1953); Shoeshine Boy, *The Patsy* (1964); Moses, *Bloody Mama* (1970) and *The Shootist* (1976); Smoke, *Chandler* (1971); Big Ben, *Lady Sings the Blues* (1972); Reverend Markham, *Detroit 9000* (1973); Duke, *Truck Turner* (1974); Pop, *Black Belt Jones* (1974).

2. See Edwards, "Louis Armstrong and the Syntax of Scat," 622.

3. Mackey, *Bedouin Handbook*, 83.

4. This underground and aboveground distinction incurs an association with the spatial tropes of blackness central to work such as Richard Wright's "The Man Who Lived Underground" (1942) and Ralph Ellison's *Invisible Man* (1952).

5. The prison scenes were shot at the Macalester State Penitentiary in Oklahoma.

6. Phillip Thomas would eventually add his middle name (Michael) to his billing and achieve some celebrity as Ricardo Tubbs on *Miami Vice* (1984–89). Sampson/Bear is played and voiced by Barry White, the singer, songwriter, and producer. Charles Gordone performs and voices the roles of Preacher/Preacher Fox. He had previously done voice-over work on Bakshi's *Heavy Traffic* (1973). A playwright and

actor, Gordone had a successful off-Broadway run at the Public Theater in New York City with his play *No Place to Be Somebody* (1969). In 1970 he became the first African American to receive the Pulitzer Prize for drama. His ambivalence toward the idea of black theater and his opinions of black art more generally have a special correspondence to *Coonskin*'s enactment of blackness. See Charles Gordone, "Yes, I Am a Black Playwright, But . . . ," *New York Times*, 25 January 1970.

7. Max Fleischer created the Rotograph in 1925 at Fleischer Studios, an early rival of Walt Disney Studios. The Rotograph was an advance on his invention of the Rotoscope in 1914 that was first used in the *Koko the Clown* series. Considered the process of painting on film, rotoscoping quickly became the industry standard, most prominently at Disney. While rotoscoping was a process by which film frames were projected onto the surface of a stand (a rotoscope stand) so that a set of animation frames could be drawn or traced over the film images, the Rotograph allowed for the use of animation over live images as opposed to an animated image derived from a live image. My thanks to Nicholas Sammond for helping me understand the distinction.

8. Kotlarz, "The Birth of a Notion," 22. For more on blackness and animation, see Sampson, *That's Enough, Folks*; Lindvall and Eraser, "Darker Shades of Animation"; Lehman, *The Colored Cartoon*; Sammond, *Birth of an Industry*.

9. Wright, "Big Boy Leaves Home," 239–75.

10. For more on the "cult of true womanhood," see Carby, *Reconstructing Womanhood*. The sheriff's daughter is modeled on the title character from Harvey Kurtzman's popular *Playboy* strip, *Little Annie Fanny* (1962–88). Kurtzman would later become the founding editor of *Mad* (1952). *Coonskin* makes intertextual gestures toward several pivotal figures in the history of animation and comics, such as George Herriman, Tex Avery, Isadore ("Friz") Freleng, Bob Clampett, Don Marquis, and R. Crumb. As Pappy's tale first introduces Rabbit, Bear, and Fox through animation, it occurs against a backdrop of inflated and colorful concentric circles, a direct reference to the proscenium that opened Warner Bros.' Merrie Melodies. The poster for *Coonskin* featured Rabbit in a white suit (circa *Super Fly* [Gordon Parks Jr., 1972]) backed by the Merrie Melodies circles with the phrase "This Is It Folks," a nod to the Looney Tunes standard "That's All Folks."

11. Carpio, *Laughing Fit to Kill*, 22.

12. Morrison, *Playing in the Dark*, 38, 90. Also see Nericcio, *Tex[t]-Mex*, 111–52.

13. Mikhail M. Bakhtin, "Discourse in the Novel," in *The Dialogic Imagination*, 421.

14. Bakhtin, *Rabelais and His World*, 19.

15. Ahmed, *The Cultural Politics of Emotion*, 45.

16. Ngai, *Ugly Feelings*, 124.

17. My framing of *Coonskin* as a metapicture draws from W. J. T. Mitchell's conception of the idea in the context of his consideration of Spike Lee's *Bamboozled* (2000) as a metapicture. *Coonskin* and *Bamboozled* share a similar reflexive impulse in regard to history, antiblack visual culture, and American popular culture. As Mitchell writes,

"*Bamboozled* is a metapicture—a picture about pictures, a picture that conducts a self-conscious inquiry into the life of images, especially racial images, and the way they circulate in media and everyday life" ("Living Color," 301).

18. Busack, "Here He Comes to Save the Day." For a review of Bakshi's life and career in animation, see McGilligan, "A Talk with Ralph Bakshi"; Gibson and McDonnell, *Unfiltered*.

19. Notably, Albert S. Ruddy was retained as the film's producer. His previous Paramount Pictures films, *The Godfather* (1972) and *The Longest Yard* (1974), assured the studio that the film was a viable project.

20. Originally scheduled for 12 November, the work-in-progress screening of *Coonskin* occurred at the Museum of Modern Art on 24 November 1974 as part of Cineprobe. A screening program started by the MoMA Film Department in 1968, Cineprobe was devoted to fostering an informal dialogue with young independent filmmakers. The audio recording from that evening opens with prescreening introductory comments by Adrienne Mancia and Bakshi before a cut to the beginning of the postscreening conversation. There are two prominent sounds: the agitated tones of Mancia and Bakshi imploring the audience to be respectful and civil, and off-microphone shouts. Members of CORE who had protested before and during the screening were still in attendance. After a question about whether he used LSD, the next question came from a woman who walked to the stage to directly address Bakshi. Her voice builds to a crying scream: "You wrote it. You put it up there. I have black kids out here. My black kids don't take dope. They don't live in ghettos, they live in communities." Building on her distinguishing of communities from ghettos, she mentions the origins of the ghetto with the Jews in Europe. "When are you going to laugh at them [Jews]? Goddamnit, man!!! You don't laugh at my people. You don't laugh at black people." Al Sharpton can be heard after the woman walks away, quipping, "You're just a pimp." Sharpton also calls for a boycott of Barry White's music. Incensed, Bakshi goes on the offensive in his response to some of the questions as a group of men surround him at the table on the stage. Someone in the audience says, "Either kick his ass or let him speak." Someone else asks, "What was the purpose of making this film?" Bakshi responds, "*Coonskin* was made because . . . the Black revolution has sold out. The Black revolution has done nothing. CORE does nothing better but attack my film." Another audience member asks, "Who appointed you as the Messiah to speak for black people?" Bakshi answers, "I'm not the Messiah. I'm a director who has tried not to cop out. I'm a director who has tried not to take easy sugar-coated Hollywood pills and deliver it to the public which is usually a lot of bullshit." In response to the Preacher Fox character, someone asks, "When was the last time you saw a minister use 'motherfucker'?" Bakshi quips, "When was the last time you saw God help your people?" The rest of the session continues with angry shouts, yelling, and Bakshi antagonizing the crowd (e.g., "Is the black man afraid of the truth?"; "Have you turned so middle class that you can't see the truth?"). Sound Recordings of Museum-Related Events, "An Evening with Ralph Bakshi."

21. Whitney Williams, "Blacks Blast 'Coonskin,'" *Variety*, 15 January 1975, 34.

22. Stephen Farber, "The Campaign to Suppress 'Coonskin,'" *New York Times*, 20 July 1975.

23. In an attempt to preemptively reduce the perception of the film as racist and correct some pronunciation issues, a great deal of Barry White's dialogue was overdubbed by a different actor in the months leading up to the film's opening. CORE's protest campaign included meetings between Paramount officials and regional CORE leaders in Los Angeles as well as picketing of the New York offices of Gulf and Western, the conglomerate of which Paramount was a part. The studio was inundated by requests for preview screenings by various black newspapers, NAACP and Urban League chapters across the country, and many prominent black entrepreneurs, including Frederick S. Weaver, the great-grandson of Frederick Douglass. The majority of people who commented on the film over the course of the year leading up to its August premiere had never seen it. Most criticism drew on the reports of the small CORE contingent at the MoMA screening. One NAACP official endorsed the film as "difficult satire" but overall a "positive film." Bakshi vigorously defended the film rather problematically as simply "truth" throughout the year. See "Black Leaders Say Movie 'Coonskin' Is Racist," *San Francisco Sun Reporter*, 16 November 1974; Farber, "Campaign to Suppress 'Coonskin.'"

24. Bakshi had negotiated a release from Paramount as changes in the studio brass resulted in the arrival of new studio heads with less favorable interest in *Coonskin*. In particular, Bakshi has claimed that Barry Diller, who became Paramount's new chairman and CEO around the time of the film's MoMA screening, was the figure most responsible for the studio's change of interest in the film (Busack, "Here He Comes to Save the Day").

25. Bryanston Distributors was an independent distributor whose first title and hit was *Return of the Dragon* (Bruce Lee, 1972). Notably the company had successes with cult and midnight movies and programming (e.g., Andy Warhol's *Flesh for Frankenstein* [Paul Morrissey and Antonio Margheriti, 1974] and *The Texas Chainsaw Massacre* [Tobe Hooper, 1974]), a screening practice that contributed to the strong gross of Bakshi's first two feature films, *Fritz the Cat* (1972) and *Heavy Traffic* (1973). See Hoberman and Rosenbaum, *Midnight Movies*.

26. Commenting on the smoke bomb incidents, Bakshi has stated: "Martin Scorsese was driving around filming second-unit stuff for *Taxi Driver* near Times Square, just random New York mania he was trying to catch. He happened to have the camera going right at the same time someone threw a smoke bomb into the theater showing *Coonskin*. He sent me this roll of film showing people running out of the theater. I didn't know whether to laugh or cry, but it's OK now" (Busack, "Here He Comes to Save the Day").

27. Significant literature on *Coonskin* includes the following: McGilligan, "A Talk with Ralph Bakshi"; Holte, "Ethnicity and the Popular Imagination"; Kotlarz, "The Birth of a Notion"; Sabin, *Adult Comics*; James, *That's Blaxploitation!*; Cohen, "Racism and Resistance" and *Forbidden Animation*; Kanfer, *Serious Business*; Neal, *Soul*

Babies; Randolph, "On the Blackhand Side"; Gibson and McDonnell, *Unfiltered*; Sperb, *Disney's Most Notorious Film*. In the wake of an extended version of *Coonskin* screened in conjunction with the awarding of the Cinequest Maverick Spirit award to Bakshi at the San Jose Film Festival in March 2003, there has been a great deal of renewed interest in *Coonskin*. The version of the film screened in San Jose is reportedly the longest version. Much of the additional footage is of live-action sequences (admittedly, the weakest parts of the film). This footage is readily available on the Internet but curiously only in German. *Coonskin* and Bakshi's work in general have been discovered by a new generation of filmgoers due to the popularity of Peter Jackson's *Lord of the Rings* trilogy (2001–3), spurring interest in Bakshi's animated adaptation of *Lord of the Rings* (1978). *Coonskin* was officially released on DVD in 2012. Most recently Bakshi participated in a postscreening discussion of the film at the Brooklyn Academy of Music with Darius James (10 May 2014).

28. Snead, *White Screens/Black Images*, 89. For a thorough history of *Song of the South* and its circulation, see Sperb, *Disney's Most Notorious Film*.

29. Goings, *Mammy and Uncle Mose*, 9.

30. Houston Baker elaborates on the neoclassical design of the New South: "The Plantation tradition consists of white American literary works which project a southern ideal based on a somewhat ad hoc model of the enlightened Greek city-state. In order to achieve the tradition's fictively projected ideal, southern society must be divided into discrete classes with white masters at the helm, black slaves in the galley, and all voyagers aware of the boundaries and duties of their respective positions. Shored up by Walter Scott's romantic chivalry, the plantation prospect produced literary narratives that represent kind masters, gracious manor houses, chastely elegant southern belles, and obediently happy dark servants who are given to a life of mindless labor and petty high jinks" (*Blues, Ideology, and Afro-American Literature*, 130).

31. Levine, *Black Culture and Black Consciousness*, 116–17.

32. Fanon, *Black Skin, White Masks*, 174.

33. *Coonskin* and its transgressive tone of revolution and retaliation tacitly pose a critique of the ways these tales were used in concert with institutional policies of antiblack violence. In *Disturbing the Peace*, Bryan Wagner astutely considers the context in which Joel Chandler Harris's Uncle Remus tales circulated in the *Atlanta Constitution* during the late 1870s. He identifies how these early Remus tales functioned as observational pieces of the perceived urban crisis of black vagrancy and criminality with the arrival of ex-slaves and free blacks to the city. Wagner astutely centers on how the tales were effectively staged as New South propaganda for the newspaper's advocacy of expanded powers for the Atlanta Municipal Police, the city's modern police force that was established in 1874. He writes, "Harris does more than put editorial opinions in Uncle Remus's mouth. He crafts interlocutory scenes where the repetition of these opinions becomes meaningful in relation not only to their speaker but also to their listeners" (157–58).

34. For more on the Second Reconstruction, see Marable, *Race, Reform, and Rebellion*; Woodward, *The Strange Career of Jim Crow*.

35. In spite of Bakshi's intention to pose *Coonskin* as an indictment of Disney's *Song of the South* and the cultural nostalgia surrounding the film, part of the backlash against Bakshi and the film resulted in a valorization of *Song of the South* as the "good object" to *Coonskin* as "bad object." In *Disney's Most Notorious Film*, Jason Sperb richly examines how the tone of the backlash echoed growing white opposition of the post–civil rights era of the Second Reconstruction: "In the void of liberal disagreements over Bakshi's film grew an unchallenged conservatism. The criticism of *Coonskin* was used to implicitly discredit the larger civil rights movement for greater equality in cinematic representation.... Once devised as a particular kind of critique of *Song of the South*, *Coonskin's* failure and de facto censorship became appropriated by Disney supporters and a vindication of the 1946 film's innocence and entertainment value, and as a deflection from the controversies Disney's movie had incited" (137).

36. Ngai, *Ugly Feelings*, 117.

37. See Green and Guillory, "Question of a 'Soulful Style,'" 250–65.

38. For more on the significance of the Biograph films in relation to *The Birth of a Nation*, see Bernardi, "The Voice of Whiteness." For an invaluable assessment of the legacy of *The Birth of a Nation*, see McEwan, "Racist Film."

39. David R. Roediger identifies how "coon" initially circulated as a term for a "white country person" before becoming related to the Whig Party in the 1840s. The term's circulation as racial slur is derived from Zip Coon and the blackface minstrel conceit of "coon-hunting" and "eating coons." See *Wages of Whiteness*, 97–99.

40. Gilroy, *Against Race*, 46.

41. Fanon, *Black Skin, White Masks*, 112, 122.

42. With the shadow of blackface minstrelsy in play during Tom's monologue, this moment touches on the enduring legacy of blackface minstrelsy and the history of American animation. On this point Nicholas Sammond's work is crucial. This work was released while I was in the very final stages of this book, but I look forward to more fully engaging with it in my future work on animation. Sammond writes, "American animation, which had its origins and developed many of its enduring conventions on the vaudeville stage, is not merely one more in a succession of textual forms; it is also a performative tradition that is indebted to and imbricated in blackface minstrelsy and vaudeville. Commercial animation in the United States didn't borrow from blackface minstrelsy and vaudeville, nor was it simply influenced by it. Rather, American animation is actually in many of its most enduring incarnations an integral part of the ongoing iconographic and performative traditions of blackface. Mickey Mouse isn't *like* a minstrel; he is a minstrel" (*Birth of an Industry*, 5).

43. Mikhail M. Bakhtin, "Forms of Time and *Chronotope* in the Novel," in *The Dialogic Imagination*, 84.

44. Robert Stam comments, "The chronotope mediates between two orders of experience and discourse: the historical and the artistic, providing fictional environments where historically specific constellations of power are made visible" (*Subversive Pleasures*, 11).

45. Ralph Ellison, "Twentieth-Century Fiction and the Black Mask of Humanity," in *Shadow and Act*, 29.

46. This interplay of benevolence and rebellion recalls what Eric Lott says about Sambo in the nineteenth century: "Rebellion tears the mask off the happy slave, exposing the angry face of a violent, frequently desperate captive. Admitting the rebel's existence as anything but an unnatural exception to the norm means not only the destruction of the Sambo stereotype but also the unraveling of the master's own self-construction as a benevolent father figure, an image whose coherence depends on the (imagined) happiness of the slave" (*Love and Theft*, 163).

47. Du Bois, *The Souls of Black Folks*, 364–65.

48. Smith, *Photography on the Color Line*, 25.

49. Bakhtin, *Rabelais and His World*, 24.

50. Cassuto, *The Inhuman Race*, 11, 9.

51. Writing on the work of Michael Ray Charles and Kara Walker in terms of "dreadful beauty," Rachael Ziady DeLue explains, "The imagery deployed by Walker and Charles has accumulated over time an aura of untouchability that inspires a kind of negative reverence. This is a condition of thrall that hinges, not on the transfer of desire or relationality to an object or group of objects—that is, one that relies on the translation of the subjective into the objective—but, rather, on the ascription of special subjectivity to a set of images and artifacts, special in that this subjectivity is of a nonhuman, inhuman sort, not God's superhumanity, but slavery's and racism's traumatic breaching of human limits" ("Dreadful Beauty and the Undoing of Adulation in the Work of Kara Walker and Michael Ray Charles," 78).

52. See Gayle, *The Black Aesthetic*.

53. Benston, *Performing Blackness*, 3.

54. See Ongiri, *Spectacular Blackness*.

55. Glaude, "Introduction," 5.

56. See Schaefer, *Bold! Daring! Shocking! True!* As Amy Ongiri observes, "In creating the genre of Blaxploitation, the film industry took a spectatorial community that had been and was being constituted by the political and cultural configurations of Black Power discourse and simply commodified it into an audience for Blaxploitation. That process of commodification opened new opportunities for the representation of a Black Power discourse on film, but it set significant limitations on the shape of the representation as well" (*Spectacular Blackness*, 168).

57. Sound Recordings of Museum-Related Events, "An Evening with Ralph Bakshi."

58. For more on the political critique of 1970s American cinema, see Kellner and Ryan, *Camera Politica*; Hoberman, *The Dream Life*.

59. See Guerrero, *Framing Blackness*.

60. Keeling, *The Witch's Flight*, 101.

61. Notably Bakshi's force of a difference exploits the folds of blaxploitation with an amplification of intertextual gestures to *Superfly*, *Across 110th Street* (Barry Shear, 1972), and *The Spook Who Sat by the Door* (Ivan Dixon, 1973).

62. Blaxploitation nostalgia in the sense of the vernacular cosmopolitanism of minori-

tarian cool reduces cultural nationalism to the tropological redundancy of the fly of future past. The pleasure it continues to provide occurs in the absence of a contextualization of cultural politics and the resignifying of racialization that fueled the film cycle.

63. See Massood, *Making a Promised Land*; Shukla, "Loving the Other in 1970s Harlem."

64. Locke, *The New Negro*, 5.

65. "With the visual arts of the 1920s and 1930s anchored by black peoples, we can recollect and reimagine this twentieth century moment when Harlem was not only 'in vogue,' or 'on the minds' of a complacent few, but also a geo-political metaphor for modernity and an icon for an increasingly complex black diasporal presence in the world" (Powell, "Re/Birth of a Nation," 18).

66. Maxwell, "Harlem Polemics, Harlem Aesthetics," 46.

67. See Baker, *Modernism and the Harlem Renaissance*.

68. Dinerstein, *Swinging the Machine*, 5.

69. Coombe, *The Cultural Life of Intellectual Properties*, 169.

70. Witt, *Black Hunger*, 36.

71. Berlant, *The Female Complaint*, 122.

72. McPherson, *Reconstructing Dixie*, 7.

73. Chandler, "Xenophobes, Visual Terrorism and the African Subject," 26.

74. As Eden Osucha notes of the proliferation of antiblack iconography in the emerging mass culture of the twentieth century, "postbellum commodity racism tendered more figurative correspondences between the look of the commodity and its content or function" ("The Whiteness of Privacy," 81).

75. "Ontological residue" is derived from Bill Brown's consideration of antiblack collectibles with particular attention to *Bamboozled* (Spike Lee, 2000). Brown examines the relationship between these collectibles and the historicity of slavery. In "Reification, Reanimation, and the American Uncanny" he writes, "Even as we point to a certain moment in a certain place when and where it is no longer possible for a person to be a slave (to be someone's property, to be . . . a thing), we nonetheless find, in the post-history of that moment, residues of precisely that possibility—in other words, an ongoing record of the ontological effects of slavery" (182).

76. Stephen Vincent Benét, "John Brown's Body" (1927) (as cited in Patton, "Mammy"). Also consider the character Dr. Martin Luther King Jr. in the *Boondocks* episode "Return of the King." King awakens from a thirty-year coma following an assassination attempt in Memphis on 4 April 1968. King as Rip Van Winkle discovers that in this "new world" his image sells computers and fast food. His solemn refrain is telling: "I really should have approvals over this kind of thing."

77. This reading of *Coonskin*'s Aunt Jemima is informed by Betye Saar's *The Liberation of Aunt Jemima* (1972) and *Workers and Warriors: The Return of Aunt Jemima*, Michael Rosenfeld Gallery, New York, 10 September–31 October 1998. A mixed-media assemblage, *The Liberation of Aunt Jemima* centrally features a ceramic collectible of a mammy set in a small display cabinet with a broom and a rifle. The front of the

ceramic mammy has a card that depicts another mammy holding a child, and the background of the cabinet is tiled by images of Aunt Jemima. Saar has stated that her motivation was to combat the devaluation of a history of black domestic labor as dishonorable work: "My intention was to transform a negative demeaning figure into a positive, empowered woman who stands confrontationally with one hand holding a broom and the other armed for battle. A warrior ready to combat servitude and racism" ("Unfinished Business," 3). Kobena Mercer considers Saar's practice of the racial grotesque with attention to how the cabinet base acts as a container of mammy signifiers and notably functions as a tomb: "When seen as a vitrine or a 'cabinet of curiosities,' *The Liberation of Aunt Jemima* acts as a coffin that metaphorically 'buries' the stereotype as a historical artefact. The dialogic juxtaposition of elements inside the box interrupts the semantic currency of the stereotype" ("Tropes of the Grotesque in Black Avant-Garde," 143). Also see Jones, "To/From Los Angeles with Betye Saar."

78. Robyn Wiegman discusses how the emergence of new yet familiar forms of anti-black iconography in mass media is evidence of the continued legacy of slavery. As she notes, "Here one turns to cinema, television, and video where circulation of representational images partake in a panoptic terrain by serving up bodies as narrative commodities, detached from the old economy of corporeal enslavement and situated instead in the panoply of signs, texts, and images through which the discourse of race functions now to affirm the referential illusion of an organic real" (*American Anatomies*, 41). Two men claiming to be descendants of Anne Harrington, the woman who played the role of Aunt Jemima from 1935 to 1950, filed a $2 billion lawsuit in August 2014 against Quaker Oats, the current owner of the Aunt Jemima brand. The lawsuit claimed that Harrington's heirs were due royalties for the continued use of her name, voice, and likeness with the brand products. In particular the plaintiffs sought inventor compensation per the advertising claim that Green and Harrington created the pancake mix "secret recipe." In February 2015 a judge dismissed the suit when the plaintiffs could not prove their relation to Harrington.

79. Baker, *Blues, Ideology, and Afro-American Literature*, 7, 8.

80. Woods, *Development Arrested*, 36.

81. Ellison, *Invisible Man*, 13.

82. Judy, "On the Question of Nigga Authenticity," 225.

83. The "blow me anymore in the wind" reference is multiple as it alludes to "Strange Fruit" and the civil rights movement by way of reference to Bob Dylan's "Blowin' in the Wind" from *The Freewheelin' Bob Dylan* (1963). The song circulated as one of the folk movement's anthems of allegiance to the movement. Greil Marcus writes, "More than its own art movement, its own social movement, or its own fact, the folk revival was part of something much bigger, more dangerous, and more important: the civil rights movement. That is where its moral energy came from—its sense of a world to rediscover, to bring back to life, and to win. The two movements were fraternal twins, for the civil rights movement was also a rediscovery, a revival: of the

Constitution" (*The Old Weird America*, 22). Also see Margolick, *Strange Fruit*; Eyerman and Berretta, "From the 30s to the 60s"; Shank, "'That Wild Mercury Sound.'"

84. Moten, *In the Break*, 13.

85. Wiegman, *American Anatomies*, 13.

86. Victor Burgin suggests that lynching functions as a moral imperative to protect white women from black male rapists that acts on the psychic level as a projection: "He [the white male racist] represses the fantasy in which he himself is a rapist; the emotional investment in the unconscious fantasy forces it back into consciousness but now in an acceptable disguise: the rapist is identified as Black, absolving the subject of the fantasy of any culpability in the imaginary crime" ("Paranoiac Space," 238).

87. Writing on the ensuing controversy surrounding a public school teacher reading Carolivia Herron's *Nappy Hair* (1997) to a class of third graders, Mikko Tuhkanen considers the "knee jerk" reaction of the children's parents in terms of "cultural reflex": "If the response is a kind of cultural reflex, as is suggested here, recognizing racist images and recoiling from them are precisely not without base but, rather, constitute a response according to a deeply—even *organically*—lodged cultural memory. Of course, one may even argue that, as a reflex, such a 'knee-jerk' reaction is also potentially life-saving." Tuhkanen, *The American Optic*, 31.

88. For example, President Barack Hussein Obama has been accused of being a Socialist, a Nazi, a Muslim terrorist, foreign-born, uncircumcised, a hater of American democracy, and a proponent of white slavery, among other things. The only thing more dubious than these claims is the belief that the motivation behind them has nothing to do with race and antiblack racism. For a thorough accounting of the many inventive and delirious conspiracy theories about President Obama, see Asawin Suebsaeng and Dave Gilson, "Chart: Almost Every Obama Conspiracy Theory Ever," *Mother Jones*, 2012, http://www.motherjones.com/politics/2012/10/chart-obama-conspiracy-theories. Also see Parks and Heard, "'Assassinate the Nigger Apes.'"

89. I particularly have in mind the work of contemporary artists that traffic in the racial grotesque, such as Robert Colescott, Kara Walker, Michael Ray Charles, Lyle Ashton Harris, Gary Simmons, Wangechi Mutu, Renée Cox, Hank Willis Thomas, Trenton Doyle Hancock, Elizabeth Axtman, Mark Steven Greenfield, William Villalongo, Sanford Biggers, Travis Somerville, and Dawolu Jabari Anderson. Greenfield explicitly evoked *Coonskin* in his work featured in the *Animalicious* exhibit at the Offramp Gallery (3 March–14 April 2013). Also consider Terrance Hughes's invocation of Bakshi's film and Ishmael Reed's *Flight to Canada* (1976) in his *Coonskin 2: Flight to Canada* exhibition at Graphite Gallery in Brooklyn (8–16 October 2011). See Gillespie, "Dirty Pretty Things."

90. I am referring here to what I consider a genealogy of blackness and the art of the racial grotesque in the late twentieth century that includes Ishmael Reed's *Mumbo Jumbo* (1972), Bakshi's *Coonskin*, George Wolfe's *The Colored Museum* (1986),

Darius James's *Negrophobia: An Urban Parable* (1993), and Spike Lee's *Bamboozled* (1999).

91. James, *That's Blaxploitation!*, 121.

TWO. Smiling Faces

1. Street's invocation of this title is a direct reference to Ferdinand Waldo Demara, the renowned and notorious impersonator portrayed by Tony Curtis in *The Great Impostor* (Richard Mulligan, 1961).

2. See Patricia Edmonds, "Super Duper Imposter Says He Aided in Surgeries," *Detroit Free Press*, 16 March 1985.

3. In September 1989 *Chameleon Street* premiered at the Venice Film Festival and was screened shortly afterward at the Toronto International Film Festival. The film did not premiere in the United States until January 1990, at the Sundance Film Festival. Most of the production information in this essay is culled from my conversations with Harris; Moon, *Reel Black Talk*; Rex Weiner, "One Way Street," *Variety*, 22 January 1996, 13.

4. Moon, *Reel Black Talk*, 150–51.

5. Later posing as a Red Sox official, Street attempted to get a World Series ring from the team's 1975 run.

6. Street was released from prison not long before *Chameleon Street* was screened at the Venice and Toronto film festivals in late 1989. Harris and Street appeared together on an episode of *The Geraldo Rivera Show* devoted to con men. Not long after the broadcast, Street began serving his sixth stint in prison for check forgery.

7. Ginsberg, "Introduction," 2. Also see Wald, *Crossing the Line*.

8. Smith, "Reading the Intersection of Race and Gender in Narratives of Passing," 45. Smith examines the passing narrative in literature (e.g., James Weldon Johnson's *Autobiography of an Ex-Coloured Man* [1912], Nella Larsen's *Passing* [1929], Jessie Fauset's *Plum Bun* [1928]) and film (John Stahl's [1934] and Douglas Sirk's [1959] adaptations of Fannie Hurst's *Imitation of Life* [1933] and Julie Dash's *Illusions* [1982]). Smith's discussion of "contemporary revisions of the passing plot" includes *True Identity* (Charles Lane, 1991), which offers an additional complication to the revision impulse due to the lead actor, Lenny Henry. Henry's Miles Pope must pass as the Italian hit man sent to murder him. While passing as his own assassin, Pope is cast as James Earl Jones's understudy in a production of *Othello*. Significantly the film's fatal weakness is a result of the Black British Henry's performance as an African American. As a result the film's extradiegetic issue of cross-cultural casting undercuts the success of the diegetic conceit.

9. Smith, *Enacting Others*, 13.

10. Robinson, "Forms of Appearance of Value," 250.

11. Berlant, "She's Having an Episode." Thanks to Lauren Berlant for our conversation about *Chameleon Street* and for sharing this piece with me.

12. Thompson, "'Is Race a Trope?,'" 132.

13. Harris, "'That Nigger's Crazy,'" 27. My focus on passing through the lens of performativity draws inspiration from Muñoz's emphasis on racial performativity as "a doing." He writes, "To look at race as a performative enterprise, one that can best be accessed by its effects, may lead us out of political and conceptual impasses that have dogged racial discourse. A critical project attuned to knowing the performativity of race is indeed better suited to decipher what work race does in the world" ("Feeling Brown, Feeling Down," 679).

14. The source material of *Chameleon Street* was gathered from interviews of Douglas Street conducted by Harris and several long, handwritten letters Street wrote to Harris between 1985 and 1988. Harris has stated that much of the film's dialogue is directly from Street. As a way of acknowledging the derivation from the "true story" and as a sign of his creative license, he created the pseudonym "Erik Dupin." Wendell B. Harris Jr., email interview, 4 December 2011.

15. The presence of the primary colors, or painter's primaries, expresses an affinity for Jean-Luc Godard, modernist art, and art cinema. For a fuller explanation of the cinematic legacy of the painter's primaries, see Branigan, "The Articulation of Color in a Filmic System"; Price, "Color, the Formless, and Cinematic Eros." To further pursue Godard's use of color, its significance for *Chameleon Street*, and questions of abstraction, consider Robert Stam's comments on this point: "Godard insisted on the two-dimensionality of the screen surface through the compositional use of color, arranging colors in blocks or in polar opposites. Godard's preference for simply defined primary colors, meanwhile, reminded the spectator of the differences between natural and screen color. Whereas in nature color nuances are endless and inexhaustible, Godard closes off his inexhaustibility by the rigorous selection. He manipulates advancing and receding colors, juxtaposing highly saturated reds and greens with blues, so that the contrasting colors rise to the screen surface as abstract patterns" (*Reflexivity in Film and Literature*, 256).

16. Mills, "Non-Cartesian Sums," 9.

17. Johnson, "A Phenomenology of the Black Body," 603.

18. Griffiths, "Copy Wright," 321–22.

19. The film adaptation portrays Street's blackmail note as an attempt to ultimately get a tryout with the Tigers. There is no reference to the death threat.

20. While the film comically details Street's one surgery, a hysterectomy, the real Street performed several successful hysterectomies before being exposed as an impersonator.

21. Gilroy, *Black Atlantic*, 133.

22. Michel de Certeau, "Railway Navigation and Incarceration," in *The Practice of Everyday Life*, 113.

23. Moten, *In the Break*, 68.

24. My sense of strategic (in)visibility is directly informed by Homi K. Bhabha's "Interrogating Identity: Frantz Fanon and the Postcolonial Prerogative," in *The Location of Culture*, 40–65. Also I have in mind a scene from the *Autobiography of Malcolm X* (1964). Malcolm and his cohorts have just robbed a home in Roxbury and are now

being tailed by a police car. With the stolen goods in the car trunk, Malcolm recognizes that a car load of blacks in an all-white neighborhood late at night is grounds for a great deal of suspicion and acts quickly: "But I knew that the white man is rare who will ever consider that a Negro can outsmart him. Before their lights began flashing, I told Rudy to stop. I did what I'd done once before—got out and flagged them, walking toward them. When they stopped I was at their car. I asked them, bumbling my words like a confused Negro, if they could tell me how to get to a Roxbury address. They told me, and we, and they, went on about our respective businesses" (167).

25. Ralph Ellison, "Change the Joke and Slip the Yoke," in *Shadow and Act*, 55.

26. In a speech given to the Justice Department staff as part of Black History Month (18 February 2009), Attorney General Eric Holder made observations of America that I have appended to Ellison's masking jokers' comment: "Though this nation has proudly thought of itself as an ethnic melting pot, in things racial we have always been and continue to be, in too many ways, essentially a nation of cowards."

27. Mullen, "Optic White," 72.

28. Homi K. Bhabha, "Of Mimicry and Man," in *The Location of Culture*, 88.

29. Guerrero, "The Black Man on Our Screens and the Empty Space in Representation," 187.

30. Roger Rouse notes that *Chameleon Street* "addresses the growing sense that signs of professional and social savoir-faire that now mark the boundaries between the bottom of the class structure and its upper reaches are so readily simulated that they cannot act as effective criteria of distinction" ("Thinking through Transnationalism," 391).

31. Huh, "Whispers of Norbury," 570. The noir inflection of the voice-over narration greatly enables the film's autobiographical conceit. This is to say that *Chameleon Street*'s voice-over bears a resemblance to the general division of body and voice that has characterized the use of voice-over narration in film noir. The disconnection between the voice and the body of the noir protagonist engages as a battle for authority that propels and structures the narrative toward resolution and unification (see Hollinger, "Film Noir, Voice Over, and the Femme Fatale"). The disembodiment crisis of the noir protagonist in general explores the question of a complete persona as a central conceit of noir. The black voice(-over) will be a key feature of the analysis in chapter 3.

32. Smith, *How Race Is Made*, 106–14.

33. Guerrero, "The Black Man on Our Screens and the Empty Space in Representation," 183.

34. This sequence is one of the many Walter Mitty moments of film blackness, scenes involving black characters that lack obvious cues of interiority and instead portray a sharp wit and/or fantastical vengeance. They include Dorothy cracking a bottle over the head of her social worker in *Bush Mama* (Haile Gerima, 1976), Malcolm Little smearing cake in the faces of condescending white patrons while working on the train in *Malcolm X* (Spike Lee, 1992), and Pierre Delacroix's accelerated slapping

of Thomas Dunwitty in *Bamboozled* (Spike Lee, 2000). Also see *Top of the Heap* (Christopher St. John, 1972) and *Hollywood Shuffle* (Robert Townsend, 1986).

35. As Susan Gubar writes, "[Racechange] is meant to suggest the traversing of race boundaries, racial imitation or impersonation, cross-racial mimicry or mutability, white posing as black passing as white, pan-racial mutuality" (*Racechanges*, 5).

36. Tate, "Nigs R Us," 2.

37. See Benamou, "The Artifice of Realism and the Lure of the 'Real' in Orson Welles's *F for Fake* and Other T(r)eas(u)er(e)s."

38. Miller, *Slaves to Fashion*, 221.

39. Gates, "The Passing of Anatole Broyard," 200.

40. Caughie, "Passing as Modernism," 387.

41. My thinking about chameleonism as intertextuality is derived from Ella Shohat and Robert Stam's work on Woody Allen's *Zelig* (1983). They write, "In *Zelig*, chameleonism comes to make a metaphor of intertextuality itself, as the film, like its protagonist, assumes the coloration of its interlocutory texts" ("*Zelig* and Contemporary Theory," 199).

42. See Shohat and Stam, *Unthinking Eurocentrism*, 251; Vann, "The Colonial Casbah on the Silver Screen."

43. Harris said, "The evening of the fourth day when the beast mask was taken off my face by the make-up man, it unfortunately also started taking off layers of skin. The adhesive used to make the mask adhere to my skin was as damaging to the face as what they put on to take it off. I went home that night and looked in the mirror and thought my face looked like the final *Portrait of Dorian Grey* [*sic*]" (Moon, *Reel Black Talk*, 157).

44. Martin Rich, "Toronto Film Fest Reviews: *Chameleon Street*," *Variety*, 27 September 1989, 40; Kennedy, "Gondola Wind," 74.

45. See Levy, *Cinema of Outsiders*.

46. Moon, *Reel Black Talk*, 151. As Steven Soderbergh later revealed, the awarding of the Grand Prize to *Chameleon Street* required some behind-the-scenes negotiations: "Sunday, 31 March 1996. Cognac. Jury deliberations. We gave the prize to Stacy Title's *The Last Supper*, basically because it was liked by everyone and hated by no one. That's usually the way these things work, although when I was on the Jury at Sundance in 1990 I refused to leave the room unless we gave the Grand Prize to *Chameleon Street*. Before you leap to the conclusion that this was a heroic act on my part, you should be aware that this situation arose because the Festival had made the mistake of selecting an even number of Jurors without designating someone as Jury President (the President's vote is weighted in case of a deadlock)" (Soderbergh and Lester, *Getting Away with It*, 9).

47. Pierson, *Spikes, Mikes, Slackers, and Dykes*, 208. Harris would later characterize Pierson's account as "mean-spirited, mendacious, brazenly erroneous, slanted, and resplendently racist at its core" (in Weiner, "One Way Street," *Variety*, 22 January 1996, 13).

48. Peter Travers, "Independents Day," *Rolling Stone*, 22 March 1990, 35.

49. Eleanor Ringel, "'Chameleon Street': Comedy with Intriguing Tint," *Atlanta Journal-Constitution*, 27 July 1990. I first saw *Chameleon Street* in Atlanta during this National Black Arts Festival in 1990. It screened as part of the "Independent Strut" series, which included Charles Burnett's *To Sleep with Anger* (1990), the premiere of Julie Dash's *Daughters of the Dust*, and Robert Gardner's *King James Version* (1988). My memory of the series is the buzz surrounding the film program that suggested that the showcase was literally the avant-garde, or advanced guard, of an upcoming crop of black films. Of course that upcoming crop would be the "black film explosion" of 1991, the beginning of a new black cinema. Digital Library of Georgia, Auburn Avenue Research Library, Historica African American Education Collections: 1990 National Black Arts Festival, http://dlg.galileo.usg.edu/cgi/aaed?item=aarl90.005-002-045;format=pdf.

50. Vincent Canby, "The Multiple Masks of a Compulsive Imposter," *New York Times* 24 April 1991.

51. Georgia Brown, "The Word Is Lout," *Village Voice*, 30 April 1991, 54. Daryl Chin's comparative analysis of the reception history of *Chameleon Street* and *Metropolitan* in the wake of their showings at Sundance is worth noting. Chin's language differs from mine, but we ultimately share the same motivation to speak on the film: "My claim is that there should be more people who are willing to grant *Chameleon Street* the same attention as *Metropolitan*. An important note should be made of the fact that, though *Chameleon Street* is an African-American film, in that it was made by an African-American and the main characters are African-American, it is not a 'typical' black film. It is not a film about a black family, or the struggles of black ghetto life, or a comedy about black teenagers. Instead, it is a decidedly quirky character study of a black con-man's varied attempts at social betterment, set within a notably middle-class background" ("Multiculturalism and Its Masks," 7).

52. The film's two-week run garnered $7,772.00 in the first week and $7,791.50 in the second. Publicists at Northern Arts commented that it placed in the "top of the low third." Representatives at Film Forum said it did "very poorly."

53. Abiola Sinclair, "'Chameleon Street': A Review," *New York Amsterdam News*, 25 May 1991.

54. David Sterritt, "Freeze Frames: A Weekly Update of Film Releases—*Chameleon Street*," *Christian Science Monitor*, 7 May 1991; Hal Hinson, "*Chameleon Street*," *Washington Post*, 31 May 1991.

55. Hinson, "*Chameleon Street*."

56. Kenneth Turan, "Harris' 'Chameleon Street' an Interesting Try," *Los Angeles Times*, 19 July 1991; Terry Clifford, "Movie about a Role-Player Seems Unsure of Its Own," *Chicago Tribune*, 16 August 1991.

57. Karen Grigsby, "'They've Gotta Have Us': Hollywood's Black Directors," *New York Times Magazine*, 14 July 1991.

58. Tony Moor, "'They've Gotta Have Us,'" *New York Times*, 11 August 1991.

59. Steve Weinstein, "Maybe He Should Have Impersonated a White Studio Boss," *Los Angeles Times*, 14 July 1991.

60. Stuart Klawans, "Films: *Requiem for Dominic/Chameleon Street*," *Nation*, 27 May 1991, 715.

61. Mazor said that Gene Siskel and Roger Ebert expressed high praise for *Chameleon Street* "off the record," but they refused to review the film on their nationally syndicated television program. According to Mazor, while Siskel and Ebert were great admirers of *Chameleon Street* and independent film in general, their long-standing policy at the time was to remain fairly quiet about independent film out of concern about harming the growth of this cinema. Mazor concluded that Siskel and Ebert would have considered reviewing *Chameleon Street* only if it looked to be "the next *sex, lies, and videotape*." David Mazor, telephone interview, March 1996.

62. White, "Underground Man," 4, 6. The essay was the only critical treatment of *Chameleon Street* since Clyde Taylor's essay in *Black Film Review*.

63. Armond White, "Condition Critical," *Village Voice*, 4 June 1991. White commented that the problem with the film began with the "familiar cultural unease" that he claimed resulted in its rejection by MoMA and Lincoln Center in 1989. However, when considering whether films with a complex enactment of blackness were welcome, it should be noted that the New York Film Festival that year did feature Isaac Julien's *Looking for Langston* and Charles Burnett's *To Sleep with Anger*.

64. A longer version of this segment entitled "*Chameleon Street*: The Black Film They Could Not Sell" aired on ABC's *20/20* a few months earlier than the *Edge* broadcast. My discussion deals with the shorter *Edge* version because it has a more singular focus on *Chameleon Street*.

65. "Episode 102," *Edge*, PBS, WNET, New York City, 6 November 1991. In the segment Mitchell disparagingly notes that Will Smith was the planned lead of the Warner Bros. remake. Arsenio Hall and Wesley Snipes were later associated with the project, and Warner Bros. still listed the remake as being in active development in the late 1990s.

66. Guerrero, *Framing Blackness*, 174.

67. White, "Apostasy," 281, 282. Also in 1992 *Chameleon Street* was an Independent Spirit Award nominee for Best First Feature, along with Todd Haynes's *Poison*, Michael Tolkin's *The Rapture*, Richard Linklater's *Slackers*, and Matty Rich's *Straight out of Brooklyn* (the eventual winner).

68. Kobena Mercer, "Black Art and the Burden of Representation," in *Welcome to the Jungle*, 239.

69. This is not to completely dismiss the connections between *Chameleon Street* and the film adaptation (Fred Schepisi, 1993) of John Guare's *Six Degrees of Separation* (1990) and the films' protagonists, Douglas Street and David Hampton, the con man who impersonated Sidney Poitier's son in the 1980s and conned his way through the Upper East Side in 1983. In his first major film role Will Smith starred as David Hampton. Warner Bros. claimed early on after purchasing *Chameleon Street*'s indefinite remake rights that they hoped the remake would be a Will Smith vehicle. Thus MGM and Warner Bros. both courted Smith with impersonation projects. The relationship between the films grows muddy with closer inquiry, because *Six*

Degrees of Separation reveals a distinctly different focalization of race that has less depth than *Chameleon Street*. This is most evident with regard to issues of empathy, desire, whiteness, and privilege. Interestingly some have speculated via YouTube videos about how Smith has played characters who solve a Rubik's cube as something lifted from the scene in *Chameleon Street* where Douglas Street solves a Rubik's cube during his residency interview at Wayne State Medical School. For more on the connection between *Chameleon Street* and *Six Degrees of Separation*, see Chin, "Multiculturalism and Its Masks."

70. Financially speaking, keep in mind that until the close of 1990 the top grossing black film director cumulatively was Sidney Poitier: *Buck and the Preacher* (1972, $3.1 million), *Uptown Saturday Night* (1974, $7.4 million), *A Piece of the Action* (1977, $6.7 million), *Stir Crazy* (1980, $58.4 million), *Hanky Panky* (1982, $5.12 million), *Ghost Dad* (1990, $11.3 million). The total gross of Poitier's film rentals generated at theaters in the United States and Canada far exceeded the closest second, Michael Schultz's films. All figures were obtained from Lawrence Cohn, "Blacks Take the Helm," *Variety*, 18 March 1991.

71. Cohn, "Blacks Take the Helm." Compare to "Youthful Black Helmers Fear a Hollywood Backlash," *Variety*, 21 February 1990, published following Sundance 1990.

72. De Certeau, "History," 201.

73. See Hagopian, "Black Cinema Studies," which reviews Thomas Cripps's *Making Movies Black: The Hollywood Message Movie from World War II to the Civil Rights Era*, Manthia Diawara's edited *Black American Cinema* anthology, Ed Guerrero's *Framing Blackness*, William Jones's *Black Cinema Treasures: Lost and Found*, Mark Reid's *Redefining Black Film*, and James Snead's *White Screens, Black Images: Hollywood from the Dark Side*. This body of work was released in 1993. For another review of black cinema studies and the industrial state of affairs in the wake of the 1991 explosion and the 1993 scholarly wave, see Guerrero, "A Circus of Dreams and Lies."

74. Cripps, *Black Film as Genre*, 12.

75. Lott, "A No-Theory Theory of Contemporary Black Cinema," 223.

76. Lott, "A No-Theory Theory of Contemporary Black Cinema," 228.

77. Lott, "A No-Theory Theory of Contemporary Black Cinema," 232.

78. Ralph Ellison, "The Art of Fiction: An Interview," in *Shadow and Act*, 181.

79. Benston, *Performing Blackness*, 161.

80. Bell, *Ashes Taken for Fire*, 168–69.

81. Jackson, "Ralph Ellison, Sharpies, Rinehart, and Politics in *Invisible Man*," 84.

82. Bell, *Ashes Taken for Fire*, 168–69.

83. The fable's use in *Chameleon Street* functions as a citation of a scene from *Mr. Arkadin/Confidential Report* (Orson Welles, 1955) in which Mr. Arkadin (Welles) tells the parable to guests gathered at his Spanish castle. Finished with the recitation, he raises his glass and toasts, "Let's drink to character." Considering Welles's conflicted comments on morality and judgment, Deleuze puts him in conversation with Nietzsche: "Nietzsche said: behind the truthful man, who judges life, there is the sick man, sick with life itself. And Welles adds: behind the frog, the epitome of

the truthful animal, there is the scorpion, the animal sick with itself. The first is an idiot and the second is a bastard" (*Cinema*, 141). Moreover the tale serendipitously addresses Richard Wright's refabulation of the Nietzschean "frog perspective" as emblematic of the psychology of the oppressed. In *White Man Listen* he writes, "This is a phrase that I've borrowed from Nietzsche to describe someone looking from below upward, a sense of someone who feels himself lower than others. The concept of distance involved here is not physical; it is psychological. It involves a situation in which for moral or social reasons, a person or a group feels that there is another person or group above it. Yet physically they all live on the same general, material plane. A certain degree of hate combined with love (ambivalence) is always involved in this looking from below upward and the object against which the subject is measuring himself undergoes constant change. He loves the object because he would like to resemble it; he hates the object because his chances of resembling it are remote, slight" (6). Wright's visualization of the black existential condition in the terms of the frog perspective links the philosophical with the experiential to identify a perspectival nexus, a "dreadful objectivity" (Gilroy, "Cruciality and the Frog's Perspective," 171).

84. Edmonds, "Super Duper Imposter Says He Aided in Surgeries."

85. In the years that followed its theatrical run, *Chameleon Street* was sporadically shown at Black History Month festivals around the country before being picked up for a season run on the Independent Film Channel and later for a season on the African Heritage Movie Network. The expression "not another *Chameleon Street*" circulated in the trade press coverage of Sundance following the 1990 festival. Harris wrote a screenplay entitled *Negropolis* with the idea of its becoming a Spike Lee project and was in talks with Milos Forman on a proposed Joe Louis biopic or project. Neither came to fruition. He has appeared in two films since his own *Chameleon Street*, as a Detroit detective in *Out of Sight* (Steven Soderbergh, 1998) and a philosophy professor in *Road Trip* (Todd Phillips, 2000). Through his Prismatic Productions, Harris has been working to complete a UFO-themed drama, *Arbiter Roswell*. In 2007 he was an honorable mention on the British Film Institute's list of "100 Black Screen Icons." Long out of print, the film was released on DVD in 2007. In 2009 *Chameleon Street* and Harris were invited back to Sundance as part of the twenty-fifth anniversary of the festival and the film's inclusion in the Sundance Collection, a film preservation project established with the UCLA Film and Television Archive. Harris and the film have consistently appeared at festivals and screening events across the country over the years. Ironically the film has covertly circulated for some time through hip-hop. A sampling of dialogue from the film by producer J. Rawls acts as the intro to "Brown Skin Lady" on *Mos Def and Talib Kweli Are Black Star* (1998): "I'm a victim of four hundred years of conditioning. The Man has programmed my conditioning. Even my conditioning has been conditioned." Significantly *Chameleon Street* was the closing film for the Indie 80s film series at the Brooklyn Academy of Music (27 August 2015). As for William Douglas Street, he continued a life of petty crime for decades, until the summer of 2015, when he

again achieved national notoriety following his arrest and charges in federal court of mail fraud and aggravated identity theft. Street had taken the identity of a Defense Department contractor who was a graduate of West Point by procuring a diploma, transcripts, and a duplicate class ring. Street even appeared at speaking events as this person. He faced twenty years in prison if convicted. As a result of a plea deal his sentence was twenty-eight to thirty-four months. See Robert Snell, "Game May Be Up for 'The Great Imposter,'" *Detroit News*, 5 June 2015, http://www.detroitnews .com/story/news/local/wayne-county/2015/06/04/epic-con-artist-chameleon -strikes-feds-say/28515197/.

THREE. Voices Inside

1. Snead, *White Screens/Black Images*, 123.
2. For elaboration on "hidden polemics," see Bakhtin, "Discourse Typology in Prose," 190.
3. Naremore, *More Than Light*, 11.
4. Naremore, *More Than Light*, 224.
5. See Pratt, *Imperial Eyes*, 7.
6. In *Noir Anxiety*, Kelly Oliver and Benigno Trigo discuss this anxious core of noir that dictates the generic mode's ethical and epistemological rationale: "It is not simply that film noir absolves whites of their moral ambiguity by making them black. Rather, the moral ambiguity of the narrative noir covers over a source of even greater ambiguity that is displaced onto the style of noir: racial ambiguity. Racial ambiguity, not the fear of blackness, is the real anxiety of noir. The anxiety over racial ambiguity manifest in noir cannot be reduced to a simple association between blackness and evil. Rather, the 'evil' or threat of these films is a complicated fear of racial ambiguity, the fear of not being able to tell the difference between black-ness and whiteness. If moral ambiguity causes anxiety, racial ambiguity may be its source" (5).
7. Elsaesser, *Weimar Cinema and After*, 420.
8. Diawara, "*Noir* by Noirs," 263, 262.
9. Lott, "The Whiteness of Film Noir," 551.
10. Lott writes, "Raced metaphors in popular life are as indispensable, and rendered as invisible, as the colored bodies who give rise to and move in the shadows of those usages" ("The Whiteness of Film Noir," 542).
11. Diawara, "*Noir* by Noirs," 263.
12. Eburne, "The Transatlantic Mysteries of Paris," 812.
13. Marc Vernet identifies noir as a critical love object: "Film noir thus finds itself to be literally (but also in all senses of the term) a critical object: invented by French crit-icism, it allows one to love the United States while criticizing it, or more exactly to criticize it in order to be able to love it, in a relation that is not without connection with, on the one hand, the conflicts inherent in the Oedipal relation and, on the

other (by the split that such an attitude implies), a fetishistic economy" ("Film Noir on the Edge of Doom," 6).

14. Margolies and Fabre, *The Several Lives of Chester Himes*, 103.

15. Robin Kelley comments, "Surrealism may have originated in the West, but it is rooted in a conspiracy against Western civilization." He continues, "Juxtaposing surrealism and black conceptions of liberation is no mere academic exercise; it is an injunction, a proposition, perhaps even a declaration of war. . . . Surrealism recognizes that any revolution must begin with thought, with how we imagine a New World, with how we reconstruct our social and individual relationships, with unleashing our desire and building a new future on the basis of love and creativity rather than rationality (which is like *rationalization*, the same word they use for improving capitalist production and limiting people's needs)" ("Keepin' It [Sur]real," in *Freedom Dreams*, 159, 192, 193).

16. McCann, *Gumshoe America*, 4–5.

17. See Eburne, *Surrealism and the Art of Crime.*

18. This attractiveness is a reference to Robyn Wiegman's identification of America as hegemonic seduction: "The strength and cultural attractiveness of the belief in a transcendent America is not simply that it veils the material relations at work in contemporary culture, allowing us the easy assumption that democracy has finally been achieved, but that through this posture the discourses of dissent, particularly those of black power and feminism, can be rendered obsolete, no longer pertinent to the needs of our society" (*American Anatomies*, 209n17).

19. Margolies, *Which Way Did He Go?*, 69, 70. Ever disingenuous about his contribution to the hard-boiled tradition, Himes claimed in an interview, "The detective story originally in the plain narrative form—straightforward violence—is an American product. So I haven't created anything whatsoever; I just made the faces black" (in Williams, "My Man Himes," 49).

20. As Anne Friedburg states, "Nostalgia can hide the discontinuities between the present and the past; it falsifies, turning the past into a safe, familiar place" (*Window Shopping*, 188).

21. James Brown, "Down and Out in New York City," on *Black Caesar*, Polydor, 1973.

22. This is a point made by Henry Louis Gates Jr. to distinguish and retrieve the black expressive tradition of signifyin(g) from the misequivalence of pastiche. As he cleverly states, "Pastiche only renders explicit that which any literary history implies: that tradition is the process of formal revision. Pastiche is literary history naming itself, pronouncing its surface content to be the displaced content of intertextual relations themselves, the announcement of ostensibly concealed revision. Pastiche is an act of literary 'Naming'; parody is an act of 'Calling out of one's name'" (*The Signifying Monkey*, 124).

23. Porter, *The Pursuit of Crime*, 121. Slavoj Žižek contends that the detective of the hard-boiled tradition functions as a "subject supposed to know." The detective's task of solving the crime is tied to the desire for the return to normality of the social

order through his allegorical search for a scapegoat to delimit the scope of the crisis precipitated by the act of the crime itself. In the detective's search for truth and the assigning of guilt "lies the fundamental untruth, the existential falsity of the detective's 'solution': the detective plays upon the difference between the factual truth (the accuracy of facts) and the 'inner' truth concerning our desire. . . . In regard to the libidinal economy, the detective's 'solution' is therefore nothing but a kind of realized hallucination. . . . He guarantees precisely that we will be discharged of any guilt, that the guilt for the realization of our desire will be 'externalized' in the scapegoat and that, consequently, we will be able to desire without paying the price for it" (*Looking Awry*, 59).

24. Breu, *Hard-Boiled Masculinities*, 143–44.

25. Before *Deep Cover*, Bill Duke had directed a film adaptation of Himes's *For the Love of Immabelle: A Rage in Harlem* (1991). The other Himes Harlem adaptations are *Cotton Comes to Harlem* (Ossie Davis, 1970), *Come Back, Charleston Blue* (Mark Warren, 1972), and "Tang" from *Cosmic Slop* (Kevin Rodney Sullivan, 1994). My decision to discuss a non-Himes film through a Himes lens rather than any of these works results from their collective lack of a substantial sense of the black absurd. They all to a great extent represent the absurd as more carnivalesque slapstick than brutal allegory of vicious irrationality.

26. Patrick Pacheco, "Fighting the 'John Singleton Thing,'" *Los Angeles Times*, 12 April 1991. The screenplay was cowritten with Michael Tolkin. Tolkin's other screenwriting and direction during the 1990s includes *The Rapture* (Michael Tolkin, 1991), *The Player* (Robert Altman, 1992), and *The New Age* (Michael Tolkin, 1994). Collectively this body of work represents an intriguing deviation from the conventional rhetoric surrounding genre and entertainment.

27. Pacheco, "Fighting the 'John Singleton Thing.'" The article also mentions that the lead role was first offered to Eddie Murphy and then Denzel Washington. Although each declined, it is important to note that industry attitudes at this time presumed that Murphy and Washington were the only black actors capable of carrying the film.

28. Harris, "Black Crossover Cinema," 259.

29. Harris, "Black Crossover Cinema," 260.

30. The father is played by Glynn Turman, who starred as Leroy "Preach" Jackson in Michael Schultz's *Cooley High* (1975) and thus offers an intertextual marker of the distance between distinct iterations of black youth and coming-of-age stories, a distance between blaxploitation optimism and new black cinema horror.

31. Johnson, "A Phenomenology of the Black Body," 603.

32. Johnson, "A Phenomenology of the Black Body," 608–10.

33. Guerrero, *Framing Blackness*, 208.

34. Two other instances of hypothetical "nigger naming" inform my reading of *Deep Cover*. On 28 August 1945 Branch Rickey interviewed Jackie Robinson. Taking on the persona of a peckerwood ballplayer, Rickey employed hypothetical "nigger naming" to determine whether Robinson had the right character to integrate Major

League Baseball; that is, Robinson needed to demonstrate that he would not engage with antiblack speech or respond with anger. On 13 December 1975 Richard Pryor appeared on *Saturday Night Live*; in one skit Pryor is Mr. Wilson, a job applicant, meeting with Chevy Chase, the interviewer. What begins as a perfunctory word-association test (*dog, tree, fast, rain*) escalates to *negro*. The formality of the interview quickly drops as each man grows louder and Pryor's face shows annoyance, then anger, and eventually rage. The exchange of *tar baby/ofay, colored/redneck, jungle bunny/peckerwood, burrhead/cracker, spearchucker/white trash, jungle bunny/honky, spade/honky-honky* builds to a hysterically sharp point: the interviewer yells "Nig-ger," to which the now spastic Pryor, his face flinching uncontrollably, exclaims, "Dead Honky!"

35. Tasker, *Spectacular Bodies*, 36.

36. Manthia Diawara identifies black rage as a core element of his "noir by noirs" concept: "By black rage, I mean a set of violent and uncontrollable relations in black communities induced by a sense of frustration, confinement and white racism" (*"Noir* by *Noirs,"* 266). Also see Grier and Cobbs, *Black Rage*.

37. Jacquie Jones reads Hull/Stevens in terms of these contradictory purposes: "For an African American to embrace public law and to further pledge to uphold the law means sacrificing on some level a commitment to Black nationalist loyalty" ("Under Cover of Blackness," 31). Also see Sexton, "The Ruse of Engagement."

38. Fanon, *Black Skin, White Masks*, 134. Also see Berrettini, "Transgression, Racialized Policing, and the Limits of Identity," 151.

39. Ralph Ellison, "Twentieth-Century Fiction and the Black Mask of Humanity," in *Shadow and Act*, 28. See previous discussion of stereotypicality and social instrumentality in chapter 1 on *Coonskin*.

40. Kozloff, *Invisible Storytellers*, 44.

41. Hollinger, "Film Noir, Voice Over, and the Femme Fatale," 245.

42. Oliver and Trigo, *Noir Anxiety*, 169.

43. Telotte, *Voices in the Dark*, 15.

44. Lubiano, "Don't Talk with Your Eyes Closed," 192–93.

45. Lewis Gordon argues that anonymity acts as a relativizing gesture of antiblackness: "The black is marked by the dehumanizing bridge between individual and structure posed by anti-black racism; the black is, in the end, 'anonymous,' which enables 'the black' to collapse into 'blacks.' Whereas 'blacks' is not a proper name, anti-black racism makes it function as such, as a name of familiarity that closes off the need to further knowledge. Each black is, thus, ironically nameless by virtue of being named 'black'" ("A Questioning Body of Laughter and Tears," 12).

46. The distinction between a black film with and without voice-over echoes Henry Louis Gates Jr.'s observations about voice in the context of literature. In detailing this distinction between Wright's *Native Son* and Ellison's *The Invisible Man*, Gates suggests that Bigger Thomas's lack of voice marks him as reactive and lacking agency in a way quite different from the nameless voice of *The Invisible Man* that informs my concerns for the voice of *Deep Cover*. Gates writes, "Ellison Signifies upon Wright's

distinctive version of naturalism with a complex rendering of modernism; Wright's re-acting protagonist, voiceless to the last, Ellison Signifies upon with a nameless protagonist. Ellison's protagonist is nothing but voice, since it is he who shapes, edits, and narrates his own tale, thereby combining action with the representation of action and defining reality by its representation" (*The Signifying Monkey*, 106). It is the degree to which voice-over and its measure as the grain of authenticity is pursued in such distinct (and consistent) ways as to be a fundamental characteristic of the hood strain of new black cinema in the 1990s.

47. Gates, *The Signifying Monkey*, 131.

48. Clarence Williams III offers an interesting intertextual tremor as Taft, the father figure and savior, in light of his role as Father to the Kid (Prince) in *Purple Rain* (Albert Magnoli, 1984). And there is Williams's Linc ("Solid!") Hayes from *The Mod Squad* (1968–73) television show. Born and raised in Watts, Linc is arrested during the riots and eventually becomes a countercultural and multicultural agent of the law. The squad consisted of three troubled kids who had fallen from or dropped out of straight society into the counterculture; they infiltrated counter-cultural communities as undercover operatives capable of channeling their youthful rebellion predisposition into the productive task of crime fighting. They are the use-oriented cream of a spoiled crop. Prescribing a use-value for the abject resonates with Stevens/Hull. See Bodroghkozy, *Groove Tube*.

49. Wahneema Lubiano writes that *Deep Cover* functions as "the nexus of a conven-tional master narrative of identity, family, and the making of a good patriarch, and a *black nationalist* narrative of identity, family, and the making of a good *black* patri-arch, set within a realistic urban terrain" ("Don't Talk with Your Eyes Closed," 187). Her substantial work on *Deep Cover* deliberates on black nationalism as "a sign, an analytic, that describes a range of historically manifested ideas about black Amer-ican possibilities" that operates as a form of common sense, "ideology lived and articulated in everyday understandings of the world and one's place in it" ("Black Nationalism and Black Common Sense," 232). Thus black nationalist common sense is "a name for a range of cultural and material activities and behaviors from vague feelings of black racial solidarity in the face of white supremacist worldview and white dominance, to various cultural and behavioral manifestations of that soli-darity, ... to programs designed to intervene materially along black racial lines in order to achieve some economic and political advances" ("Don't Talk with Your Eyes Closed," 188). Taft does best epitomize this common sense in concert with his providential proclamations. But while I agree with Lubiano about the consequential way that black nationalist common sense contributes to the ideological mapping of the film narrative, it is not the sole mitigating pitch of the film, as the noir idea, the social problem film, and the interracial male coupling bear out an equally significant inflection in the film. In particular, as I will discuss later, the film disputes patriarchal and heteronormative recuperation. For more on black nationalist common sense, see Keeling, *The Witch's Flight*, 101.

50. In "No Bad Nigger," K. Anthony Appiah's discussion of the syndrome of the black

saint or angel character in American film parallels this chapter's consideration of the black archangel. Appiah recognizes how the black becomes the ultimate Faulknerian witness or participant in the roles of Sidney Poitier: "Is there, in fact, somewhere in the Saint's background a theodicy that draws on the Christian notion that suffering is ennobling? So that the black person who represents undeserved suffering in the American imagination can also, therefore, represent moral nobility? Does the Saint exist to address the guilt of white audiences, afraid that black people are angry at them, wanting to be forgiven, seeking a black person who is not only admirable and lovable, but who loves white people back? Or is it simply that Hollywood has decided, after decades of lobbying by the NAACP's Hollywood chapter that, outside crime movies, blacks had better project good images, characters who can win the NAACP's 'image awards'?"(83).

51. My use of the expression "interracial male coupling" comes from a Kobena Mercer lecture in his Examining Masculinities seminar at NYU. I am as well indebted to his discussion of the pietà scenes from *The Defiant Ones* and *Lethal Weapon 2* during this lecture. My analysis later in this chapter builds on Mercer's reading.

52. Guerrero, "Black Image in Protective Custody," 240.

53. See Bogle, *Toms, Coons, Mulattoes, Mammies, and Bucks*, 140. Also see Wiegman's critique of Leslie Fiedler's *Love and Death in the American Novel* in *American Anatomies*, 149–78.

54. Rogin, *Blackface, White Noise*, 221.

55. Krutnik, *In a Lonely Street*, 209. This point is clear in *One False Move* (Carl Franklin, 1992) and *Devil in a Blue Dress* (Carl Franklin, 1995) by the way each film disputes noir modality with the redirected function of the tragic mulatto trope of the melodrama (Lila "Fantasia" Walker and Daphne Monet). In each instance the melodrama actant complicates the social problem-solving tendency while raising issues of complicity, ideological sedimentation, and whiteness. See Nieland, "Race-ing Noir and Replacing History."

56. Wiegman, *American Anatomies*, 131–32. Also see Fuchs, "The Buddy Politic"; Susan Willis, "Mutilated Masculinities and Their Prostheses: Die Hards and Lethal Weapons," in *High Contrast*; Fred Pfeil, "From Pillar to Postmodern: Race, Class, and Gender in the Male Rampage Film," in *White Guys*.

57. Lubiano, "Don't Talk with Your Eyes Closed," 191.

58. For more on transtextuality and its legacy in literary criticism and cinema studies, see Stam, *Reflexivity in Film and Literature*, 22–27. Also see Manthia Diawara's transtextual commentary about the roles of John Travolta (in Kolbowski, "Homeboy Cosmopolitanism," 51).

59. Rogin, *Blackface, White Noise*, 169, 166.

60. Also see the crisis of Jewish embodiment, deracinated modernism, and the phenomenological imperative of noir detection in *Homicide* (David Mamet, 1991). Kendall Thomas succinctly identifies a parallelism between *Homicide* and *Deep Cover*: "As film texts on the relationship between legality and masculinity, *Deep Cover* and *Homicide* suggest that the myth of masculinity is unable fully or finally to serve as

law's enabling ideological fiction. This is not simply because the regime of masculinity cannot tame the force of the constituent violence that the law must repress
in order to establish its legitimacy. This failure may be traced as well to a congenital
defect which is lodged in the heart of the language of masculinity *as such*. *Deep
Cover* and *Homicide* bear witness to the whole of meaning in the symbolic order
which is supposed not only to serve as a figure and ground for the rule of law, but to
authorize the masculinist myths on which the law is founded" ("'Masculinity,' 'The
Rule of Law,' and Other Legal Fictions," 234).

61. Mailer, *The White Negro*, 3–4.

62. In *Racechanges: White Skin, Black Face in American Culture*, Susan Gubar uses the
term *racechange* as a critical trope in the following way: "The term is meant to suggest the traversing of race boundaries, racial imitation or impersonation, cross-racial
mimicry or mutability, white posing as black or black passing as white, pan-racial
mutuality. . . . Racechange provides artists in diverse media a way of thinking about
racial parameters. Just as the Tarquinian urn can be said to stress the rigid borders
separating the races as well as the easy commerce between them, representations
of racechange test the boundaries between racially defined identities, functioning
paradoxically to reinforce and challenge the Manichean meanings Western societies
give to color" (5–6).

63. As Andrea Levine notes, "The White Negro's fetishization of an aggressive African
American response to a history of persecution is in part an effort to obscure the
image of the cowed, impotent Jew, going meekly to the gas chamber: an image that
nonetheless haunts the essay" ("The (Jewish) White Negro," 61). James Baldwin's
self-described "love letter" to Mailer decisively assessed *The White Negro*: "'Man,'
said a Negro musician to me once, talking about Norman, 'the only trouble with
that cat is that he's white.' This does not mean exactly what it says—or rather, it
does mean exactly what it says, and not what it might be taken to mean—and it
is a very shrewd observation. What my friend meant was that to become a Negro
man, let alone a Negro artist, one had to make oneself up as one went along. This
had to be done in the not-at-all metaphorical teeth of the world's determination
to destroy you. The world had prepared no place for you, and if the world had its
way no place would ever exist. Now, this is true for everyone, but, in the case of the
Negro, this truth is absolutely naked: if he deludes himself about it, he will die. This
is not the way this truth presents itself to white men, who believe the world is theirs
and who, albeit unconsciously, expect the world to help them in the achievement
of their identity" ("The Black Boy Looks at the White Boy," 183). As Levine points
out, while Baldwin identifies Mailer as a "white boy" in the title, in the text he identifies Mailer as a "middle class Jew," which "subjects Mailer to precisely the kind of
raced and gendered scrutiny that 'The White Negro' aims to deflect" ("The (Jewish)
White Negro," 75). Also see Campbell, *Paris Interzone*; Rux, "Eminem."

64. Jonathon P. Eburne writes, "This dowry—literally the object of exchange in
this eroticized instance of homosexual/cross-racial desire appears as some essence
intrinsic to race for which blackness is the synecdoche and whose power is the sub-

lime. Moreover, the 'sublime' registers as an inflated, accelerated version of [Lionel] Trilling's sublime effect: it has the power not merely to critique society but to evoke total removal of all social restraint. This makes Mailer's White Negro literally a psychopath whose sublime power — repositioned as 'hip' and avant-garde — fulfills the role of the specter plaguing the National Security State: psychopath, sexual deviant, juvenile delinquent, drug user" ("Trafficking in the Void," 70–71). Also see Baldwin, "The Black Boy Looks at the White Boy"; Levine, "The (Jewish) White Negro."

65. My thanks to Dr. I. Nyoman Sedana for his insights and William Condee for putting us in contact. A *wayang dalang* (shadow puppet master), Dr. Sedana identified the mask and explained that in the *Ramayama* the wanara monkeys serve Prince Rama in his attack on the demon king, Ravana, who kidnapped Princess Sita.

66. See Homi K. Bhabha, "The Other Question," in *The Location of Culture*.

67. Thanks to Alessandra Raengo for her thoughts on this sequence that informed my analysis.

68. Wright, *Becoming Black*, 91.

69. As Hazel Carby writes, Betty's place within the narrative has much to do with the necessary exclusion of women from interracial male couplings in film. Carby's comments on women in the *Lethal Weapon* films resonate with Betty's role in *Deep Cover*: "These intimate black and white male partnerships, which exclude women, project the masculinity imagined by white male liberals in quest of perfect partners. Together and alone, these race men of Hollywood dreams promise to annihilate what ails this nation and resolve our contemporary crisis of race, of nation, and of manhood" (*Race Men*, 191).

70. The voice-over lines are from a vernacular toast entitled "The Fall" or "The Fall of Jezebel." Some of the lines can be heard in the opening voice-over of "Cleveland, 1972" and in a conversation between Hull and Taft. The toast was first transcribed in the collection *The Life: The Lore and Folk Poetry of the Black Hustler* (1976) and was recorded on albums by Iceberg Slim and Big Brown in the 1970s. Dan Flory notes, "This vernacular toast projects a sense of fatalistic authority on the main character as a source of knowledge regarding his saga of duplicity, manipulation, and the struggle to remain nonetheless human, giving his account undertones informed by sorrow, foreboding, and abiding humanity. . . . As cautionary *noir* tale, then, *Deep Cover's* narrative voice is substantially enhanced by recitation from this poem. It adds an air of sad wisdom to the knowledge the protagonist conveys about his misadventures within white power structures" (*Philosophy, Black Film, Film Noir*, 196, 197).

71. On set during the shooting of this scene, Patrick Pacheco reported the following variation of the dialogue: "'In three years, both of us will be worth half-a-billion dollars apiece,' says Jeff Goldblum as David Jason, a lawyer–turned–drug kingpin to his would-be partner. 'You know what happens when you're worth a half-billion dollars? You won't be a nigger anymore. Your children will never be niggers. They won't be black. They'll only be green'" ("Fighting the 'John Singleton Thing,'" *Los Angeles Times*, 12 April 1991).

72. "You shouldn't have done that, David" and "But I did, so get in the fucking van" are sampled by Prince Paul for De La Soul's "3 Days Later" on *De La Soul Is Dead* (1993).

73. Could Stevens be Moss from *Home of the Brave* being forced to get up and walk? "Get up, you yellow-bellied nigger." The scene serendipitously alludes to Fishburne's character Dap and the call "WAKE UP!" in *School Daze* (Spike Lee, 1988).

74. Lubiano, "Don't Talk with Your Eyes Closed," 194.

75. Rogin, *Blackface, White Noise*, 239–42. While Rogin suggests that Moss is "playing mammy," I prefer the feminine or maternal designation. Also, even though I am arguing that the interracial pietà is dependent on a gender binary to displace the possibility of homoeroticism between black and white men, Rogin does note that the pietà of *Home of the Brave* sparks "nervousness about homoeroticism" (241). For a consequential consideration of the sociopolitical uses of the pietà with regard to motherhood, race, and citizen, see Tapia, *American Pietas*.

76. Pfeil, "From Pillar to Postmodern," 17.

77. Rogin, *Blackface, White Noise*, 225.

78. My sense of the doppelganger differs from Mark Berrettini's discussion of the embodiment crisis of Hull/Stevens: "*Deep Cover* foregrounds Stevens as his own doppelganger, where questions about conflicting identities are internalized within the 'raced' roles of law enforcement and criminal work; and as a cop corrupted by the system, not by his own desire for money or status. When he begins to transgress the institutional practice of his profession and becomes a successful criminal, he not only begins to view himself as a criminal—the way that most of the characters view him—but also to consent to the damaging, essentialist notions of race that guides this perspective" ("Transgression, Racialized Policing, and the Limits of Identity," 149).

79. Andrea Slane writes, "The genteel, 'feminized' Black man is a staple of the literary tradition of antiracism and abolitionism—the most celebrated example being Harriet Beecher Stowe's maternal Uncle Tom, who sacrifices himself for the lost child Little Eva in *Uncle Tom's Cabin* (1851). This image attempts to counteract the image of the hypersexualized (and thus hypermasculinized) Black man by aligning him with the nobler view of feminine 'nature.' The same strategy might be read in several of Kramer's social-problem films where Black men are portrayed as caring for their white companions, including Moss in *Home of the Brave* and Poitier's character in *The Defiant Ones*. Each of these films even similarly contain scenes where the Black man cradles the dying white man in his arms. But this combination of tendencies—the unconscious conceptual association of Black masculine hypersexuality with feminine hypersexuality, and the attempt to counter the image of Black hypermasculinity with an image of the maternal Black man—results in two converging iconographic codes that associate the Black man with femininity and femininity with long-suffering selflessness and weakness" ("Pressure Points," 90).

80. Sedgwick, *The Epistemology of the Closet*, 166. Susan Willis writes, "Such wit . . . seems designed to diffuse and contain the overtly homoerotic charge these scenes produce—to offer and then withdraw the lure of homoeroticism" (*High Contrast*,

29). This showdown sequence avoids the regrettable homophobic histrionics of the murder of Ivy in a club bathroom. In this scene Hull's hesitation in shooting is read by Ivy as a sign of emasculation: "Do you want to suck it, bitch?" As Ivy urinates on the shoes of the hesitant Hull, a luridly obvious image of ejaculation, Hull's pulling of the trigger tactlessly alludes to repressed homosexuality and justifiable violence.

81. Baldwin, *The Devil Finds Work*, 80–81.

82. In an interview on acting Bill Duke quotes Jeff Goldblum's assessment of the death scene: "This is the culmination of a relationship that we've seen throughout the entire film; it's like two lovers saying goodbye. Even in death they would say goodbye properly, they would take the time; it's quality time between them." Duke continues, "So we began to explore what quality time would be, and what we found was that all the things they felt, they had never said, and now it was too late to say. That was the exchange between them as Larry's walking toward Jeff when he's dying. Larry, if you notice in that sequence, has no sense of triumph in his face when he kills him; it's a sense of loss, an irrevocable loss, and Jeff feels the same way" (in Zucker, "Bill Duke," 310).

83. Jones, "Under the Cover of *Blackness*," 30.

84. See Churchill, "'To Disrupt, Discredit, and Destroy.'"

85. Webb endured an extensive campaign mounted by major media organizations across the country that sought to discredit him and his story. Yet while minor points about the story were rigorously attacked, the central thesis remained sound. The *San Jose Mercury* eventually issued a semi-retraction of Webb's story and reassigned him to the suburban bureau, a post that required a 150-mile commute. Webb resigned. All undistributed CD-ROMs and paper reprints, along with the series record on the *San Jose Mercury* website, were destroyed or deleted by the newspaper in what some have called the first Internet book burning. A film based on Nick Schou's *Kill the Messenger: How the CIA's Crack-Cocaine Controversy Destroyed Journalist Gary Webb* (2006) was released in 2014, with Jeremy Renner starring as Gary Webb. See Webb, *Dark Alliance*. Also see the recent *Los Angeles Magazine* profile of "Freeway" Rick Ross upon his release from prison. Ross was the central figure in the drug network established by the U.S. involvement in cocaine trafficking. The piece was written by Jesse Katz, a vocal critic of Webb's "Dark Alliance" series while working at the *Los Angeles Times*. Katz admitted some culpability in destroying Webb's career and ignoring the validity of Webb's claims. Jesse Katz, "Freeway Rick Is Dreaming," *Los Angeles Magazine*, June 2013, 108–12, 145–50.

86. Cockburn and St. Clair, *Whiteout*, 2.

87. Ray Pratt offers two points that lend themselves to the general conspiratorial tone of the film: "The title of the film is the same as that of undercover narc Michael Levine's memoir *Deep Cover* (New York: Delacorte, 1990), a scathing indictment of the Reagan-Bush and earlier drug wars that considers the whole U.S. effort — essentially the background of the film — a grotesque failure. . . . The name John Hull might resonate in some readers' minds as a character out of the Iran-Contra hearings. He was a U.S. citizen with a ranch in Costa Rica, near the Nicaraguan border,

purportedly involved in smuggling arms to the CIA-controlled Contra rebels" (*Projecting Paranoia*, 290n49, 291n50).

88. See Williams, *The Man Who Cried I Am* and *Captain Blackman*; Himes, *Plan B*; Schuyler, *Black No More*; Griggs, *Imperium in Imperio*; Greenlee, *The Spook Who Sat by the Door* (and Greenlee's coproduction of Ivan Dixon's film adaptation [1973]).

89. Russel Reising writes, "By thus reifying closural moments, traditional narrative theory has unnecessarily constructed endings as the embedded and fully coherent essence of the narrative act, which, given the numerous energies and agendas driving toward some perfectly revelatory, demystifying closural epiphany, can only be imagined as fully sufficient as both origin and telos of narrativity" (*Loose Ends*, 8).

90. Dr. Dre's "Deep Cover (187 on an Undercover Cop)" plays over the closing credits of the film. California Penal Code Section 187 defines murder. The song features an early debut of Snoop Dogg before his showcase presence on Dr. Dre's *The Chronic*, released later that year, and the subsequent crossover importance of Snoop Dogg's *Doggystyle* (1993).

91. Sharon Holland's reading of the silencing of the voice-over in *Menace II Society* (Albert and Allen Hughes, 1993) with the murder of Caine at the film's close offers a nuanced sense of what death and life mean for a text enfolded in the voicing and engendering of blackness. She writes, "Lost in Caine's narration of the film, we are quick to believe that he escapes the 'hood and lives happily thereafter. The smugness of this evaluation is repudiated by the film's ending—and Caine's narrative, his ability to *speak for himself*, is demonstrated in his dying. No longer the borrowed or stolen language of the state, his words reach from the place of the dead into the space of the living. He dies, but his narrative is now *his* in a way that it could not be had he lived. As intellectuals and consumers of popular culture we are left to think very differently and deeply about what meaning a narrative-in-death has for black subjects *and* representations of blackness in the popular national imagination" (*Raising the Dead*, 28).

92. David Bowie, "Blackstar," on *Blackstar*, Columbia, 2016.

93. I have in mind Kevin Bell's assessment of Chester Himes and blackness: "[Himes's] literary project seeks to activate an aesthetical-political engagement of a delegitimated and outcast sensibility, whose ineffable and ineradicable *blackness* is at once anterior to the logic of racialization, and at the same time, augmented, reshaped, and intensified exactly by those dimensions of lived experience unique to the scene of public fascination and public abjection (or exclusion from zones of thought, value, and history) that is cultural blackness" (*Ashes Taken for Fire*, 196).

FOUR. Black Maybe

1. For more production detail about the film, see Macaulay, "The Urban Condition."

2. Kevin Quashie writes, "Quiet is antithetical to how we think about black culture, and by extension, black people. So much of the discourse of racial blackness imagines black people as public subjects with identities formed and articulated and

resisted in public. Such blackness is dramatic, symbolic, never for its own vagary, always representative and engaged with how it is imagined publicly. . . . The idea of quiet, then, can shift attention to what is interior. This shift can feel like a kind of heresy if the interior is thought of as apolitical or inexpressive, which it is not: one's inner life is raucous and full of expression, especially if we distinguish the term 'expressive' from the notion of public. Indeed the interior could be understood as the source of human action—that anything we do is shaped by the range of desires and capacities of our inner life. . . . Silence often denotes something that is suppressed or repressed, and is an interiority that is about withholding absence, and stillness. Quiet, on the other hand is presence . . . and can encompass fantastic motion" (*The Sovereignty of Quiet*, 8, 22).

3. Hall, "Cultural Identity and Diaspora," 394.

4. Jackson continues, "Analyses that deal exclusively with discussions of 'racial scripts' dehumanize. Much like the processes they ostensibly critique. They turn us all into mere objects of our own discourses, less the actors who read and interpret scripts than the inert pages themselves" (*Real Black*, 15).

5. Thanks to Stewart Griffin at Final Frame for his color insights.

6. In *Who Can Afford to Improvise?*, Ed Pavlić comments, "After noticing one of the working women in Jean-Luc Godard's *Two or Three Things I Know about Her* [1967] reading a translation of Ray Bradbury's book, *Medicine for Melancholy*, I thought about the role of the city as language and the language of the city in Barry Jenkins's eponymous film. Jenkins confirmed that he'd titled his film after remarking that phrase while viewing Godard's film in San Francisco. It strikes me that much of what Jenkins does with the music of the soundtrack can be considered a musical translation of the semiotic and linguistic treatise Godard laces into his film about the role of the city in the language of its inhabitants and vice versa" (317n6). While we ultimately differ in our reading of *Medicine*, Pavlić's work on the film is a valuable difference of opinion.

7. Berlant, *Desire/Love*, 71–72.

8. Berlant, *Desire/Love*, 76–77.

9. Jon Anderson's characterization of the cultural geographer parallels the narrativization of San Francisco in *Medicine for Melancholy*: "When cultural geographers study place they study material objects, cultural activities, social ideas and geographical contexts. They investigate how these material and non-material traces, these emotions and ideologies, come together with spatial contexts to constitute particular places in time, and how these places impact on other sites that may be geographically or temporally disparate" (*Understanding Cultural Geography*, 10).

10. Personal communication, 29 February 2016.

11. Les Roberts defines cinematic geography as a consideration of "the temporal layers of visuality and urban form" and of cinema's capacity to detail a present that contains active residuals of the past. In this way cinema can compel an understanding of how "the absent geographies of a city's past confront the material and symbolic landscapes of present and future urban spaces" (*Film, Mobility and Urban Space*, 5).

12. I have in mind Foucault's third principle of heterotopias that in the context of *Medicine* and San Francisco means a diegetic place "capable of juxtaposing in a single real place several spaces, several sites that are in themselves incompatible" ("Of Other Spaces," 25).

13. Benjamin, "Thesis on the Philosophy of History," 9. David Eng and David Kazanjian instructively frame this passage: "Reliving an era is to bring the past to memory. It is to induce actively a tension between the past and present, between the dead and the living. In this manner, Benjamin's historical materialist establishes a continuing dialogue with loss and its remains—a flash of emergence, an instant of emergency, and most important a moment of production" ("Introduction," 1).

14. The tonal quality, camera work, and abbreviated dialogue have often led to *Medicine for Melancholy*'s being characterized as a "mumblecore film." While I appreciate that mumblecore was one of the influences on the conception of *Medicine*, the film's fundamental amending of the mumblecore form—a form whose elements are by no means discrete in terms of the history of independent and global cinema—with a racial, cultural, and historical context antithetical to mumblecore disallows the labeling reduction and exaggeration. As Aymar Jean Christian notes, "The movie took the stylistic conventions of mumblecore—overuse of close-ups, handheld camera work, poor sound quality and sometimes stunted dialogue—and reinterpreted with a message of some social import. . . . But in *Medicine* that inability to communicate has a whole lot to do about [an] inability to talk constructively about race and class" (personal communication, 7 April 2008). For more on mumblecore, see Christian, "Joe Swanberg, Intimacy, and the Digital Aesthetic."

15. See Dickel's "Between Mumblecore and Post-Black Aesthetics" for an interesting take on the significance of gallery spaces in the film and what he identifies as the film's intertextual regard for contemporary art.

16. Catanese, "'When Did You Discover You Are African?,'" 94.

17. Lord and Lord, *Artists, Patrons, and the Public*, 74.

18. Brand, *A Map to the Door of No Return*, 24–25.

19. Clifford, "Diasporas," 308.

20. "Slavery Passages" features testimonials from Olaudah Equiano, Mary Prince, Juan Francisco Manzano, Harriet Jacobs, Mahommahgardo Baquaqua, Esteban Motejo, Francis Bok, Tempe Herndon Durham, and Fountain Hughes.

21. Equiano, *The Interesting Narrative of the Life of Olaudah Equiano*, 56.

22. For a consideration of how recent scholarship that has raised questions about the validity of Equiano's claims of African birth might impact Middle Passage epistemology, see Wright, *Physics of Blackness*, 22–25.

23. Wilderson, *Red, White and Black*, 279.

24. As Michelle Wright argues, "To date, discourses on Middle Passage Blackness that account for its formation through . . . spacetime are stuck in [a] baffling state of affairs: how can one retain the historical continuity (and thus be able to point to the existence and pedigree of Black culture, Black politics, Black music, Black literature,

etc.) of Middle Passage Blackness *and* accurately represent all its many manifestations?" (*Physics of Blackness*, 18–19).

25. Catanese, "'When Did You Discover You Are African?,'" 93. Also see Ruffins, "Revisiting the Old Plantation."

26. Wright, *Becoming Black*, 2.

27. Catanese, "'When Did You Discover You Are African?,'" 92.

28. "Monuments that resist transformation risk losing their significance to future generations" (Wilson, "Between Rooms 307," 20). Also see Romano and Raiford, *The Civil Rights Movement in American Memory*; Gooden, "The Problem with African American Museums."

29. Leigh Raiford and Michael Cohen query, "What are we doing when we frame African American history as a progressive journey from enslavement to the White House, as a heroic narrative of struggle, unity and racial progress?" ("Black History Month and the Uses of the Past," *Al Jazeera*, 28 February 2012, http://www.aljazeera .com/indepth/opinion/2012/02/2012226922224952.html).

30. Thanks to Brian Harnetty for his thoughts on the musical arrangement.

31. Created in 1906, the Zeum Carousel was first installed at the ocean-side amusement park Playland-at-the-Beach in 1913. It remained there until the park closed in 1972 and was eventually refurbished and installed at the Yerba Buena Gardens in 1998. It is now known as the LeRoy King Carousel in honor of the former San Francisco redevelopment commissioner and is part of the Children's Creativity Museum. It suggests a sense of how the past is refurbished and revised as an active relic for the purposes of a new San Francisco landscape.

32. Claire Denis made these remarks for the *Friday Night* DVD commentary to explain her choice to not use voice-over in the film (in Mayne, *Claire Denis*, 121).

33. Del Rio, *Deleuze and the Cinemas of Performance*, 165.

34. In a postscreening discussion at the Northwest Film Forum (25 February 2009) Barry Jenkins described an interesting distinction between *Friday Night* and *Medicine for Melancholy*. Denis's film opens with the city crisis of the transit strike before shifting to the specific and intimate encounter between the characters. *Medicine* operates in reverse, moving from the intimate encounter to the city crisis of housing rights, displacement, and black erasure. Northwest Film Forum, "Q&A with Barry Jenkins, *Medicine for Melancholy*," YouTube, 6 March 2009, https://www.youtube .com/watch?v=DboWil5pdmU.

35. Goyal, *Romance, Diaspora, and Black Atlantic Literature*, 10, 15.

36. Rebecca Wanzo writes, "The problem with normative claims is that they are inherently disciplinary, although the regulatory nature of normative models is sometimes masked by a progressive sheen" ("Black Love Is Not a Fairytale," 12). My sense of respectability in this instance comes directly from Jenkins, *Private Lives, Proper Relations*.

37. Leigh Raiford contends that critical black memory "names an ongoing, engaged practice through which a range of participants speak back to history and assess on-

going crises faced by black subjects" ("Photography and the Practices of Critical Black Memory," 114–15). Her conception of critical black memory as "a mode of historical interpretation and political critique that has functioned as an important resource for framing African American social movements and political identities" has particularly informed my reading of Micah's memory and historical conscious- ness (*Imprisoned in a Luminous Glare*, 16). In *Affective Mapping*, Jonathan Flatley argues that modernist "melancholizing" occurs as a form of melancholy distinct from the more common characterization of melancholy as faulty mourning or de- bilitating loss. Instead Flatley proposes that nondepressive forms of melancholy function as an epistemological practice, a production of knowledge: "Melancholiz- ing is something one does: longing for lost loves, brooding over absent objects and changed environments, reflecting on unmet desires, and lingering on events from the past. It is a practice that might, in fact, produce its own kind of knowledge" (2). Also see Muñoz, *Disidentifications*.

38. See the following for elaboration on the history of African Americans in San Fran- cisco: Broussard, *Black San Francisco*; Crowe, *Prophets of Rage*; Miller, *Postwar Struggle for Civil Rights*; Banks et al., *Black California Dreamin'*. In tandem with the gentrification wave of accelerated redevelopment, the displacement of local communities is occurring with the execution of evictions as a result of the Ellis Act (1985), a provision that allows for landlords to "go out of business" short of declar- ing bankruptcy and to remove occupants. Landlords have used this provision as a way of circumventing rent control statutes and evicting occupants. See the work of the Anti-Eviction Mapping Project, "a data visualization, data analysis, and digital storytelling collective documenting the SF Bay Area eviction crisis." The project has mapped in detail the increased use of the Ellis Act and the rate of evictions from 1997 to 2013 at http://www.antievictionmappingproject.net/serialevictions.html. In ad- dition there is a crowdsourced map that allows displaced residents to upload their personal narratives at "Anti-Eviction Mapping Project: Narratives of Displacement and Loss," Crowdmap, https://crowdmap.com/map/narrativesofdisplacement/. For a personal account of gentrification and Marcus Book Store, the oldest black bookstore in America and last black-owned business in the Fillmore, see Johnson, "Dear Khary (An Autobiography of Gentrification)." Marcus Book Store was shut- tered and the Johnson family evicted in March 2014.

39. See Jackson and Jones, "Remember the Fillmore."

40. Rebecca Solnit explains how redevelopment in San Francisco recodes the ideal of social justice: "The city's redevelopment manifestoes seem at least implicitly a counter argument to the Civil Rights Movement; they argue a different set of causes than racism, exclusion and poverty for the condition of nonwhite inner-city inhabi- tants, and a different cure than social justice — or argue that modernist architecture is social justice, a shaky premise even then" (*Hollow City*, 47).

41. Marcuse, "Gentrification, Abandonment and Displacement," 196.

42. Shukla, "Harlem's Pasts in Its Present," 179. Also see Shukla, "Loving the Other in 1970s Harlem."

43. Elena Gorfinkel and John David Rhodes contend that there are primarily three ways that the cinematic place occurs: "Place seems to reside in three spatiotemporal registers at once: (1) in its own obstinately distinct world that exceeds the borders of the film frame, (2) in a world furnished for our immersed view, and (3) in a realm that exists somewhere between (and in tension with) the first two registers. It is in this dialectical third term that we can conceive of place as a product of an agnostic relation, instead of an essence, truth, or pure matter that needs to be properly preserved, rescued, or excavated" ("Introduction," xvii). I am arguing that *Medicine for Melancholy*'s San Francisco resonates with this dialectical third term of place. For a wide survey of San Francisco in cinema, see Harris, ed., *World Film Locations: San Francisco*. For an alternative emplotting of the history of San Francisco in a fiction film, see Spike Lee's *Sucker Free City* (2004). Conceived as the pilot episode for a series on Showtime devoted to San Francisco, the film focuses on the communities of Hunter's Point and Chinatown and the growing gentrification of the city. To articulate the spatial histories of the city, the film employs maps superimposed with historical text. Also see the teaser for *The Last Black Man in San Francisco*, circulating on the Internet. The short film was made to attract investors for a feature-length project that promises to be a significant examination of San Francisco.

44. This historical review is drawn from Hartman, *City for Sale*; Hartman et al., *Displacement*; Smith and Williams, *Gentrification of the City*; Brook et al., *Reclaiming San Francisco*.

45. As David Delaney notes about contemporary geographical theories of space and race, "Elements of the social (race, gender, and so on) are not simply reflected in spatial arrangements; rather, spatialities are regarded as constituting and/or reinforcing aspects of the social. . . . This suggests that race—in all of its complexity and ambiguity, as ideology and identity—is what it is and does what it does precisely because of how it is given spatial expression" ("The Space That Race Makes," 7).

46. See Puwar, *Space Invaders*.

47. Sassen, *Globalization and Its Discontents*, xxxiii.

48. The comments made during this meeting echo the concerns of the community housing activists of the 1970s and 1980s. For example, "Moving people involuntarily from their homes or neighbourhoods is wrong. Regardless of whether it results from government or private market action, forced displacement is characteristically a case of people without the economic and political power to resist being pushed out by people with greater resources and power, people who think they have a 'better' use for a certain building, piece of land, or neighborhood. The pushers benefit. The pushees do not. [It is also] fundamentally wrong to allow removal of housing units from the low-moderate income stock, for any purpose, without requiring at least a one-for-one replacement. Demolition, conversion, or 'upgrade' rehab of vacant private or publicly owned lower-rent housing should be just as vigorously opposed as when those units are occupied" (Hartman et al., *Displacement*, 4–5).

49. See Smith, *The New Urban Frontier*; Slater, "Gentrification of the City."

50. Smith, *The New Urban Frontier*, 23.
51. Cheng, *Melancholy of Race*, 3.
52. See Butler, *The Psychic Life of Power*.
53. Cheng, *Melancholy of Race*, 8.
54. The difference in bicycles is noteworthy. Jo with her multigear and Micah with his fixed-gear bike suggest "something about the ways in which fixed and optioned speeds calibrate their movements in the city differently, and how the codes of bicycles are cool/hip/generational codes of navigation and pace linked to the body" (Lokeilani Kaimana, personal communication, 30 April 2015).
55. Thanks to Tehama Bunyasi Lopez for aiding me in the tabulation of these numbers.
56. City and County of San Francisco, Mayor's Office of Housing and Community Development, "African American Out-Migration," http://sf-moh.org/index.aspx ?page=649 (last updated 25 January 2008).
57. In fact the cover of the report is a cropped version of the cover for Howard Dodson and Sylviane A. Diouf's *In Motion: The African-American Migration Experience* (Washington: National Geographic Society, 2004), a book that accompanied the exhibition of the same name at The Schomburg Center for Research in Black Culture. The exhibit, book, and Internet database represent an initiative to reenvision African American history.
58. Jenkins noted, "The music playing in the club that night was what the English call Northern Soul, Chuck Berry, Otis Redding, James Brown, etc. I chose this club and that music specifically because like everything else, it was a place I hung out and danced at a lot with my then girlfriend, who was white (this woman broke up with me and thus I decided to finally put pen to paper and write this film). There were nights where I was the only person of color in the club, yet all the music playing on the speakers—and all vinyl, very tactile—was the voices, the 'souls of black folks.' That shit did a number on me, absolutely did a number on me. It crystallized something about displacement, about gentrification and representation and appropriation. I set the scene there because I wanted to reclaim that space through these characters, so to speak. Or at least to have them *share* in the representation of those souls. . . . [But] the *intent* of the scene, reclaiming that space as I put it, proved impossible because of the ways in which those black voices on vinyl were controlled by corporate licensing" (personal communication, 29 February 2016).
59. Neal, *Soul Babies*, 3. Nelson George first used the term *post-soul* to identify the period immediately after the civil rights era and the subsequent rise of blaxploitation cinema. In particular George argues that the 1970s was a "germinating" period for four emergent types of blackness: the buppie, the b-boy, the bap (black American prince or princess), and the boho. While the historicization of George's typology might be debatable, the marking of a period after and distinguishable from the civil rights movement is an important qualifier. See George, *Buppies, B-Boys, Baps, and Bohos*, 1–40. Also see Ashe, "Theorizing the Post-Soul Aesthetic."
60. Neal, *Soul Babies*, 3.
61. My address of *Medicine for Melancholy* and its post-soul overtones is in deliberate

opposition to considerations of the film as *postblack*. I particularly appreciate the meanings attributed to the term by Thelma Golden and Glenn Ligon, and the curatorial stagings of the idea at the Studio Museum of Harlem beginning with the *Freestyle* exhibit (2001) and across the *Frequency* (2005–6) and *Flow* (2008) shows. As art studies critique, curatorial practice, a remediation of reception, the antiessentialist conception of an art practice, and savvy marketing, *postblack* has an indisputable value, but it does not adequately account for my interest in *Medicine for Melancholy*. Ultimately, it strikes me as too circumstantial a claim that the exchanges and modulations between Micah and Jo are emphatically postblack. See Campbell, "African American Art in a Post-Black Era"; Copeland, "Post/Black/Atlantic"; Adusei-Poku, "The Multiplicity of Multiplicities."

62. Dickel also labels *Medicine for Melancholy* as a post-soul film, but his motivation differs from mine, as he positions the film as between postblack and mumblecore. See "Between Mumblecore and Post-Black Aesthetics."

63. The film soundtrack includes music by The Answering Machine, Au Revoir Simone, Bloodcat Love, Canoe, Casiotone for the Painfully Alone, The Changes, Gypsophile, Igor Romanov, Ivana XL, The Octopus Project, Oh No! Oh My!, Saturday Looks Good to Me, Tandemoro, Tom Waits, Total Shutdown, White Denim, and Yesterday New Quartet.

64. My thinking about this authenticity point is directly informed by Barry Shank's address of the 1980s indie music scene that developed around the band Beat Happening. As opposed to the Washington hardcore circles of the 1980s, with figures such as Minor Threat and Bad Brains, the Beat Happening scene did not insist on the dissolution between the scene and the world outside and beyond the stage. Rather this indie music's sense of authenticity was predicated on the affective dynamics of "emotional honesty" in ways less discretely tied to a conclusive praxis: "Indie's authenticity proceeds from the self-conscious rejection of virtuosity and the illusions it fosters. . . . This version of authenticity, which does not provide much for the foundation on which to build a political stance, synthesizes amateurism and artistry and serves instead to allow the music's political community to interrogate its own divisions, to inquire into its ability to produce a chain of equivalences capable of mediating agnostic difference. The community should not resolve difference away but allow it to engender new problems from its momentary incomplete solutions. . . . The indie scene distributes an anxious sense of ambiguity, contradiction, and uncertainty that derives from its founding illusion, the primary importance of emotional honesty" (*The Political Force of Musical Beauty*, 190–91, 192). Characterized by a disavowal of virtuosity and the elevation of an amateurism/artistry dialectic, this indie scene espoused a politics of pleasure that neither concretized the terms of allegiance nor sought to discourage the possibility of a self-critique.

65. Thanks to Dana Seitler for her thoughts on a politics of pleasure.

66. As Ernest Hardy astutely surmises, "[Micah's] love of indie music . . . is not a desire to escape or deny blackness: Immersion in a scene whose default setting is 'white' is paradoxically rooted in his hunger to embody and live a more complex, dynamic

blackness than that which pop barons market. The irony crushes him" ("Medicine for Melancholy Both Political and Graceful," *Village Voice*, 28 January 2009, http://www.villagevoice.com/2009-01-28/film/medicine-for-melancholy-both-political-and-graceful/).

67. Broyard, "A Portrait of a Hipster," 49.

68. Solnit, *Hollow City*, 19.

69. Also see Grief et al., *What Was the Hipster?*, and Michael Cohen's recuperation of the hipster in nongentrifier terms in "Douchebag: The White Racial Slur We've All Been Waiting For."

70. For more on race and the indie scene, see the discussion that developed across the following pieces: Sasha Frere-Jones, "A Paler Shade of White: How Indie Rock Lost Its Soul," *New Yorker*, 22 October 2007, 176–81; Ann Powers, "Hail Indie Rock, in All Its Diversity," *Los Angeles Times*, 24 November 2007; Tate, "Black Rockers vs. Blackies Who Rock."

71. I am thinking here of Kobena Mercer's address of key aspects of the Black British film collectives, Sankofa and Black Audio Film Collective. Mercer writes, "What is in question is not the expression of some lost origin or uncontaminated essence in black film language, but the adoption of a critical voice that promotes consciousness of the collision of cultures and histories that constitute our very conditions of existence" ("Diaspora Culture and the Dialogic Imagination: The Aesthetics of Black Independent Film in Britain," in *Welcome to the Jungle*, 63).

72. "To return . . . is not only a trip to a no-longer-existing past, but also involves an encounter with a no-longer existing self" (Wilson, "Looking Backward," 131).

73. Ed Pavlić contends that Jo's refusal to engage with Micah's point demonstrates her "reject[ion] of a racial point of view" (*Who Can Afford to Improvise?*, 216). Pavlić states: "Pushed to racial extremes in (by?) indie-isolation, the two find themselves nose to nose on opposite sides of the post-racial membrane of the dream bubble. There is obviously important living experience between Micah's passionate, racial simplicity and Joanne's detached universals, but they don't have the words to go there" (239). While I agree with his reading of a diasporic anxiety permeating *Medicine*, I disagree with his assessment of their respective ideological positions and the characterization of their division as concentrated around a postracial divide.

74. Berlant writes, "In the popular rhetoric of romance, love is a most fragile thing, a supposed selflessness in a world full of self; its plots also represent the compulsion to repeat scenes of transgression, ruthlessness, and control, as well as their resolution into something transcendent, or at least consoling, still, stabilized—at least for a moment" (*Desire/Love*, 89–90).

75. "Peoples whose sense of identity is centrally defined by collective histories of displacement and violent loss cannot be 'cured' by merging into a new national community. This is especially true when they are the victims of ongoing, structural prejudice. Positive articulations of diaspora identity reach outside the normative territory and temporality (myth/history) of the nation-state" (Clifford, "Diasporas," 307).

76. Thanks to Ayesha K. Hardison for this consideration of lamentations.

77. Sharon Van Etten, "Give Out," on *Tramp*, Jagjaguwar, 2012.

CODA

1. In addition to all of these films, it is important to note recent occasions when new programming and archiving has produced vital revisions of black film historiography. This includes the UCLA Film and Television Archive's LA Rebellion initiative led by Allyson Nadia Field, Jan-Christopher Horak, and Jacqueline Stewart; the formation of the Black Cinema House as part of Theaster Gates's Dorchester Project in Chicago; the *Cinema Remixed and Reloaded: Black Women Artists and the Moving Image since 1970* exhibition co-organized by Valerie Cassel Oliver and Dr. Andrea Barnwell Brownlee; the Black Radical Imagination touring programs curated by Emir Christovale and Amir George; the Liquid Blackness project at Georgia State University coordinated by Alessandra Raengo; and the Tell It Like It Is: Black Independents in New York, 1968–1986 film series at Lincoln Center (6–19 February 2015) programmed by Jake Perlin and Michelle Materre.

2. See Alexander, *The New Jim Crow*.

3. Personal communication, 4 June 2011.

BIBLIOGRAPHY

Adusei-Poku, Nana. "The Multiplicity of Multiplicities: Post-Black Art and Its Intri-
cacies." *Dark Matter*, 29 November 2012. http://www.darkmatter101.org/site/2012
/11/29/the-multiplicity-of-multiplicities—post-black-art-and-its-intricacies/.
Ahmed, Sara. *The Cultural Politics of Emotion*. New York: Routledge, 2004.
Alexander, Michelle. *The New Jim Crow: Mass Incarceration in the Age of Colorblind-
ness*. New York: New Press, 2010.
Alexie, Sherman. "The Unauthorized Autobiography of Me." In *One Stick Song*, 13–25.
Brooklyn: Hanging Loose, 2000.
Altman, Rick. "Reusable Packaging: Generic Products and the Recycling Process."
In *Refiguring American Film Genres: Theory and History*, ed. Nick Browne, 1–41.
Berkeley: University of California Press, 1998.
Anderson, Jon. *Understanding Cultural Geography: Places and Traces*. New York:
Routledge, 2010.
Appiah, K. Anthony. "No Bad Nigger: Blacks as the Ethical Principle in Movies." In
Media Spectacles, ed. Marjorie Garber, Jann Matlock, and Rebecca L. Walkowitz,
77–90. New York: Routledge, 1993.
Ashe, Bertram D. "Theorizing the Post-Soul Aesthetic: An Introduction." *African
American Review* 41.4 (2007): 609–23.
Baker, Houston. *Blues, Ideology, and Afro-American Literature: A Vernacular Theory*.
Chicago: University of Chicago Press, 1984.
———. *Modernism and the Harlem Renaissance*. Chicago: University of Chicago
Press, 1990.
Bakhtin, Mikhail M. *The Dialogic Imagination: Four Essays*. Ed. Michael Holquist. Trans.
Caryl Emerson and Michael Holquist. Austin: University of Texas Press, 1981.
———. "Discourse Typology in Prose." In *Readings in Russian Poetics: Formalist and
Structuralist Views*, ed. Ladislav Matejka and Krystyna Pomorska, 176–96. Cam-
bridge, MA: MIT Press, 1971.
———. *Rabelais and His World*. Trans. Hélène Iswolsky. Bloomington: Indiana Uni-
versity Press, 1984.

Baldwin, James. "The Black Boy Looks at the White Boy." In *Nobody Knows My Name*, 169–90. New York: Dell, 1961.

———. *The Devil Finds Work: An Essay*. New York: Dial, 1976.

———. "Many Thousands Gone." In *Notes of a Native Son*, 24–45. New York: Bantam Books, 1955.

Banks, Ingrid, Gaye Johnson, George Lipsitz, Ula Taylor, Daniel Widener, and Clyde Woods, eds. *Black California Dreamin': The Crises of California's African-American Communities*. Santa Barbara: UCSB Center for Black Studies Research, 2012.

Bell, Kevin. *Ashes Taken for Fire: Aesthetic Modernism and the Critique of Identity*. Minneapolis: University of Minnesota Press, 2007.

———. "The Embrace of Entropy: Ralph Ellison and the Freedom Principle of Jazz Invisible." *boundary 2* 30.2 (2003): 21–45.

———. "Fugitivity and Futurity in the Work of Chester Himes." *Modern Fiction Studies* 51.4 (2005): 846–72.

Benamou, Catherine L. "The Artifice of Realism and the Lure of the 'Real' in Orson Welles's *F for Fake* and Other T(r)eas(u)er(e)s." In *F Is for Phony: Fake Documentary and Truth's Undoing*, ed. Alexander Juhasz and Jesse Lerner, 143–70. Minneapolis: University of Minnesota Press, 2006.

Benjamin, Walter. "Thesis on the Philosophy of History." In *Illuminations*, 253–64. New York: Schocken Books, 1968.

Benston, Kimberly. "I Yam What I Am: The Topos of Un(naming) in Afro-American Literature." In *Black Literature and Literary Theory*, ed. Henry Louis Gates Jr., 151–72. New York: Methuen, 1984.

———. *Performing Blackness: Enactments of African-American Modernism*. New York: Routledge, 2000.

Berlant, Lauren. *Desire/Love*. Brooklyn: Punctum Books, 2012.

———. *The Female Complaint: The Unfinished Business of Sentimentality in American Culture*. Durham, NC: Duke University Press, 2008.

———. "National Brands/National Body: *Imitation of Life*." In *Comparative American Identities: Race, Sex, and Nationality in the Modern Text*, ed. Hortense J. Spillers, 51–72. Durham, NC: Duke University Press, 1991.

———. "She's Having an Episode: Patricia Williams' Poetics." Paper presented to Symposium Honoring the Contributions of Patricia Williams. Columbia University Law School, 1 March 2013.

Berlant, Lauren, and Elizabeth Freeman. "Queer Nationality." In Lauren Berlant, *The Queen of America Goes to Washington City: Essays on Sex and Citizenship*, 145–74. Durham, NC: Duke University Press, 1997.

Bernardi, Daniel. "The Voice of Whiteness: D.W. Griffith's Biograph Films (1908–1915)." In *The Birth of Whiteness: Race and the Emergence of U.S. Cinema*, ed. Daniel Bernardi, 103–28. New Brunswick, NJ: Rutgers University Press, 1998.

Berrettini, Mark. "Transgression, Racialized Policing, and the Limits of Identity: *Deep Cover*." *Journal of Criminal Justice and Popular Culture* 10.3 (2003–4): 148–60.

Bhabha, Homi K. *The Location of Culture*. New York: Routledge, 1994.

———. "Unsatisfied: Notes on Vernacular Cosmopolitanism." In *Text and Nation: Cross-Disciplinary Essays on Cultural and National Identities*, ed. Laura García-Moreno and Peter C. Pfeiffer, 191–207. Columbia, SC: Camden House, 1996.

Bodroghkozy, Aniko. *Groove Tube: Sixties Television and the Youth Rebellion*. Durham, NC: Duke University Press, 2001.

Bogle, Donald. *Toms, Coons, Mulattoes, Mammies, and Bucks: An Interpretative History of Blacks in American Film*. New York: Continuum, 1995.

Bowdre, Karen. "Romantic Comedies and the Raced Body." In *Falling in Love Again: Romantic Comedy in Contemporary Cinema*, ed. Stacey Abbott and Deborah Jermyn, 105–16. New York: I. B. Taurus, 2009.

Brand, Dionne. *A Map to the Door of No Return: Notes to Belonging*. Toronto: Random House, 2001.

Branigan, Edward. "The Articulation of Color in a Filmic System: *Deux ou trois choses que je sais d'elle*." In *Color: The Film Reader*, ed. Angela Dalle Vacche and Brian Price, 170–82. New York: Routledge, 2006.

Breu, Christopher. "Freudian Knot or Gordian Knot? The Contradictions of Racialized Masculinity in Chester Himes' *If He Hollers Let Him Go*." *Callaloo* 26.3 (2003): 766–95.

———. *Hard-Boiled Masculinities*. Minneapolis: University of Minnesota Press, 2005.

Brook, James, Chris Carlsson, and Nancy J. Peters, eds. *Reclaiming San Francisco: History, Politics, Culture*. San Francisco: City Lights, 1998.

Broussard, Albert S. *Black San Francisco: The Struggle for Racial Equality in the West, 1900–1954*. Lawrence: University Press of Kansas, 1993.

Brown, Bill. "Reification, Reanimation, and the American Uncanny." *Critical Inquiry* 32.2 (2006): 175–207.

Brown, Kate E., and Howard I. Kushner. "Eruptive Voices: Coprolalia, Malediction, and the Poetics of Cursing." *New Literary History* 32.3 (2001): 537–62.

Broyard, Anatole. "A Portrait of a Hipster." 1948. In *Beat Down to Your Soul: What Was the Beat Generation?*, ed. Ann Charters, 42–48. New York: Penguin Books, 2001.

Burgin, Victor. "Paranoiac Space." In *Visualizing Theory*, ed. Lucien Taylor, 230–41. New York: Routledge, 1994.

Busack, Richard von. "Here He Comes to Save the Day: An Interview with Cinequest Maverick Spirit Honoree Ralph Bakshi." *Metroactive*, 27 February 2003. http://www.metroactive.com/papers/metro/02.27.03/bakshi-0309.html.

Butler, Judith. "Competing Universalities." In Judith Butler, Ernesto Laclau, and Slavoj Žižek, *Contingency, Hegemony, Universality: Contemporary Dialogues on the Left*, 136–81. London: Verso, 2000.

———. *Gender Trouble: Feminism and the Subversion of Identity*. New York: Routledge, 1990.

———. *The Psychic Life of Power: Theories in Subjection*. Stanford, CA: Stanford University Press, 1997.

Campbell, James. *Paris Interzone: Richard Wright, Lolita, Boris Vian and Others on the Left Bank 1946–1960*. New York: Literary Classics, 1998.

Campbell, Mary Schmidt. "African American Art in a Post-Black Era." *Women and Performance: A Journal of Feminist Theory* 17.3 (2007): 317–30.

Camus, Albert. *The Rebel*. New York: Vintage Books, 1956.

Carby, Hazel V. *Race Men*. Cambridge, MA: Harvard University Press, 1998.

———. *Reconstructing Womanhood: The Emergence of the Afro-American Woman Novelist*. Oxford: Oxford University Press, 1987.

Carpio, Glenda. *Laughing Fit to Kill: Black Humor in the Fictions of Slavery*. Oxford: Oxford University Press, 2008.

Cassuto, Leonard. *The Inhuman Race: The Racial Grotesque in American Literature and Culture*. New York: Columbia University Press, 1997.

Catanese, Brandi Wilkins. "'When Did You Discover You Are African?' MoAD and the Universal, Diasporic Subject." *Performance Research* 12.3 (2007): 91–102.

Caughie, Pamela. *Passing and Pedagogy: The Dynamics of Responsibility*. Urbana: University of Illinois Press, 1999.

———. "Passing as Modernism." *Modernism/Modernity* 12.3 (2005): 385–406.

Chandler, Robin M. "Xenophobes, Visual Terrorism and the African Subject." *Third Text* 35 (Summer 1996): 15–28.

Chapman, Abraham, ed. *New Black Voices*. New York: New American Library, 1972.

Cheng, Anne Anlin. *Melancholy of Race: Psychoanalysis, Assimilation, and Hidden Grief*. New York: Oxford University Press.

Chin, Daryl. "Multiculturalism and Its Masks: The Art of Identity Politics." *Performing Arts Journal* 14.1 (1992): 1–15.

Christian, Aymar Jean. "Joe Swanberg, Intimacy, and the Digital Aesthetic." *Cinema Journal* 50.4 (2011): 117–35.

Churchill, Ward. "'To Disrupt, Discredit, and Destroy': The FBI's Secret War against the Black Panther Party." In *Liberation, Imagination, and the Black Panther Party*, ed. Kathleen Cleaver and George Katsiaficas, 78–117. New York: Routledge, 2001.

Clifford, James. "Diasporas." *Cultural Anthropology* 9.3 (1994): 302–38.

Cockburn, Alexander, and Jeffrey St. Clair. *Whiteout: The CIA, Drugs and the Press*. New York: Verso, 1998.

Cohan, Steven. *Masked Men: Masculinity and Movies in the Fifties*. Bloomington: Indiana University Press, 1997.

Cohen, Karl. *Forbidden Animation: Censured Cartoons and Blacklisted Animators in America*. Jefferson, NC: McFarland, 1997.

———. "Racism and Resistance: Black Stereotypes in Animation." *Animation Journal* 4.2 (1996): 43–68.

Cohen, Michael Mark. "Douchebag: The White Racial Slur We've All Been Waiting For." *Medium*, 14 October 2014. https://medium.com/human-parts/douchebag-the-white-racial-slur-weve-all-been-waiting-for-a2323002f85d.

Cole, C. L., and Samantha King. "The New Politics of Urban Consumption: *Hoop Dreams, Clockers*, and 'America.'" In *Sporting Dystopias: The Making and Meanings of Urban Sport Cultures*, ed. Ralph C. Wilcox, David L. Andrews, Robert Pitter, and Richard L. Irwin, 221–46. Albany: SUNY Press, 2003.

Coombe, Rosemary J. *The Cultural Life of Intellectual Properties: Authorship, Appropriation, and the Law*. Durham, NC: Duke University Press, 1998.

Copeland, Huey. *Bound to Appear: Art, Slavery, and the Site of Blackness in Multicultural America*. Chicago: University of Chicago Press, 2013.

———. "Post/Black/Atlantic: A Conversation with Thelma Golden and Glenn Ligon." In *Afro Modern: Journeys in the Black Atlantic*, ed. Tanya Barson and Peter Gorschlüter, 76–81. Liverpool, England: Tate, 2010.

Corbusier, Le. *When the Cathedrals Were White*. New York: Reynal and Hitchcock, 1947.

Cripps, Thomas. *Black Film as Genre*. Bloomington: Indiana University Press, 1979.

Crowe, Daniel Edward. *Prophets of Rage: The Black Freedom Struggle in San Francisco, 1945–1969*. New York: Routledge, 2009.

Davis, Angela Y. "Black Nationalism: The Sixties and the Nineties." In *Black Popular Culture*, ed. Gina Dent, 317–24. Seattle: Bay Press, 1992.

———. *Blues Legacies and Black Feminism: Gertrude "Ma" Rainey, Bessie Smith, and Billie Holiday*. New York: Vintage Books, 1998.

de Certeau, Michel. "History: Science and Fiction." In *Heterologies: Discourse on the Other*, 199–221. Trans. Brian Massumi. Minneapolis: University of Minnesota Press, 1986.

———. "Making History: Problems of Method and Problems of Meaning." In *The Writing of History*, 19–55. Trans. Tom Conley. New York: Columbia University Press, 1988.

———. *The Practice of Everyday Life*. Trans. Steven Rendall. Berkeley: University of California Press, 1984.

Delaney, David. "The Space That Race Makes." *Professional Geographer* 54 (2002): 6–14.

Deleuze, Gilles. *Cinema: The Time Image 2*. Trans. Hugh Tomlinson and Robert Galeta. Minneapolis: University of Minnesota Press, 1989.

Del Rio, Elena. *Deleuze and the Cinemas of Performance: Powers of Affection*. Edinburgh: Edinburgh University Press, 2008.

DeLue, Rachael Ziady. "Dreadful Beauty and the Undoing of Adulation in the Work of Kara Walker and Michael Ray Charles." In *Idol Anxiety*, ed. Josh Ellenbogen and Aaron Tugendhaft, 74–96. Stanford, CA: Stanford University Press, 2011.

Diawara, Manthia. "*Noir* by *Noirs*: Towards a New Realism in Black Cinema." In *Shades of Noir: A Reader*, ed. Joan Copjec, 261–78. London: Verso, 1993.

Dickel, Simon. "Between Mumblecore and Post-Black Aesthetics: Barry Jenkins's *Medicine for Melancholy*." In *Understanding Blackness through Performance: Contemporary Arts and the Representation of Identity*, ed. Anne Cremieux, Xavier Lemoine, and Jean-Paul Rocchi, 109–23. New York: Palgrave Macmillan, 2013.

Dinerstein, Joel. *Swinging the Machine: Modernity, Technology, and African American Culture between the World Wars*. Amherst: University of Massachusetts Press, 2003.

Donaldson, Melvin. *Black Directors in Hollywood*. Austin: University of Texas Press, 2003.

Du Bois, W. E. B. *The Souls of Black Folks*. 1903. In *Du Bois: Writings*, 357–548. Ed. Nathan Huggins. New York: Library of America, 1986.

Eburne, Jonathan P. *Surrealism and the Art of Crime*. Ithaca: Cornell University Press, 2008.

———. "Trafficking in the Void: Burroughs, Kerouac, and the Consumption of Otherness." *Modern Fiction Studies* 43.1 (1997): 53–92.

———. "The Transatlantic Mysteries of Paris: Chester Himes, Surrealism, and the Série noire." *PMLA* 120.3 (2005): 806–21.

Edmondson, Belinda. "The Black Romance." *Women's Studies Quarterly* 35.1–2 (2007): 191–211.

Edwards, Brent Hayes. "Louis Armstrong and the Syntax of Scat." *Critical Inquiry* 28 (Spring 2002): 618–49.

Eisenstein, Sergei. *Film Form: Essays in Film Theory*. Trans. Jay Leyda. New York: Harcourt, Brace, Jovanovich, 1949.

Ellison, Ralph. *Invisible Man*. 1947. New York: Random House, 1972.

———. *Shadow and Act*. New York: Vintage Books, 1953.

Elsaesser, Thomas. *Weimar Cinema and After: Germany's Historical Imaginary*. New York: Routledge, 2000.

Eng, David, and David Kazanjian. "Introduction: Mourning Remains." In *Loss: The Politics of Mourning*, ed. David Eng and David Kazanjian, 1–25. Berkeley: University of California Press, 2002.

English, Darby. *How to See a Work of Art in Total Darkness*. Cambridge, MA: MIT Press, 2007.

Enwezor, Okwui. "Repetition and Differentiation: Lorna Simpson's Iconography of the Racial Sublime." In *Lorna Simpson*, 102–31. New York: Harry N. Abrams and American Federation of Arts, 2006.

Equiano, Olaudah. *The Interesting Narrative of the Life of Olaudah Equiano, Or Gustavus Vassa, the African*. 1789. New York: Penguin Books, 2003.

Eyerman, Ron, and Scott Berretta. "From the 30s to the 60s: The Folk Music Revival in the United States." *Theory and Society* 25.4 (1996): 501–43.

Fanon, Frantz. *Black Skin, White Masks*. 1952. Trans. Charles Lam Markmann. New York: Grove, 1967.

———. *Toward the African Revolution*. Trans. Haakon Chevalier. New York: Grove, 1969.

Ferguson, Roderick. *Aberrations in Black: Toward a Queer of Color Critique*. Minneapolis: University of Minnesota Press, 2004.

Flatley, Jonathan. *Affective Mapping: Melancholia and the Politics of Modernism*. Cambridge, MA: Harvard University Press, 2008.

Fleetwood, Nicole R. *Troubling Vision: Performance, Visuality, and Blackness*. Chicago: University of Chicago Press, 2010.

Flory, Dan. *Philosophy, Black Film, Film Noir*. University Park: Pennsylvania State University Press, 2008.

Foucault, Michel. "Of Other Spaces." Trans. Jay Miskowiec. *Diacritics* 16.1 (1986): 22–27.

Freud, Sigmund. "Mourning and Melancholia." In *General Psychological Theory: Papers on Metapsychology*, 161–78. New York: Collier Books, 1963.

Friedburg, Anne. *Window Shopping: Cinema and the Postmodern*. Berkeley: University of California Press, 1993.

Fuchs, Cynthia. "The Buddy Politic." In *Screening the Male: Exploring Masculinities in Hollywood Cinema*, ed. Steven Cohan and Ina Rae Hark, 194–210. New York: Routledge, 1993.

Fusco, Coco. "Racial Time, Racial Marks, Racial Metaphors." In *Only Skin Deep: Changing Visions of the American Self*, ed. Coco Fusco and Brian Wallis, 13–48. New York: International Center of Photography and Harry N. Abrams, 2003.

Gabbard, Krin. *Black Magic: White Hollywood and African American Culture*. New Brunswick, NJ: Rutgers University Press, 2004.

Gaines, Charles. "The Theatre of Refusal: Black Art and Mainstream Criticism." In *The Theater of Refusal: Black Art and Mainstream Criticism*, ed. Catherine Lord, 12–20. Irvine: Fine Arts Gallery and University of California, Irvine, 1993.

Gates, Henry Louis, Jr. "The Passing of Anatole Broyard." In *Thirteen Ways of Looking at a Black Man*, 180–214. New York: Random House, 1997.

———. *The Signifying Monkey*. Oxford: Oxford University Press, 1988.

Gayle, Addison, Jr., ed. *The Black Aesthetic*. New York: Doubleday, 1971.

George, Nelson. *Buppies, B-Boys, Baps, and Bohos: Notes on Post-Soul Black Culture*. Boston: Da Capo, 1992.

Gibson, Jon M., and Chris McDonnell. *Unfiltered: The Complete Ralph Bakshi*. New York: Universe, 2008.

Gilbert, Thomas. *Baseball at War: World War II and the Fall of the Color Line*. New York: Grolier, 1997.

Gillespie, Michael B. "Dirty Pretty Things: The Racial Grotesque and Contemporary Art." In *Post-Soul Satire: Black Identity after Civil Rights*, ed. Derek Maus and James Donahue, 68–84. Jackson: University Press of Mississippi, 2014.

———. "*Do the Right Thing*." In *The Routledge Encyclopedia of Films*, ed. John White, Sarah Barrow, and Sabine Haenni, 208–12. New York: Routledge, 2015.

———. "Reckless Eyeballing: *Coonskin*, Film Blackness, and the Racial Grotesque." In *Contemporary Black American Cinema: Race, Gender and Sexuality at the Movies*, ed. Mia Mask, 56–86. New York: Routledge, 2012.

———. "Smiling Faces: *Chameleon Street*, Racial Passing/Performativity, and Film Blackness." In *Passing Interest: Racial Passing in U.S. Fiction, Memoirs, Television, and Film, 1990–2010*, ed. Julie Cary Nerad, 255–82. Albany: SUNY Press, 2014.

Gilman, Sander L. *Difference and Pathology: Stereotypes of Race, Sexuality, and Madness*. Ithaca: Cornell University Press, 1985.

Gilroy, Paul. *Against Race: Imagining Political Culture beyond the Color Line*. Cambridge, MA: Harvard University Press, 2000.

———. *Black Atlantic: Modernity and Double Consciousness*. Cambridge, MA: Harvard University Press, 1992.

———. "Cruciality and the Frog's Perspective: An Agenda of Difficulties for the Black

Arts Movement in Britain." In *Small Acts: Thoughts on the Politics of Black Cultures*, 97–114. New York: Serpent's Tale, 1993.

Ginsberg, Elaine K. "Introduction: The Politics of Passing." In *Passing and the Fictions of Identity*, ed. Elaine K. Ginsberg, 1–18. Durham, NC: Duke University Press, 1996.

Girard, René. *Violence and the Sacred*. Trans. Patrick Gregory. Baltimore: Johns Hopkins University Press, 1977.

Glaude, Eddie S., Jr. "Introduction: Black Power Revisited." In *Is It Nation Time: Contemporary Essays on Black Power and Black Nationalism*, ed. Eddie S. Glaude Jr., 1–21. Chicago: University of Chicago Press, 2001.

Goings, Kenneth W. *Mammy and Uncle Mose: Black Collectibles and American Stereotyping*. Bloomington: Indiana University Press, 1994.

Gooden, Mario. "The Problem with African American Museums." *Avery Review*, no. 6 (March 2015). http://www.averyreview.com/issues.

Gordon, Lewis. *Bad Faith and Anti-Black Racism*. Amherst, NY: Humanity Books, 1995.

———. "A Questioning Body of Laughter and Tears: Reading *Black Skin, White Masks* through the Cat and Mouse of Reason and a Misguided Theodicy." *Parallax* 8.2 (2002): 10–29.

Goyal, Yogita. *Romance, Diaspora, and Black Atlantic Literature*. New York: Cambridge University Press, 2010.

Gray, Herman. "Black Masculinity and Visual Culture." *Callaloo* 18.2 (1995): 401–5.

Green, Richard C., and Monique Guillory. "Question of a 'Soulful Style': Interview with Paul Gilroy." In *Soul: Black Power, Politics, and Pleasure*, ed. Monique Guillory and Richard C. Green, 250–65. New York: New York University Press, 1998.

Greenlee, Sam. *The Spook Who Sat by the Door*. 1969. Detroit: Wayne State University Press, 1989.

Grief, Mark, Kathleen Ross, and Dayna Tortorici, eds. *What Was the Hipster? A Sociological Investigation*. Brooklyn: n+1 Foundation, 2010.

Grier, William H., and Price M. Cobbs. *Black Rage*. New York: Basic Books, 1968.

Griffin, Farah Jasmine. *"Who Set You Flowin'?" The African-American Migration Narrative*. New York: Oxford University Press, 1995.

Griffiths, Frederick T. "Copy Wright: What Is an (Invisible) Author?" *New Literacy History* 33 (Summer 2002): 315–41.

Griggs, Sutton E. *Imperium in Imperio*. 1899. New York: Modern Library Classics, 2004.

Gubar, Susan. *Racechanges: White Skin, Black Face in American Culture*. New York: Oxford University Press, 1997.

Guerrero, Ed. "Black Image in Protective Custody: Hollywood's Biracial Buddy Films of the Eighties." In *Black American Cinema*, ed. Manthia Diawara, 237–46. New York: Routledge, 1993.

———. "The Black Man on Our Screens and the Empty Space in Representation."

In *Black Male: Representations of Masculinity in Contemporary American Art*, ed. Thelma Golden, 181–90. New York: Whitney Museum of American Art, 1994.

———. "A Circus of Dreams and Lies: The Black Film Wave at Middle Age." In *New American Cinema*, ed. John Lewis, 328–52. Durham, NC: Duke University Press, 1998.

———. *Framing Blackness: The African-American Image in Film*. Philadelphia: Temple University Press, 1993.

Gussow, Adam. *Seems Like Murder Here: Southern Violence and the Blues Tradition*. Chicago: University of Chicago Press, 2002.

Hagopian, Kevin. "Black Cinema Studies: Shadows and Acts." *Journal of Communication* 45.3 (1995): 177–85.

Hall, Stuart. "Cultural Identity and Diaspora." In *Colonial Discourse and Post-Colonial Theory: A Reader*, ed. Patrick Williams and Laura Chrisman, 392–401. London: Harvester Wheatsheaf, 1993.

———. *Stuart Hall: Critical Dialogues in Cultural Studies*. Ed. David Morley and Kuan-Hsing Chen. New York: Routledge, 1996.

Harney, Stefano, and Fred Moten. *The Undercommons: Fugitive Planning & Black Study*. Brooklyn, NY: Autonomedia, 2013.

Harris, Keith. "Black Crossover Cinema." In *The Wiley-Blackwell History of American Film*. Vol. 4: *1976 to the Present*, ed. Cynthia Lucia, Roy Grundmann, and Art Simon, 255–71. Oxford: Wiley-Blackwell, 2012.

———. *Boys, Boyz, Bois: An Ethics of Black Masculinity in Film and Popular Media*. New York: Routledge 2006.

———. "*Clockers*: Adaptations in Black." In *The Spike Lee Reader*, ed. Paula Massood, 128–41. Philadelphia: Temple University Press, 2008.

———. "'That Nigger's Crazy': Richard Pryor, Racial Performativity, Cultural Critique." In *Richard Pryor: The Life and Legacy of a "Crazy" Black Man*, ed. Audrey Thomas McCluskey, 23–38. Bloomington: Indiana University Press, 2008.

Harris, Scott Jordan, ed. *World Film Locations: San Francisco*. Chicago: Intellect Books, 2013.

Hartman, Chester. *City for Sale: The Transformation of San Francisco*. Revised and updated edition. Berkeley: University of California Press, 2002.

Hartman, Chester, Dennis Keating, and Richard LeGates, eds. *Displacement: How to Fight It*. Berkeley, CA: National Housing Law Project, 1982.

Himes, Chester. *My Life of Absurdity: The Later Years*. New York: Thunder's Mouth, 1976.

———. *Plan B*. Jackson: University of Mississippi Press, 1983.

Hoberman, J. *The Dream Life: Movies, Media, and the Mythology of the Sixties*. New York: New Press, 2003.

Hoberman, J., and Jonathan Rosenbaum. *Midnight Movies*. New York: Da Capo, 1983.

Holland, Sharon Patricia. *Raising the Dead: Readings of Death and (Black) Subjectivity*. Durham, NC: Duke University Press, 2000.

Hollinger, Karen. "Film Noir, Voice Over, and the Femme Fatale." In *Film Noir Reader*, ed. Alain Silver and James Ursini, 243–59. New York: Limelight Editions, 1996.

Holte, James Craig. "Ethnicity and the Popular Imagination: Ralph Bakshi and the American Dream." *MELUS* 8.4 (1981): 105–13.

hooks, bell. "States of Desire: An Interview with Isaac Julien." *Transition* 52 (1991): 168–84.

Huh, Jinny. "Whispers of Norbury: Sir Arthur Conan Doyle and the Modernist Crisis of Racial (Un)Detection." *Modern Fiction Studies* 49.3 (2003): 550–80.

Iton, Richard. *In Search of the Black Fantastic: Politics and Popular Culture in the Post–Civil Rights Era*. New York: Oxford University Press, 2008.

Jackson, Christina, and Nikki Jones. "Remember the Fillmore: The Lingering History of Urban Renewal in Black San Francisco." In *Black California Dreamin': The Crises of California's African-American Communities*, ed. Ingrid Banks, Gaye Johnson, George Lipsitz, Ula Taylor, Daniel Widener, and Clyde Woods, 57–74. Santa Barbara: UCSB Center for Black Studies Research, 2012.

Jackson, John. *Real Black: Adventures in Racial Sincerity*. Chicago: University of Chicago Press, 2005.

Jackson, Lawrence. *Ralph Ellison: Emergence of Genius*. New York: Wiley, 2002.

———. "Ralph Ellison, Sharpies, Rinehart, and Politics in *Invisible Man*." *Massachusetts Review* 40.1 (1990): 71–95.

James, Darius. *That's Blaxploitation! Roots of the Baadasssss 'Tude (Rated X by an All-Whyte Jury)*. New York: St. Martin's Griffin, 1995.

JanMohamed, Abdul R. *The Death-Bound-Subject: Richard Wright's Archaeology of Death*. Durham, NC: Duke University Press, 2005.

Jenkins, Candice. *Private Lives, Proper Relations: Regulating Black Intimacy*. Minneapolis: University of Minnesota Press, 2007.

Johnson, Charles. "A Phenomenology of the Black Body." *Michigan Quarterly Review* 32.4 (1993): 595–614.

Johnson, James Weldon. *The Autobiography of an Ex-Coloured Man*. 1912. New York: Hill and Wang, 1960.

Johnson, Jasmine Elizabeth. "Dear Khary (An Autobiography of Gentrification)." *Gawker*, 31 August 2013. http://gawker.com/dear-khary-an-autobiography-of-gentrification-1227561902.

Jones, Jacquie. "Under the Cover of Blackness." *Black Film Review* 7.3 (1993): 30–33.

Jones, Kellie. "To/From Los Angeles with Betye Saar." In *EyeMinded: Living and Writing Contemporary Art*, 165–76. Durham, NC: Duke University Press, 2011.

Judy, Ronald A. T. "On the Question of Nigga Authenticity." *boundary 2* 21.3 (1994): 211–30.

Julien, Isaac, and Kobena Mercer. "Introduction: De Margin and de Centre." *Screen* 29.4 (1988): 2–11.

Kanfer, Stefan. *Serious Business: The Art and Commerce of Animation in America from Betty Boop to Toy Story*. New York: Scribner, 1997.

Keeling, Kara. *The Witch's Flight: The Cinematic, the Black Femme, and the Image of Common Sense*. Durham, NC: Duke University Press, 2007.

Kelley, Robin D. G. *Freedom Dreams: The Black Radical Imagination*. Boston: Beacon, 2002.

Kellner, Douglas, and Michael Ryan. *Camera Politica: The Politics and Ideology of Contemporary Hollywood Film*. Bloomington: Indian University Press, 1988.

Kelly, John. "Integrating America: Jackie Robinson, Critical Events and Baseball Black and White." *International Journal of the History of Sport* 22.6 (2005): 1011–35.

Kennedy, Harlan. "Gondola Wind: Report from the 46th Venice Mostra." *Film Comment* 25.6 (1989): 74.

Kennedy, Liam. "Black Noir: Race and Urban Space in Walter Mosley's Detective Fiction." In *Criminal Proceedings: The Contemporary American Crime Novel*, ed. Peter Messent, 42–61. London: Pluto, 1997.

Klein, Norman. *Seven Minutes: The Life and Death of the American Animated Cartoon*. New York: Verso, 1993.

Kolbowski, Silvia. "Homeboy Cosmopolitanism: Manthia Diawara Interviewed by Silvia Kolbowski." *October* 83 (Winter 1998): 51–70.

Kotlarz, Irene. "The Birth of a Notion." *Screen* 24.2 (1983): 21–29.

Kozloff, Sarah. *Invisible Storytellers: Voice-Over Narration in American Fiction Film*. Berkeley: University of California Press, 1988.

Krutnik, Frank. *In a Lonely Street: Film Noir, Genre, Masculinity*. New York: Routledge, 1991.

Kun, Josh. *Audiotopia: Music, Race, and America*. Berkeley: University of California, 2005.

———. "Two Turntables and a Social Movement: Writing Hip-Hop at Century's End." *American Literary History* 14.3 (2002): 580–92.

Lehman, Christopher P. *The Colored Cartoon: Black Representation in American Animated Short Films, 1907–1954*. Amherst: University of Massachusetts Press, 2007.

Levine, Andrea. "The (Jewish) White Negro: Norman Mailer's Racial Bodies." *MELUS* 28.2 (2003): 59–81.

Levine, Lawrence. *Black Culture and Black Consciousness: Afro-American Folk Thought from Slavery to Freedom*. Oxford: Oxford University Press, 1977.

Levy, Emanuel. *Cinema of Outsiders: The Rise of American Independent Film*. New York: NYU Press, 1999.

Lindvall, Terry, and Ben Fraser. "Darker Shades of Animation." In *Reading the Rabbit: Explorations in Warner Bros. Animation*, ed. Kevin S. Sandler, 121–36. New Brunswick, NJ: Rutgers University Press, 1998.

Locke, Alain. *The New Negro*. 1925. New York: Athenaeum, 1968.

Lord, Barry, and Gail Dexter Lord. *Artists, Patrons, and the Public: Why Culture Changes*. Lanham, MD: AltaMira, 2010.

Lott, Eric. *Love and Theft: Blackface Minstrelsy and the American Working Class*. Oxford: Oxford University Press, 1993.

———. "The Whiteness of Film Noir." *American Literary History* 9.3 (1997): 542–66.

Lott, Tommy. "A No-Theory Theory of Contemporary Black Cinema." *Black American Literature* 25.2 (1991): 221–36.

Lubiano, Wahneema. "Black Nationalism and Black Common Sense: Policing Ourselves and Others." In *The House That Race Built*, ed. Wahneema Lubiano, 232–52. New York: Pantheon, 1997.

———. "'But Compared to What': Reading Realism, Representation, and Essentialism in *School Daze, Do the Right Thing*, and the Spike Lee Discourse." In *Representing Black Men*, ed. M. Blount and G. P. Cunningham, 173–204. New York: Routledge, 1996.

———. "Don't Talk with Your Eyes Closed: Caught in the Hollywood Gun Sights." In *Borders, Boundaries, and Frames*, ed. Mae G. Henderson, 185–201. New York: Routledge, 1996.

Macaulay, Scott. "The Urban Condition." *Filmmaker* 17.2 (2009): 60–63, 122.

Mackey, Nathaniel. *Bedouin Handbook*. Los Angeles: Sun and Moon, 1997.

———. *Discrepant Engagement: Dissonance, Cross-Culturality, and Experimental Writing*. Cambridge: Cambridge University Press, 1993.

Mailer, Norman. *The White Negro: Superficial Reflections on the Hipster*. San Francisco: City Lights Books, 1957.

Malcolm X. *The Autobiography of Malcolm X as Told to Alex Haley*. New York: Ballantine Books, 1964.

Marable, Manning. *Race, Reform, and Rebellion: The Second Reconstruction in Black America, 1945–1990*. Jackson: University Press of Mississippi, 1991.

Marcus, Greil. *The Old Weird America: The World of Bob Dylan's Basement Tapes*. New York: Picador, 2001.

Marcuse, Peter. "Gentrification, Abandonment and Displacement: Connections, Causes and Policy Responses in New York City." *Journal of Urban and Contemporary Law* 28 (1985): 195–240.

Margolick, David. *Strange Fruit: Billie Holiday, Café Society, and an Early Cry for Civil Rights*. Philadelphia: Running Press, 2000.

Margolies, Edward. *Which Way Did He Go? The Private Eye in Dashiell Hammett, Raymond Chandler, Chester Himes, and Ross Macdonald*. New York: Holmes and Meier, 1982.

Margolies, Edward, and Michel Fabre. *The Several Lives of Chester Himes*. Jackson: University Press of Mississippi, 1997.

Massood, Paula. *Black City Cinema: African American Urban Experiences in Film*. Philadelphia: Temple University Press, 2003.

———. *Making a Promised Land: Harlem in Twentieth-Century Photography and Film*. Philadelphia: Temple University Press, 2003.

Maxwell, William J. "Harlem Polemics, Harlem Aesthetics." In *Teaching the Harlem Renaissance*, ed. Michael Soto, 37–46. New York: Peter Lang, 2008.

Mayne, Judith. *Claire Denis*. Champaign: University of Illinois Press, 2005.

McCann, Sean. *Gumshoe America: Hard-Boiled Crime Fiction and the Rise and Fall of New Deal Liberalism*. Durham, NC: Duke University Press, 2000.

McEwan, Paul. "Racist Film: Teaching *The Birth of a Nation*." *Cinema Journal* 47.1 (2007): 98–101.

McGilligan, Patrick. "A Talk with Ralph Bakshi." In *The American Animated Cartoon: A Critical Anthology*, ed. Danny Peary and Gerald Peary, 269–79. New York: E. P. Dutton, 1980.

McPherson, Tara. *Reconstructing Dixie: Race, Gender, and Nostalgia in the Imagined South*. Durham, NC: Duke University Press, 2003.

Medvoi, Leerom. *Rebels: Youth and the Cold War Origins of Identity*. Durham, NC: Duke University Press, 2005.

Mercer, Kobena. "Tropes of the Grotesque in Black Avant-Garde." In *Cosmopolitan Modernisms*, ed. Kobena Mercer, 136–59. Cambridge, MA: Institute of International Visual Arts and MIT Press, 2007.

———. *Welcome to the Jungle: New Positions in Black Cultural Studies*. New York: Routledge, 1994.

Miller, Monica L. *Slaves to Fashion: Black Dandyism and the Styling of Black Diasporic Identity*. Durham, NC: Duke University Press, 2009.

Miller, Paul T. *Postwar Struggle for Civil Rights: African Americans in San Francisco: 1945–1975*. New York: Routledge, 2009.

Miller, Stephen Paul. *The Seventies Now: Culture as Surveillance*. Durham, NC: Duke University Press, 1999.

Mills, Charles W. "Non-Cartesian Sums: Philosophy and the African-American Experience." In *Blackness Visible: Essays on Philosophy and Race*, 1–20. Ithaca: Cornell University Press, 1998.

———. *The Racial Contract*. Ithaca: Cornell University Press, 1997.

Mitchell, W. J. T. "Living Color: Race, Stereotype, and Animation in Spike Lee's *Bamboozled*." In *What Do Pictures Want? The Lives and Loves of Images*, 294–308. Chicago: University of Chicago Press, 2005.

———. "Showing Seeing: A Critique of Visual Culture." *Journal of Visual Culture* 1.2 (2002): 165–81.

Moon, Spencer. *Reel Black Talk: A Sourcebook of 50 American Filmmakers*. Westport, CT: Greenwood, 1997.

Morrison, Toni. *Playing in the Dark: Whiteness and the Literary Imagination*. Cambridge, MA: Harvard University Press, 1990.

Moten, Fred. "Blackness and Nothingness (Mysticism in the Flesh)." *South Atlantic Quarterly* 112.4 (2013): 737–80.

———. *In the Break: The Aesthetics of the Black Radical Tradition*. Minneapolis: University of Minnesota Press, 2003.

Mullen, Harryette. "Optic White: Blackness and the Production of Whiteness." *diacritics* 24.2–3 (1994): 71–89.

Muñoz, José Esteban. *Disidentifications: Queers of Color and the Performance of Politics*. Minneapolis: University of Minnesota Press, 1999.

———. "Feeling Brown, Feeling Down: Latina Affect, the Performativity of Race and the Depressive Position." *Signs* 31.3 (2006): 675–88.

Naremore, James. *More Than Light: Film Noir in Its Contexts*. Berkeley: University of California Press, 1998.

Neal, Mark Anthony. *Soul Babies: Black Popular Culture and the Post-Soul Aesthetic*. New York: Routledge, 2002.

Nericcio, William Anthony. "Autopsy of a Rat: Odd, Sundry Parables of Freddy Lopez, Speedy Gonzales, and Other Chicano/Latino Marionettes Prancing about Our First World Visual Emporium." *camera obscura* 13.1 37 (1996): 187–237.

———. *Tex[t]-Mex: Seductive Hallucinations of the "Mexican" in America*. Austin: University of Texas Press, 2007.

Nieland, Justus. "Race-ing Noir and Replacing History: The Mulatta and Memory in *One False Move* and *Devil in a Blue Dress*." *Velvet Light Trap* 43 (Spring 1999): 63–77.

Ngai, Sianne. *Ugly Feelings*. Cambridge, MA: Harvard University Press, 2005.

Oliver, Kelly, and Benigno Trigo. *Noir Anxiety*. Minneapolis: University of Minnesota Press, 2003.

Ongiri, Amy. *Spectacular Blackness: The Cultural Politics of the Black Power Movement and the Search for a Black Aesthetic*. Charlottesville: University of Virginia Press, 2010.

Osucha, Eden. "The Whiteness of Privacy: Race, Media, Law." *Camera Obscura* 24.1 (2009): 67–107.

Parks, Gregory Scott, and Danielle C. Heard. "'Assassinate the Nigger Apes': Obama, Implicit Imagery, and the Dire Consequences of Racist Jokes." *Rutgers Race and Law Review* 11.2 (2010): 1–39.

Patton, Phil. "Mammy: Her Life and Times." *American Heritage* 44.5 (1993): 78–87.

Pavlić, Ed. "Speechless in San Francisco." *Transition* 110 (2013): 103–19.

———. *Who Can Afford to Improvise? James Baldwin and Black Music, the Lyric and the Listeners*. Bronx, NY: Fordham University Press, 2015.

Pfeil, Fred. *White Guys: Studies in Postmodern Domination and Difference*. London: Verso, 1995.

Pierson, John. *Spikes, Mikes, Slackers, and Dykes*. New York: Miramax/Hyperion, 1995.

Porter, Dennis. *The Pursuit of Crime: Art and Ideology in Detective Fiction*. New Haven, CT: Yale University Press, 1981.

Powell, Richard J. "Re/Birth of a Nation." In *Rhapsodies in Black: Art of the Harlem Renaissance*, ed. Richard J. Powell and David A. Bailey, 14–33. Oakland: Institute of International Visual Arts and University of California Press, 1997.

Pratt, Mary Louise. *Imperial Eyes: Travel Writing and Transculturation*. London: Routledge, 1992.

Pratt, Ray. *Projecting Paranoia: Conspiratorial Visions in American Film*. Lawrence: University of Kansas Press, 2001.

Price, Brian. "Color, the Formless, and Cinematic Eros." *Framework* 47.1 (2006): 22–35.

Puwar, Nirwal. *Space Invaders: Race, Gender, and Bodies Out of Place*. New York: Berg, 2004.

Quashie, Kevin. *The Sovereignty of Quiet: Beyond Resistance in Black Culture*. New Brunswick, NJ: Rutgers University Press, 2012.

Raiford, Leigh. *Imprisoned in a Luminous Glare: Photography and the African American Freedom Struggle*. Chapel Hill: University of North Carolina Press, 2011.

———. "Photography and the Practices of Critical Black Memory." *History and Theory* 48.4 (2009): 112–29.

Randolph, Mark. "On the Blackhand Side: Uncle Remus Wore Platforms. The Story of *Coonskin*." *Waxpoetics* 11 (Winter 2005): 64–66.

Rastegar, Roya. "Evolving Narrative Structures Forge New Cine-Love at the 2012 Sundance Film Festival." *Camera Obscura* 27.4 (2012): 149–57.

Rausch, Andrew J. "Ralph Bakshi." In *Reflections on Blaxploitation: Actors and Directors Speak*, ed. David Walker, Andrew J. Rausch, and Chris Watson, 1–10. Lanham, MD: Scarecrow, 2009.

Reed, Ishmael. *Shrovetide in New Orleans*. Garden City, NY: Doubleday, 1978.

Reid, Mark A. *Redefining Black Film*. Berkeley: University of California Press, 1993.

Reising, Russel. *Loose Ends: Closure and Crisis in the American Social Text*. Durham, NC: Duke University Press, 1996.

Rhodes, John David, and Elena Gorfinkel. "Introduction: The Matter of Places." In *Taking Place: Location and the Moving Image*, ed. John David Rhodes and Elena Gorfinkel, vii–xxix. Minneapolis: University of Minnesota Press, 2011.

Roberts, Les. *Film, Mobility and Urban Space: A Cinematic Geography of Liverpool*. Liverpool: Liverpool University Press, 2012.

Robinson, Amy. "Forms of Appearance of Value: Homer Plessy and the Politics of Privacy." In *Performance and Cultural Politics*, ed. Elin Diamond, 237–60. New York: Routledge, 1996.

Roediger, David R. *Wages of Whiteness: Race and the Making of the American Working Class*. Rev. ed. New York: Verso, 1999.

Rogin, Michael. *Blackface, White Noise: Jewish Immigrants in the Hollywood Melting Pot*. Berkeley: University of California Press, 1998.

Romano, Renee, and Leigh Raiford, eds. *The Civil Rights Movement in American Memory*. Athens: University of Georgia Press, 2006.

Rouse, Roger. "Thinking through Transnationalism: Notes on the Cultural Politics of Class Relations in the Contemporary United States." *Public Culture* 7 (1995): 353–402.

Ruffins, Fath Davis. "Revisiting the Old Plantation: Reparations, Reconciliation, and Museumizing American Slavery." In *Museum Frictions: Public Cultures/Global Transformations*, ed. Ivan Karp and Corrine Kratz, 394–434. Durham, NC: Duke University Press, 2006.

Rutledge, Gregory E. "Futurist Fiction and Fantasy: The *Racial* Establishment." *Callaloo* 24.1 (2001): 236–52.

Rux, Carl Hancock. "Eminem: The White Negro." In *Everything but the Burden: What White People Are Taking from Black Culture*, ed. Greg Tate, 15–38. New York: Broadway Books, 2003.

Saar, Betye. "Unfinished Business: The Return of Aunt Jemima." In *Betye Saar: Workers + Warriors, the Return of Aunt Jemima*, ed. Halley K. Harrisburg, 3. New York: Michael Rosenfeld Gallery, 1998.

Sabin, Roger. *Adult Comics: An Introduction*. New York: Routledge, 1993.

Sammond, Nicholas. *Birth of an Industry: Blackface Minstrelsy and the Rise of American Animation*. Durham, NC: Duke University Press, 2015.

Sampson, Henry T. *That's Enough, Folks: Black Images in Animated Cartoons, 1900–1960*. Lanham, MD: Scarecrow, 1998.

Sassen, Saskia. *Globalization and Its Discontents*. New York: New Press, 1998.

Schaefer, Eric. *Bold! Daring! Shocking! True! A History of Exploitation Films, 1919–1959*. Durham, NC: Duke University Press, 1999.

Schuyler, George S. *Black No More*. 1931. Boston: Northeastern University Press, 1999.

Sedgwick, Eve K. *Between Men: English Literature and Homosocial Desire*. New York: Columbia University Press, 1996.

———. *The Epistemology of the Closet*. Berkeley: University of California Press, 1990.

Sexton, Jared. "The Ruse of Engagement: Black Masculinity and the Cinema of Policing." *American Quarterly* 61.1 (2009): 39–63.

Shank, Barry. *The Political Force of Musical Beauty*. Durham, NC: Duke University Press, 2014.

———. "'That Wild Mercury Sound': Bob Dylan and the Illusion of American Culture." *boundary 2* 29.1 (2002): 97–123.

Sharpe, Christina A. *Monstrous Intimacies: Making Post-Slavery Subjects*. Durham, NC: Duke University Press, 2010.

Shohat, Ella, and Robert Stam. *Unthinking Eurocentrism: Multiculturalism and the Media*. New York: Routledge, 1994.

Shohat, Ella, and Robert Stam. "*Zelig* and Contemporary Theory: Meditation on the Chameleon Text." 1985. In *The Films of Woody Allen*, ed. Charles L. P. Silet, 198–216. Lanham, MD: Scarecrow, 2006.

Shukla, Sandhya. "Harlem's Pasts in Its Present." In *Ethnographies of Neoliberalism*, ed. Carol J. Greenhouse, 177–93. Philadelphia: University of Pennsylvania Press, 2010.

———. "Loving the Other in 1970s Harlem: Race, Space, and Place in *Aaron Loves Angela*." *symploke* 18.1–2 (2010): 171–88.

Slane, Andrea. "Pressure Points: Political Psychology, Screen Adaptation, and the Management of Racism in the Case-History Genre." *camera obscura* 15.3 (2000): 71–113.

Slater, Tom. "Gentrification of the City." In *The New Blackwell Companion to the City*, ed. Gary Bridge and Sophie Watson, 571–85. London: Blackwell, 2011.

Smith, Cherise. *Enacting Others: Politics of Identity in Eleanor Antin, Nikki S. Lee, Adrian Piper, and Anna Deavere Smith*. Durham, NC: Duke University Press, 2011.

Smith, Mark M. *How Race Is Made: Slavery, Segregation, and the Senses*. Chapel Hill: University of North Carolina Press, 2006.

Smith, Neil. *The New Urban Frontier: Gentrification and the Revanchist City*. London: Routledge, 1996.

Smith, Neil, and Peter Williams, eds. *Gentrification of the City*. New York: Routledge, 1986.

Smith, Shawn Michelle. *Photography on the Color Line: W. E. B. Du Bois, Race, and Visual Culture*. Durham, NC: Duke University Press, 2004.

Smith, Valerie. "The Documentary Impulse in Contemporary African-American Film." In *Black Popular Culture*, ed. Gina Dent, 56–64. Seattle: Bay Press, 1992.

———. "Reading the Intersection of Race and Gender in Narratives of Passing." *diacritics* 24.2–3 (1994): 43–57.

Snead, James. *White Screens/Black Images: Hollywood from the Dark Side*. Ed. Colin MacCabe and Cornel West. New York: Routledge, 1994.

Sobchack, Vivian. "'Lounge Time': Post-War Crises and the Chronotope of Film Noir." In *Refiguring American Film Genres: History and Theory*, ed. Nick Browne, 129–70. Berkeley: University of California Press, 1998.

Soderbergh, Steven, and Richard Lester. *Getting Away with It: Or, The Further Adventures of the Luckiest Bastard You Ever Saw*. New York: Faber and Faber, 2000.

Soitos, Stephen. *The Blues Detective: A Study of African American Detective Fiction*. Amherst: University of Massachusetts Press, 1996.

Solnit, Rebecca. *Hollow City: The Siege of San Francisco and the Crisis of American Urbanism*. London: Verso Books, 2000.

Sommerville, Siobhan B. *Queering the Color Line: Race and the Invention of Homosexuality in American Culture*. Durham, NC: Duke University Press, 2000.

Sound Recordings of Museum-Related Events. "An Evening with Ralph Bakshi." 74.21. Museum of Modern Art Archives, New York, 12 November 1974.

Sperb, Jason. *Disney's Most Notorious Film: Race, Convergence, and the Hidden Histories of* Song of the South. Austin: University of Texas Press, 2012.

Spillers, Hortense. "The Idea of Black Culture." *CR: The New Centennial Review* 6.3 (2006): 7–28.

———. "Mama's Baby, Papa's Maybe: An American Grammar Book." *diacritics* 17.2 (1987): 65–81.

Stam, Robert. *Reflexivity in Film and Literature: From Don Quixote to Jean-Luc Godard*. New York: Columbia University Press, 1985.

———. *Subversive Pleasures: Bakhtin, Cultural Criticism, and Film*. Baltimore: Johns Hopkins University Press, 1989.

Stew. *Passing Strange: The Complete Book and Lyrics of the Broadway Musical*. Milwaukee: Applause Theatre and Cinema Books, 2010.

Tal, Kali. "'That Just Kills Me': Black Militant Near-Future Fiction." *Social Text* 20.2 71 (2002): 65–91.

Tapia, Ruby. *American Pietàs: Visions of Race, Death, and the Maternal*. Minneapolis: University of Minnesota Press, 2011.

Tasker, Yvonne. *Spectacular Bodies: Gender, Genre, and the Action Cinema*. New York: Routledge, 1993.

Tate, Greg. "Black Rockers vs. Blackies Who Rock, or The Difference between Race and Music." In *Pop When the World Falls Apart: Music in the Shadow of Doubt*, ed. Eric Weisbard, 15–26. Durham, NC: Duke University Press, 2012.

———. "Nigs R Us, or How Blackfolk Became Fetish Objects." In *Everything but the Burden: What White People Are Taking from Black Culture*, ed. Greg Tate, 1–14. New York: Broadway Books, 2003.

Taylor, Clyde. "The Re-Birth of the Aesthetic." In *The Birth of Whiteness: Race and the Emergence of U.S. Cinema*, ed. Daniel Bernardi, 1–37. New Brunswick, NJ: Rutgers University Press, 1996.

———. "Two Way Street." *Black Film Review* 1.6 (1990): 8–9.

Telotte, J. P. *Voices in the Dark: The Narrative Patterns of Film Noir*. Urbana: University of Illinois Press, 1989.

Thomas, Kendall. "The Eclipse of Reason: A Rhetorical Reading of *Bowers v. Hardwick*." *Virginia Law Review* 79.7 (1993): 1805–32.

———. "'Masculinity,' 'The Rule of Law,' and Other Legal Fictions." In *Constructing Masculinity*, ed. Maurice Berger, Brian Wallis, and Simon Watson, 221–37. New York: Routledge, 1995.

Thompson, Debby. "'Is Race a Trope?' Anna Deavere Smith and the Question of Racial Performativity." *African American Review* 37.1 (2003): 127–38.

Tillet, Salamishah. *Sites of Slavery: Citizenship and Racial Democracy in the Post–Civil Rights Imagination*. Durham, NC: Duke University Press, 2012.

Tuhkanen, Mikko. *The American Optic: Psychoanalysis, Critical Race Theory, and Richard Wright*. Albany: SUNY Press, 2009.

Turvey, Malcolm. "Black Film Making in the USA: The Case of *Malcolm X*." *Wasafiri: Journal of Caribbean, African, Asian and Associated Literatures and Film* 9.18 (1993): 53–56.

U.S. Department of Justice. "Attorney General Eric Holder at the Department of Justice African American History Month Program." 18 February 2009. http://www.justice.gov/ag/speeches/2009/ag-speech-090218.html.

Vann, Michael G. "The Colonial Casbah on the Silver Screen: Using *Pepe le Moko* and *The Battle of Algiers* to Teach Colonialism, Race, and Globalization in French History." *Radical History Review* 83.1 (2002): 186–92.

Vernet, Marc. "Film Noir on the Edge of Doom." In *Shades of Noir: A Reader*, ed. Joan Copjec, 1–32. London: Verso, 1993.

Wagner, Bryan. *Disturbing the Peace: Black Culture and the Police Power after Slavery*. Cambridge, MA: Harvard University Press, 2009.

Wald, Gayle. *Crossing the Line: Racial Passing in Twentieth-Century U.S. Literature and Culture*. Durham, NC: Duke University Press, 2000.

Wanzo, Rebecca. "Black Love Is Not a Fairytale: African American Women, Romance, and Rhetoric." *POROI: An Interdisciplinary Journal of Rhetoric and Invention* 7.2 (2011): article 5. http://ir.uiowa.edu/cgi/viewcontent.cgi?article=1096&context=poroi.

Watkins, Mel. *On the Real Side: Laughing, Lying, and Signifying. The Underground*

Tradition of African-American Humor That Transformed American Culture, from Slavery to Richard Pryor. New York: Touchstone Books, 1994.

Webb, Gary. *Dark Alliance: The CIA, the Contras, and the Crack Cocaine Explosion*. New York: Seven Stories, 1998.

Weheliye, Alexander G. *Phonographies: Grooves in Sonic Afro-Modernity*. Durham, NC: Duke University Press, 2005.

Wepman, Dennis, Ronald B. Newman, and Murray B. Binderman, eds. *The Life: The Lore and Folk Poetry of the Black Hustler*. Philadelphia: University of Pennsylvania Press, 1976.

White, Armond. "Apostasy: Anti-Hype in Four Steps." In *The Resistance*, 278–82. Woodstock, NY: Overlook, 1995.

———. "Underground Man." *Film Comment* 27.3 (1991): 4.

White, Hayden. "Historiography and Historiophoty." *American Historical Review* 93.5 (1988): 1193–99.

Wiegman, Robyn. *American Anatomies: Theorizing Race and Gender*. Durham, NC: Duke University Press, 1995.

Wilderson, Frank B. *Red, White and Black: Cinema and the Structure of U.S. Antagonisms*. Durham, NC: Duke University Press, 2010.

Williams, John A. *Captain Blackman*. New York: Doubleday, 1972.

———. *The Man Who Cried I Am*. Boston: Little, Brown, 1967.

———. "My Man Himes: An Interview with Chester Himes." In *Amistad 1: Writings on Black History and Culture*, ed. John A. Williams and Charles F. Harris, 25–93. New York: Random House, 1970.

Williams, John A., and Dennis A. Williams. *If I Stop I'll Die: The Comedy and Tragedy of Richard Pryor*. New York: Thunder's Mouth, 1991.

Willis, Susan. *High Contrast: Race and Gender in Contemporary Hollywood Cinema*. Durham, NC: Duke University Press, 1997.

Wilson, Elizabeth. "Looking Backward: Nostalgia and the City." In *Imagining Cities: Scripts, Signs, Memories*, ed. Sallie Westwood, 127–51. New York: Routledge, 1997.

Wilson, Mabel O. "Between Rooms 307: Spaces of Memory at the National Civil Rights Museum." In *Sites of Memory: Perspectives on Architecture and Race*, ed. Craig Barton, 13–26. New York: Princeton Architectural Press, 2001.

Witt, Doris. *Black Hunger: Food and Politics of U.S. Identity*. Oxford: Oxford University Press, 1999.

Woods, Clyde. *Development Arrested: The Blues and Plantation Power in the Mississippi Delta*. New York: Verso, 1998.

Wright, Michelle M. *Becoming Black: Creating Identity in the African Diaspora*. Durham, NC: Duke University Press, 2004.

———. *Physics of Blackness: Beyond the Middle Passage Epistemology*. Minneapolis: University of Minnesota Press, 2015.

Wright, Richard. "Big Boy Leaves Home." 1938. In *Uncle Tom's Children. Richard Wright: Early Works*, 239–75. New York: Library of America, 1991.

———. *Native Son*. 1940. New York: Harper, 1987.

———. *The Outsider*. New York: HarperCollins, 1953.

———. *White Man Listen*. 1957. New York: Anchor Books, 1964.

Žižek, Slavoj. *Looking Awry: An Introduction to Jacques Lacan through Popular Culture*. Cambridge, MA: MIT Press, 1992.

Zucker, Carole. "Bill Duke." In *Figures of Light: Actors and Directors Illuminate the Art of Film Acting*, 299–312. New York: Plenum, 1995.

INDEX

adaptation, 23, 32, 53, 174n8; animated forms of, 15, 167–68n27; blackface minstrelsy and, 32; disobedient forms of, 26, 48; distinction from source material and, 161n4; live-action film and, 3, 15, 63, 67, 92, 175n19, 179–80n69, 184n25; narrative recoding and, 67; revisions of the black vernacular within, 26; roving as, 155; sonic forms of, 130

aesthetics, 3–7, 11–12, 77–78, 84–87, 158–59; ambition for, 65–68; black cinematic strategies and, 3, 6–7, 12, 78, 121, 158; black critical ideas of, 35, 118; craft and, 6; literary affinities and, 86, 118

Africa, 62, 130

allegory, 85, 184n25

Allen, Harry, 3–4

Allen, Lewis (Abel Meeropol), 45

Allen, Woody, 71–72

ambient sounds, 120, 127, 140

animation, 19–21, 29, 159, 165n7, 166n18; blackness and, 19, 27, 165n8; figurations of, 23; history of, 15, 165n10, 169n42; live action, 19, 27

antebellum, 21–22, 25–26, 44

antiblack: American imaginary, 19, 44, 60; belief, 97; codes, 3, 13; collectibles, 171n75; critique, 23; everyday, 89; iconography, 20–23, 27, 34, 171n74, 172n78; inscriptions, 32; intent, 96; precognition, 97; presumption, 46; racism, 6, 48, 66,

75, 90, 96, 137, 146–47, 173n88; regimes, 35; social hierarchies, 63; speech, 66, 184–85n34; standards, 60; tendencies, 19, 32, 60; terror, 22; violence, 168n33; visual culture, 20, 22–23, 27, 33, 37, 48, 158, 165–66n17; whiteness, 31; world, 61

antiblackness, 34, 91; anonymity and, 185n45; authority of, 96; systemic critique of, 101; terms of, 89

art, contemporary, 13, 173n89; filmic intertextuality and, 2, 194n15

Atlanta, 13, 70–72, 178n49

Atlanta Constitution, 168n33, 178n49

Atlanta Municipal Police, 168n33

attachment, 16, 120–21, 131–34, 153–55, 158–60; adventure plot of, 121; chronicle of, 132, 155; stakes of, 131

Aunt Jemima, 39–41, 171–72n77

auteur, 65, 74

avant-garde film, 9; black artistic gestures toward, 160; black filmmaking as, 178n49

Baker, Houston, 44, 168n30

Bakhtin, Mikhail, 22, 33–34, 162n16

Bakshi, Ralph, 15, 17, 23–24, 26–27, 35–37, 44, 48, 164–65n6, 167n24, 167n26, 169n35; black artists and, 173n89; black film and, 36, 170n61; career of, 27, 166n18, 167n25, 167–68n27; reductive views on black politics of, 36–37, 166n20

cocaine, 92–93, 99, 107, 109–10, 191n85; crack form of, 116, 118; distributors and suppliers of, 92, 116; importation of, 115–16

communities, working-class, 137–38, 140–42

Confederacy, 25, 29

conspiracy: black film and, 114–16, 191–92n87; black freedom desires as, 13; paranoia and, 115; theories of, 173n88; U.S. government and, 115

Coonskin, 15, 17–49, 158, 164–65n6, 167–68n27, 168n33, 171n77, 173n89, 173–74n90, 185n39; collusion in, 33–34; controversy of, 24, 166n20; epidermilization and, 31–32; grotesque realism of, 22–23, 27, 38–39, 41–41, 49; horror of, 20, 22, 28; ideological function of, 37, 41; intermission of, 37–39; intertextuality of, 25–26, 165n10, 169n35; metapicture and, 23, 165–66n17, 167n24; picaresque and, 21–22; racialization and, 22, 29; reanimation and, 23, 48; urbanism of, 27, 37

Copeland, Huey, 157–58

cosmopolitanism, 15–16, 65, 153; vernacular forms of, 48, 170–71n62

countercultural: agent of the law, 186n48; commix, 15; communities, 186n48; movement, 150

craft, 6, 22, 33, 38, 65, 87, 160; conflation of, 87; disobedient forms of, 55; film and video and, 160; history and, 22; mediations of, 33; performative blackness and, 65, 87, 160; political engineering of, 6; pop politics and, 37

criminality, 3, 97, 168n33

Cripps, Thomas, 76–79

critical dialogism, cinematic, 6, 15, 162n16; absurdist modalities of, 15; black enactments of, 6, 162n16; conceptions of, 162n16

Crothers, Scatman, 18, 44, 164n1

cultural nationalism, black: cinematic category of, 88; commodification of, 36; enduring lessons of, 5; filmic conversance

with, 35; patriarchal authority of, 111; pop phenomena of, 36; radical break of, 96; reductionist significations of, 35–36, 170–71n62; rhetoric of, 101

dance, black: cinematic placement of social, 13, 147–48; clubs and, 148; footage of, 35; interpretative forms of, 36; montages of, 13, 37; performance of criticality within, 38; refusal of, 45

de Certeau, Michel, 59, 76, 120

Deep Cover, 15, 84, 92–118, 158, 184n25, 184–85n34, 186n49, 187–88n60, 189n69; black embodiment and, 96, 190n78; difference in, 99, 101, 112, 158; interracial coupling of, 104, 112–13; resolution of, 115, 192n90; voice-over in, 98–99, 117–18, 185–86n46, 189n70

Defiant Ones, The, 112–13, 187n51

Deleuze, Gilles, 134, 180–81n83

Denis, Claire, 133–34, 195n32, 195n34

desire, 13, 53, 57, 60–61, 103–4, 108, 112–13, 120–23, 143, 158, 179–80n69; black characters and, 16, 120, 123, 126, 134, 152–55, 160; politics of, 6, 123; racialized power dynamics and, 113, 153

Detroit Human Rights Commission, 64, 79

Detroit Tigers, 52, 58, 175n19

diaspora, black, 129, 137–39; absence and, 16; aesthetics of, 159; anxiety of, 200n73; complexities of, 37; exile and, 153; false cures for, 154; global terms of, 131; identity dynamics within, 131; museology within, 134; negotiation of, 9; new forms of, 137; states of consciousness within, 155; subjectivity and, 127, 130; time and, 134–35, 155; transvaluation of, 139; writers of, 134

Diawara, Manthia, 15, 87–88, 186n36, 187n58

Dickel, Simon, 194n15, 199n62

discursivity, racial, 5–7, 15, 83, 121, 162n12; black films demonstrative of, 54, 118; cinematic analysis and, 87; indifference to, 7; rigor of, 6

Disney, 15–17, 75, 165n70; cultural imperialism of, 15; humanistic pandering of, 25; parodic mimicry of, 12, 25–26, 44, 169n35
Disney, Walt, 25–26
Dixie, 26, 44
documentary, 45; categorical distinctions of, 65; experimental modes of, 12; static practice of, 13
doppelganger, 113, 190n78
double consciousness, 34, 99
Dreams Are Colder Than Death, 12, 14, 163n26
drug trade, the, 4–5; Mafia control of, 21; network of, 99, 191n85; pyramid infrastructure of, 92; terminology of, 4; trafficking and, 92, 116, 191n85
Du Bois, W. E. B., 34, 49, 56, 99
Duhamel, Marcel, 89–90
Duke, Bill, 15, 84, 92, 184n25, 191n82
Dylan, Bob, 112, 172–73n83

Ellison, Ralph, 5, 20, 33, 45, 58, 79, 185–86n46; mask and, 60, 176n26; tropes of blackness and, 60, 164n4
engagement, discrepant, 162–63n17; black film and, 7, 84; black writers and, 15, 91–92, 161–62n17; creaking of Dogon weaving block and, 160; ethos of, 129; with America and, 15, 92
English, Darby, 11–12
Equiano, Olaudah, 129–30, 132, 194n22
erasure, 137–38, 140, 148; black cinematic, 158; film focus on, 143; historical forms of, 41; urban black life and, 137, 148, 195n34
existentialists, 85–86, 90, 106
expressive culture, black, 5–6, 28, 37, 92, 158–60; archive of, 118; cinematic enactment of, 6, 14, 16, 85, 116–17, 158; conceptual field of, 2, 85; emplotment of, 88; instruction in, 127; pastiche and, 185n22; possibilities of, 118
expressivity, black, 13–14, 104, 106; fetishistic designs of, 104; history of, 14; white conduits for, 106

Fanon, Frantz, 26, 31–32, 97, 106
fantasy, 16, 120–22, 152–54, 217; cinematic connotations of, 120–21, 127, 152; raced desire as, 120, 153; unraveling of, 152
FBI (Federal Bureau of Investigation), 115–16
fetish, commodity, 15, 42
Fillmore, the, 137, 196n38
film blackness, 2–16, 82–86, 155–59, 161–62n10, 162n16, 163n19; conceptual frame of, 16, 85, 118–19; enactments of, 14–16, 20, 49, 54–55, 120, 123, 176–77n34; reading practice of, 6, 83–84
Film Forum, 71, 178n52
Fleetwood, Nicole, 7, 13
Flint, 51, 58
Flying Lotus, 13, 159
folklore, 5, 22, 26, 79
form, 1–7, 38, 41–46, 73, 164n32, 194n14; artistic insistence on, 160; blackness and, 84, 151, 186n49; blues challenges and, 44; cinematic modes of, 5, 84, 194n19; commodity rebranding and, 46; common sense and, 186n49; dialogics of, 15; film as, 77, 84; hard-boiled convention as, 91–92; innocence and, 19–20; literary modes of, 1, 91–92; noir as, 3; nondepressive melancholia and, 195–96n37; nonfiction and, 13; politics of, 5; questions of, 2; scripting and, 59–60; study and, 164n32; utility and, 41
Friday Night, 133–34, 195n32, 195n34
Fritz the Cat, 23, 167n25

Ganja & Hess, 5, 36
Gates, Henry Louis, Jr., 65, 183n22, 185–86n46
genocide, 106, 115
genre, 2, 83–87, 91, 119, 158; black film as idea and, 12, 84; blackness and, 83–84, 119; conventional rhetoric surrounding, 184n26; critical function of, 83; dialogics of, 15; film and, 83; function of, 85; investment in, 83; liminality and, 105; polemics of, 85; practice of,

84; racial classification and, 84, 87–88; refabulation of, 84; studies of, 15; terms of, 102

gentrification, 16, 122, 137–39, 142–43, 197n43; intent of, 151; urban renewal and, 142, 196n38; violence of, 143

George Washington, 5, 159

Gilliam, Leah, 8–9

Goyal, Yogita, 134–35

Great Migration, 37, 146

Griffin, John Howard, 8–9

Guare, John, 71, 179–80n69

Guerrero, Ed, 61, 74, 101

Hall, Stuart, 6, 120–21

hard-boiled: form, 92; literature, 85; tone, 90; trace, 106; tradition, 15, 183n18, 183–84n23

Harlem, 37–39; cinematic representations of, 13, 37, 39; detective fiction set in, 89; figuration as Black Metropolis and, 37; filmic setting in, 23–24; interpretative measure of, 28; Jewish residents' leave-taking of, 57; landscape of, 13; novel series set in, 91; substitution in noir for beloved Americana, 89–91; Uptown and, 37

Harlem Renaissance, 37–38; critical legacy of, 38; trace of, 38

Harris, Joel Chandler, 25–26, 168n33

Harris, Keith, 92–93

Harris, Wendell B., Jr., 15, 51, 69–73, 82, 174n6, 177n47; conversations with, 174n3; criticism of, 71–73; erasure of, 158, 181–82n85; interviews conducted by, 175n14

Heavy Traffic, 23, 164–65n6, 167n25

Himes, Chester, 15, 84, 183n19, 192n93; complexity of, 88–91; film and, 88, 184n25; novels of, 90–91

hipster, the: American life and, 105–6; black characters as, 150–51; contemporary culture of, 151; Greenwich Village scene of in 1940s, 149; racial entitlement of, 106, 149; recuperation of, 69; songs and, 148

hood film, the, 69, 92–93, 115, 118; cycle of, 69, 93; drug culture of, 115; origins of, 92

Home of the Brave, 111–12, 190n73, 190n75

Horton, Willie, 52, 58

"I Have a Dream" speech, 12–13, 163n26

immateriality: blackness and, 157–58; faith and, 14; quiet contemplation and, 132; shifting state of, 120

impersonation, 51–54; film projects of, 179–80n69; impulse of, 82; sequence of, 66

Industrial Age, 38–39

industrialism, 69; de-, 148; history, 84; logic of, 76; post-, 58; urban, 148

interiority, black, 120–21, 132; characters lacking, 109, 176–77n34; narrative authority and, 98–99; social interlocutors and, 121

Invisible Man, 5, 58, 185–86n46; narrator of, 44–45, 79, 185–86n46; spatial tropes in, 79, 164n4

Jafa, Arthur, 12–14, 163n28, 163–64n29

jazz, 37–38

Jenkins, Barry, 15, 122, 133, 193n6, 195n36

Jewishness, 24, 166n20; blackface and, 105; blackness and, 37, 73, 104–6; crisis embodied by, 187–88n60

Julien, Isaac, 161n1, 179n63

King, Martin Luther, Jr., 12–14, 163n26

Latin America, 86, 109, 114–16

Lee, Spike, 75, 161n5, 165–66n17, 173–74n90, 181–82n85, 197n43; auteurist liberties of, 3; *Clockers*, 3–5; importance of, 70; successes of, 92

Lethal Weapon 2, 112–13, 187n69; pietà scene of, 113, 187n51

Liberation of Aunt Jemima, The, 171–72n77

liminality, 34, 41–42, 105

Los Angeles, 13–14, 98–99, 106, 167n23; street gangs of, 116

Los Angeles Times, 72, 191n85

Lott, Eric, 87–88

Lott, Tommy, 76–78

love, black, 14–16, 122–23, 152–55, 158–60; absolution as, 160; courting of, 143; critical devotion to, 14; diasporic distinction of, 135; failure and, 155; film plot and, 122, 143, 154–55, 158; immateriality of, 121; lore of the power of, 122–23; query of, 163n31; redemptive promise of, 152; self-sabotage of, 154

Lubiano, Wahneema, 6, 104, 186n49

lynching, 46, 173n86

Mackey, Nathaniel, 18, 162–63n17

Mailer, Norman, 105–6, 150, 188n63

mammy, 39, 41–42; collectible of, 171–72n77; intertext of, 41; signifiers of, 171–72n77

March on Washington, 147–48; fiftieth anniversary of, 163n26

market, the: American imaginary and commercial, 41; American film on European, 85–86; black film crossover and, 76; condominium projects and, 142; exclusivity and, 140; film testing on, 70–71; forces of, 137, 151; inner-city audiences as, 36; New York's importance on, 71; real estate and, 139; white audiences, 76

masculinity: cinematic black visions of, 100, 104; crisis of, 104; normative focus on white forms of, 84, 106; standards of, 109

masquerade, the, 53–54, 60; acting and, 51; ball theme of, 68; cartoon tradition of, 31; collapse of normative distinction via, 65; conditional categories of, 54; embodied forms of, 9; facial performance and, 108–9; racial mode of, 54; success of, 65

materiality: blackness and, 157–58; cinematic forms of, 4; shifting state of, 120

Mazor, David, 72, 179n61

Medicine for Melancholy, 119–55; cinematic geography of, 122, 138, 155, 159, 193n6, 197n43; inspiration for, 133–34, 195n34; mumblecore and, 194n14, 199n62; postblackness and, 198–99n61, 199n62;

post-soul enactments in, 148, 199n2; quietude of, 15–16, 155, 158; ruin in, 155; sense of acceleration in, 134

melancholia, 121–22; black memory and, 137; cinematic portrayal of black, 159; cures for, 122

melancholy, 16; nondepressive forms of, 195–96n37; shadow of, 143

melodrama, 53; family for, 25; murder melodramas variation of, 85–86; tragic mulatto trope of, 187n55

Mercer, Kobena, 74, 77, 161n1, 162n16, 171–72n77, 187n51, 200n71

Middle Passage, 86, 108, 129–32; epistemology of, 130, 194n22

mimicry, 64, 113; menace of, 55, 60

minstrel, blackface, 16–17, 39–44, 60; conceit of, 169n39; pose of, 28; shadow of, 169n42; song of, 44; stage of, 39

misrecognition, 2, 91, 122

Mission Street, 131–32

modernism, black, 38, 59

Moten, Fred, 13–14, 59, 164n32; black love query by, 164n31; capacious blackness noted by, 12; filmic appearance by, 14

Museum of Modern Art (MoMA), New York, 24, 69, 166n20

Museum of the African Diaspora (MoAD), 127–31, 134–35, 138–39

music scene, the, 145–48; black presence in, 148; indie, 148, 199n64; subcultural space of, 148

Naremore, James, 15, 85–88

narrativity, 4, 59

nationalists, black, 36, 94; common sense and, 186n49

Neal, Mark Anthony, 147–48

neoliberalism, 15–16, 138–40; age of, 16; narratives of, 138

New Deal, 90–91, 105

New Jack City, 75, 92

New South, the, 19, 25–26, 41–46; anti-, 25, 41; cinematic revitalization of, 29; hermeneutic rendition of, 42; ideal of, 25, 41; lore of, 46; neoclassical design of, 168n30; white supremacist intent of, 25, 41

New York City, 105–6, 143, 164–65n6, 167n23; backdrop of, 21; movie theaters in, 24, 71

New York Film Festival, 69, 179n63

Ngai, Sianne, 23, 26–27

1920s, 37, 86

1930s, 37, 90

1960s, 15, 51, 70, 137, 147

1970s, 17–18, 36–38, 53, 75, 198n59; black film explosion of, 75–76; cinema of, 170n58; community housing activists of, 197n48; movie theaters of, 38; reverse migration in, 146; toast recordings of, 189n70; urban dress of, 18; white conservatism of, 36

1980s, 53, 92, 115–16, 197n48; films set in, 115, 179–80n69; independent film circuit of, 70; interracial male coupling films of, 104; music in, 199n64

noir, 3, 63, 67, 83–118; blackness and, 15, 84–88, 96, 99, 116–18; film and, 83–87, 92–118; literature and, 89–92

"Noir by Noirs: Towards a New Realism in Black Cinema," 87–88, 185n36

Northern Arts Entertainment, 71–72

nostalgia, 26–27, 33–34, 85; antiblack form of, 23, 33–34

Now Pretend, 8–10

Oliver, Kelly, 98, 182n86

ontology, black, 7, 78

oral tradition, 19, 26

Paramount Pictures, 24, 92, 166n19, 167nn23–24

Paris, 85, 133–34

passing, 8, 52–54, 58–61, 105, 174n8; performative act of, 15, 54, 65–67, 175n13; tradition of, 53–54, 82, 158

pathology, black, 54, 96–97

Pavlić, Ed, 193n6, 200n73

performativity, black, 83, 158–59; alternative narratives of, 159; resistance to automation by, 39; study of, 14

philosophy, 68–69; Africana, 57; black existential forms of, 57, 108; professor of, 181–82n85

photography, 2, 13

plantation, 25–29; literary narratives of, 168n30; setting of, 25

Poitier, Sidney, 178n69, 180n70, 186–87n50, 190n79

popular culture, American, 3, 19, 41, 165–66n17; black forms of, 6; high modernism and, 85; history of, 158

postproduction, 24, 51, 121, 147; desaturation in, 121; film music and, 147; release delays and, 24

post-soul, 147–48, 198n59; black films as, 199n62; ethos of, 148; generation of, 147; moment of, 147

potentiality: blackness as, 7, 121, 131; quiet expressions of, 131

prison, 19, 27, 59, 62–63, 160, 181–82n85; cell in, 81–82; escape from, 66; plantation conceit and, 25; release from, 174n6, 191n85; scenes shot in, 164n5; term in, 51; writer of, 90

Pryor, Richard, 45–46, 63, 184–85n34

Rabelais and His World, 22, 34

racial grotesque, 33–42, 48–49, 158; black artistic practice of, 171–72n77, 173n89, 173–74n90; cinematic employment of, 23, 33; creative practice of, 15; cultural memory and, 23; film staging of, 15, 22–23, 27, 33–34, 49; indignity of, 49; semiotics of, 39; strategy of, 39; tactic of, 48

"Rallye, Le," 133–35

Reagan–Bush era, the, 88, 115–16

Reaganomics, 58, 148

Reconstruction, 21, 25–26, 39

redemption, 134, 152

Red Sox, 52, 174n5

Regents of the University of California v. Bakke, 147–48

Reid, Mark, 10–11

respectability, black, 3–4, 145, 152, 195n36

Rogin, Michael, 102, 105, 111, 190n75

romance, 106, 155; black literary tradition of, 134; capacity for black agency within, 135; conceit of, 16, 119, 122; film staging of, 134; racial calibrations of, 122, 134

Rotograph, 19, 165n7

Saar, Betye, 171–72n77

Sandyha, Shukla, 137–38

San Francisco, 119–55, 193n6, 193n9, 194n12, 197n43; African Americans in, 119–20, 143–47, 196n38; communities in, 137–38, 141; cultural geography of, 16, 120–23, 154; redevelopment in, 137–38, 195n31, 196n40; tourist imaginary of, 139; urban history of, 119–22, 140–43, 146

San Francisco Museum of Modern Art, 126–27

San Francisco Redevelopment Agency, 137–38

San Jose Mercury, 116, 191n85

Schwartz, Russell, 73–74

Second Reconstruction, 36, 168n34, 169n35

Seitler, Dana, 161n8, 188n65, 199n65

Sharpton, Al, 24, 166n20

sincerity, racial, 121, 125, 148

Six Degrees of Separation, 71, 74, 179–80n69

slavery, 29, 41–42, 45–46, 132; account of, 103–4; complicity with, 41; escape from, 129; historicity of, 171n75; legacy of, 45, 172n78; revisionism of, 26; trace of, 42

"Slavery Passages," 130–32, 194n20

Smith, Valerie, 161n2, 174n78

Smith, Will, 179n65, 179–80n69

Snead, James, 25, 84

social critique, 5, 85

Soderbergh, Steven, 73, 177n46

South, the, 8; black migration to and from, 146; imagery of, 41; romanticism of, 26

Spillers, Hortense, 12–13; thoughts on state of black cultural life by, 13, 163n27; vocal soundtrack by, 13

Spook Who Sat by the Door, The, 59, 170n61

stereotype, the, 33–34; contemporary

artists' untethering of, 21; critique of, 15; disenabling of, 33; fundamental tendencies of, 108; presumptions of, 33; radical resignification of, 15

"Strange Fruit," 45, 172–73n83

Street, William Douglas, Jr., 51–59, 66, 75, 82, 174n1, 174n6, 175n14, 175n20, 181–82n85; film portrayal of, 55–59, 66, 75, 82, 175nn19–20, 179–80n69

style, black, 2–5, 65, 84; literature and, 2, 5, 44; lyrics and, 44; music and, 44, 148; politics and, 28, 88; praxis of, 150

subjectivity, black: cycling of, 121; embodiment and, 104; film narrativization of, 127–28; production of audience via, 130; recuperation via essentialist forms of, 149; subjectification and, 48; universal forms of, 6, 127, 130

Sundance Film Festival, 51, 69–72, 174n3, 178n51, 180n71, 181–82n85

surrealism, 89, 108

surrealists, 85–86, 89–90

tableau, 21, 29, 42, 121; film timbre and, 121; profilmic form of, 21; staging of past via, 29

Talented Tenth, the, 61, 118

Task Force on African American Out-Migration, 145–46

Taylor, Clyde, 65, 179n62

texture, 15–16, 41, 84, 122; blackness and, 147; cinematic palette and, 121; cultural forms of, 16; ideological forms of, 15; racial forms of, 16

Thomas, Kendall, 162n12, 187–88n60

Toronto Film Festival, 69, 174n6

To Sleep with Anger, 70, 178n49, 179n63

trademark, 39–42

trauma, 18, 27, 129

True Identity, 75, 174n8

UCLA Film and Television Archive, 181–82n85; LA Rebellion initiative of, 201n1

underground, 19, 164n4; register of, 109; U.S. military arms in, 116

vaudeville, 37–38, 169n42
Venice Film Festival, 69, 174n3
Village Voice, 71, 73
visuality, 3, 5–6, 27, 34, 59, 158–60; blackness and, 3, 6, 27, 34, 159
voice, 8–9, 13–14, 45–46, 80–81, 98–99, 164–65n6; absence of, 98; autobiographical film form of, 9; black lack of, 185–6n46; bodily disconnect from, 99, 176n31; brand use of, 172n78; futurity of, 118; giving of, 45; indecipherability of, 56; literary context of, 185–86n46; multiplicity of, 9; namelessness and, 185–86n46; narrative authority of, 9, 98, 189n70; reunification with body and, 118; scream built from, 166n20; slave as lacking, 46; slowing and acceleration of, 8; unvoiced recuperation of, 84, 86, 127–28, 139

Walker, Kara, 13, 170n51, 173n89
Warner Bros., 70, 73, 165n10, 179n65, 179–80n69
Wayne State Medical School, 58, 179–80n69
Webb, Gary, 116, 191n85

Welles, Oscar, 65, 180–81n83
Western Addition, the, 136–39; renewal plan for, 137–38, 145
White, Armond, 72–74, 179n65
White, Barry, 164–65n6, 166n20; overdubbing of, 167n23
"White Negro, The," 105–6, 150, 188n63
white supremacy, 6, 21–22, 27, 31–34, 48, 75, 90–91, 96; collusion and, 33–34, 41; crime of, 91; critique of, 101; emplotment of, 90; visual logic of, 31
Wiegman, Robyn, 7–8, 104, 172n78, 183n18, 187n53
Workers and Warriors: The Return of Aunt Jemima, 171–72n77
World War II: film drama of, 111–12; post-, 85, 137
Wright, Michelle M., 108, 130, 194–95n24
Wright, Richard, 164n4, 180–81n83, 189–90n46

Yale University, 66–67
Yerba Buena Gardens, 131, 195n31

Zelig, 73–74, 177n41